The Prajñāpāramitā Literature

The literature on Prajñāpāramitā, vast, deep and vital to an understanding of the Mahāyāna. It has so far been neglected by European scholars. With the aim of facilitating the study, the author has set out a certain amount of information about it. Thus, this handbook records, for the use of scholars, the very limited knowledge acquired during the last century.

Edward Conze was born in London and was educated at various universities and did his Ph.D from University of Cologne in 1928. He had a talent for learning languages and picked up 14 languages including Sanskrit.

From 1933 until 1960, he lectured in psychology, philosophy, and comparative religion at the University of London and the University of Oxford.

In 1960 and 1970, he met with university students of Buddhism in Canada and lectured at several universities in the United States; he was appreciated by his students.

Dr Conze has been called "the foremost Western scholar of the Prajñāpāramita literature." It is especially significant that, as a scholar of Buddhism, he also tried to practice it, especially meditation.

The Prajñāpāramitā Literature

Edward Conze

Munshiram Manoharlal
Publishers Pvt. Ltd.

ISBN 978-81-215-0992-3
Reprinted 2000, 2008, 2012, **2017**
First published 1958

PRINTED IN INDIA
Published by
Munshiram Manoharlal Publishers Pvt. Ltd.
PO Box 5715, 54 Rani Jhansi Road, New Delhi 110 055, INDIA

www.mrmlbooks.com

PREFACE

The literature on Prajñāpāramitā, vast, deep and vital to an understanding of the Mahāyāna, has so far been somewhat neglected by European scholars. With the aim of facilitating its study, I have in this book set out a certain amount of information about it. This is a handbook which records for the use of scholars the very limited knowledge we have acquired during the last century. I am well aware that a compilation of this kind lends itself to innumerable sins of commission and omission. The critical reader will discover many of them, and I must console myself with having given him something to build on. After completing my typescript, which has slowly matured over twenty years, I find that the gaps in my treatment stand out more clearly than its contours. The Bibliography, though comprehensive, is by no means complete. I have not listed all the translations, articles and books which have appeared in Japanese, nor the numerous Chinese commentaries which are not included in the *Taishō Issaikyō*. As for the Mongol, I have ignored the Tanjur, which seems to exist only in Ulan Bator. The Manchu translations of the Kanjur, which were done between 1730 and 1790, are likewise inaccessible in Europe. Modern translations into Dutch, Italian, etc., are noted only sporadically. The treatment of the commentatorial literature is quite unsatisfactory, and generally confined to listing the bare bibliographical data. The material is so vast that no one person can be expected to do everything. Others will, I hope, take up the thread where I have left it.

London, March 1958 EDWARD CONZE

PREFACE TO THE SECOND EDITION

By 1972 the first edition of this work had been sold out. Mouton & Co., the publishers, had by then largely withdrawn from their Indological publications and returned the copyright to the author. Over the years a number of minor inaccuracies have been detected in the original text, and they have been corrected for this reprint. In addition much has been published on *Prajñāpāramitā* since 1960, and I have, as far as I could, inserted these later publications in their appropriate places in the Bibliography. In fact it appears that the *Prajñāpāramitā* writings have in recent years been explored more thoroughly than most other branches of Buddhist literature.

The Reiyukai has done wonderful work in providing us with precious materials for the study of the *Saddharmapuṇḍarīka,* and all Buddhist scholars will now be grateful to them for having brought this monograph on the *Prajñāpāramitā* back into circulation. In 1963, when I was a professor in Madison, Wisc., I tried to make up for my neglect of the Japanese contributions to this subject by supervising and directing Hanayama Shōyū's survey on what had been done in Japan up to that date (see p. 91). In the last fourteen years much more has been written in that country and I can only apologize for its omission. The simple truth is that I do not know the language and am now too old to learn it.

Sherborne, December 1977 — Edward Conze

TABLE OF CONTENTS

CHRONOLOGICAL SURVEY

A. THE DEVELOPMENTS IN INDIA

The composition of Prajñāpāramitā texts extended over about 1,000 years. Roughly speaking, four phases can be distinguished: 1. The elaboration of a basic text (ca. 100 B.C. to 100 A.D.), which constitutes the original impulse; 2. The expansion of that text (ca. 100 A.D. to 300); 3. The restatement of the doctrine in 3a. short Sūtras and in 3b. versified Summaries (ca. 300 A.D. to 500); 4. The period of Tantric influence and of absorption into magic (600 A.D. to 1200).

1. The oldest text is the *Perfection of Wisdom in 8,000 Lines,* in 32 chapters (Bibl. no. 5). Most of the Sūtras of this class, although in prose, are named after the number of lines (*ślokas* of 32 syllables) which they contain. The English translation is about 110,000 words long. Some parts of this basic Prajñāpāramitā probably date back to 100 B.C. Other sections were added at later times, and the composition of the whole may have taken over two centuries.

The *place of origin* of the Prajñāpāramitā has been the subject of some controversy. Several authors have claimed that it probably developed among the Mahāsāṅghikas in Southern India, in the Andhra country, on the Kistnā river.[1] Near Amarāvatī ("The sojourn of the immortals") and Dhānyakaṭaka (the modern Dharanikot), the Mahāsāṅghikas had two famous monasteries, which gave their names to the sects of the Pūrvaśailas and of the Aparaśailas. These sects are significant because 1) they had a Prajñāpāramitā in Prakrit,[2] they 2) spoke of the *dharmadhātu* in the same sense as the Prajñāpāramitā[3], and 3) their Buddhology prepared the way for that of the Prajñāpāramitā. The doctrines which the *Kathāvatthu* attributes to the Andhakas are so much akin to the Mahāyāna doctrines that the latter may well have developed from them.[4]

Nāgārjuna, whose name is associated with the consolidation of the Prajñā-

1 For the references see E. Lamotte, "Sur la formation du Mahāyāna", *Asiatica,* 1954, p. 386 n. 49.
2 Paramārtha; cf. Przyluski, *Rājagṛiha,* p. 304.–*Siddhi* p. 752.–According to Lamotte p. 387 the Tibetan *Grub-mtha'* is the authority for this.
3 The verses are preserved in Candrakīrti, *Prasannapadā,* p. 548.
4 So R. Sāṃkrityāyana, in *JAs,* Oct.-Dec. 1934, pp. 195–208.

pāramitā, came from the South of India, and was probably connected with Nāgārjunīkoṇḍa in the Andhra country, which is not far from Amarāvatī.[1] His *Suhṛllekha* was dedicated to Śātavāhana, king of the Dekkhan, and according to the *Harṣacarita*[2] he collected Sūtras from the Nāgas for the same king, and it is an often repeated legend that he recovered the text of the Prajñāpāramitā from the palace of the Nāgas in the Nether Regions.[3] A striking illustration of this event is found in an 11th century Ms of the *Pañcavimśatisāhasrikā*, now in the Baroda Museum.[4] Nāgārjuna lived in Dhānyakaṭaka,[5] and the name of the Bhadanta Nāgārjunācārya occurs on an inscription found in the neighbourhood of the Stūpa of Jaggayyapaṭa.[6] In this area both Dravidian and Greek influences made themselves felt, and Grousset has rightly called the Stūpa of Amarāvatī a "Dravido-Alexandrian synthesis". In view of the close analogies which exist between the Prajñāpāramitā and the Mediterranean literature on Sophia,[7] this seems to me significant. Also the Andhras were a non-Aryan people who spoke a Telugu language, and the matriarchal traditions of the Dravidians may well have something to do with the introduction of the worship of the "Mother of the Buddhas" into Buddhism.

The *Aṣṭa* (*A* x 225) states that "after the passing away of the Tathāgata" the perfection of wisdom will "proceed to the South", and from there spread first to the West, and then to the North. The different recensions of the Prajñāpāramitā, from the earliest onwards, as preserved in Chinese,[8] all agree, with one exception[9], that the itinerary of the Prajñāpāramitā began in the South, or South-East.[10] Further, the *Mañjuśrīmūlatantra,* as Obermiller points out[11], specifies four regions for the recitation of various Mahāyāna

1 P. S. Sastri, "Nagarjuna and Aryadeva", *IHQ*, XXX, 1 (1955), pp. 193–202, has provided further evidence for the thesis that Nāgārjuna was an Andhra.

2 Ed. L. Parab (Bombay, 1945), p. 250.–Cf. F. W. Thomas, *Harshacarita,* p. 252.– De La Vallée Poussin, *L'Inde au temps des Mauryas* (1930), takes on p. 207 *śāta*= *munda sata*—horse, for the Andhras treated the horse as an incarnation of a great god. See E. Lamotte, *HBI*, 1958, p. 524.

3 The Śrāvakas, according to Tāranātha p. 71, concluded that Nāgārjuna had actually written the *Śatasāhasrikā.* But that seems unlikely.

4 *Bulletin,* I, 1, (1943–4), p. 35, Figure 14, Restoration of Prajñāpāramitā.

5 Kloṅ rdol *gsuṅ-'bum* C p. 9a. Bu-ston, II, 127. Tāranātha, p. 73, 81, 303.

6 J. Burgess, *Notes on the Amarāvatī Stūpa* (1882), p. 57.

7 See E. Conze, in *Religion,* V (1975), pp. 160–167. Further interesting suggestions also in A. Migot, *BEFEO,* XLVI (1954), pp. 530–32, and cf. the literature in C. Regamey, *Buddhistische Philosophie* (1950), pp. 28–29.

8 Cf. E. Lamotte, *Le traité de la grande vertu de sagesse,* I (1944), pp. 25–26.

9 The translation of *A* by Chih-Ch'ien; see Lamotte, p. 26 n.

10 According to Hsüan-tsang's translation of *A* and *P.*

11 *Analysis of the Abhisamayālaṅkāra,* p. 346.

Sūtras, and the Prajñāpāramitā "is to be recited in the South".

We may also mention the Arapacana chapter of the large Prajñāpāramitā (*Ś* ix 1450–1453), in which 42 letters of the alphabet are illustrated by words that begin with them[1]. In its present form this chapter clearly points to the North-West of India, for it includes the letter YSA=Z, illustrates the letter ṢA by *ṣaṅga* (for *saṅga*), etc. But while the letters of the alphabet have remained substantially the same, the words used to illustrate them have undergone great changes between 200 and 900 A.D. The Sanskrit text of the Chinese translations often differed from that of the Nepalese manuscripts and the Tibetan translation. Mokṣala, for instance, has at CHA *choraṇa* for the *chedanā* of *Ś*, at SMA *śmaśāna* for *smaraṇa,* and at TSA *utsarga* (*utsādana*) for *utsāha.* It is to be hoped that a competent scholar will one day determine from all sources the development of the Arapacana alphabet.[2] What is important for our argument is that in the case of ḌA Nāgārjuna's commentary indicates that the word which illustrates it had its origin in Southern India.[3]

The evidence for the Southern origin of the Prajñāpāramitā is merely circumstantial, and by no means conclusive. The whole theory has recently been challenged by E. Lamotte[4] who is inclined to localize it in the North-West and the region of Khotan. It is, we must admit, clearly speculative in that it refers to a period antecedent to the one for which documents have

1 Translated SS no. 127. It is difficult to decide whether the Arapacana consists of 42 or 43 letters. The *Gaṇḍavyūha* and Kumārajīva have 42, and S. Lévi (*Mémorial S. Lévi,* 1937, pp. 355–363) and F. W. Thomas (*Miscellanea Academica Berolinensia,* 1950, p. 204) assume this to be the original number. This is to some extent confirmed by *P* 536b, duplicated by Gilgit *Ad* f. 282r, which speaks of 42 *akṣaras,* though not explicitly in connection with the Arapacana. On the other hand, the number is clearly 43 in Hsüan-tsang, in Ghosha's edition of *Ś* and, most important of all, in the Gilgit Ms of *P.*

2 A useful compilation of the alphabets in the Chinese translations of P. P. texts and Avataṃsaka is found in an article by Yamada Ryūjō: Shijūni jimon ni tsuite (he proposes 42 letters), *Nihon Bukkyōgaku Kyōkai Nempō,* III, 1931, pp. 201–267. see also E. Lamotte, *HBI,* 1968, pp. 549–550.

3 *Mpp-ś* T 1509 p. 408, col. 2,4 from left. "If you hear the syllable DA you at once (or: in fact) know the unburning (or: not hot) characteristic of dharmas. The word *ḍajada* (=*jaḍa*?) in South Indian usage means "unburning" or "not hot"." Prof. Burrow has kindly explained this passage to me: The usual Dravidian words for "cold", like *taṇ,* etc., cannot be in question here. Nāgārjuna therefore did not refer to a Dravidian language, but to a peculiarity of South Indian Sanskrit usage, in which *jaḍa* (usually meaning "dull" etc.) was used in the sense of "cold". Cf. F. Kittel's *Kannada Dictionary* (1894). "This meaning is only recorded in Monier-Williams' *Sanskrit Dictionary* on the authority of Wilson, who presumably got it from his South Indian pandit. It is not found in ordinary classical Sanskrit usage." The Chinese: 'are separated from the heat'.

4 See note 1 on p. 1.

survived. The new creed may well have originated in one area in which circumstances, historical and climatic, were unfavourable to the survival of documents, and then shifted from that to another area, i.e. the North-West where some documents survived the universal destruction and were preserved either in the climate of Nepal and Central Asia, or in translations into Chinese and Tibetan. It is not unreasonable to assume that the new texts existed for a time orally in the Prakrit of the regions in which they originated, and were only later on, around the beginning of the Christian era, transferred into a written language, i.e. Buddhist Hybrid Sanskrit which is unrelated to the Southern Prakrits, but has many affinities with Ardha-māgadhī and Apabhraṃśa and contains a number of Middle-Iranian words introduced by Indo-Scythians. By some chance we have, as we saw, documentary evidence to show that the Arapacana alphabet was re-modelled when it reached the North-West. The same remodelling may well have applied to the Abhidharma lists[1] and to the location of legends. In the interest of increasing the monastic income from pilgrims Buddhists everywhere were inclined to locate mythical events in places within their own neighbourhood. Lamotte makes much of the tradition according to which the Gandhavatī of the Sadāprarudita story lies in Gāndhāra. Yet the *Blue Annals*[2] in their turn assure us that "the city of Chen-tu in Szü-chuan province is believed to be Dharmodgata's residence". So no great certainty can be attained in this field. In any case, the entire story is a late *avadāna*[3] which was added to the *Aṣṭasāhasrikā* centuries after its doctrines had been quite clearly formulated. In other words I believe that Lamotte has shown no more than that the Prajñāpāramitā had a great success in the North-West at the Kushāṇa period, and that, to use his own words (p. 392), that region may well be the "fortress and hearth", though not necessarily the "cradle" of the Mahāyānistic movement. The *Mañjuśrīmūlakalpa* (LIII v. 575) says that under Kaniṣka the Prajñāpāramitā was "established" *(pratiṣṭhitā)* in the North-West, but not that it originated there, and its Southern origin has not, I think, been definitely disproved.

Two kinds of *ideas* can be distinguished in the *Aṣṭa*: The first set contrasts point by point with the *Abhidharma,* the second is newly created by the *Mahāyāna.* The persons against whom these writings are directed are perpetually referred to as the "Disciples and Pratyekabuddhas". Judging from the

1 The 119 wholesome dharmas in the commentary to Nāgārjuna's *Vigrahavyāvartanī* (v. 7) are totally different from those in the *Ta-chih-tu-lun. See IHQ* xiv, 1938, 314–323.

2 Trsl. Roerich p. 938.

3 Which has its counterpart in *Saddharmapuṇḍarīka* ch. 22 and *Samādhirāja* ch. 33.

Mahāprajñāpāramitopadeśa (no. 2 cy 1) the new ideas arose historically speaking as a reaction against the Abhidharma traditions of the Sarvāstivādins. The affiliation of the *Aṣṭa* with the same school is, however, by no means certain. No distinctive Sarvāstivādin doctrines are ever referred to, and the three references[1] to the *Buddhavacana* are, as far as I know, still untraced anywhere. The first is an allusion to the story of Śreṇika Vatsagotra, at i 8–9, which seems to presuppose a scriptural basis other than *Saṃyuktāgama* no. 105 (pp. 31c–32). The second is at iv 94; i.e. *uktaṃ hy etad Bhagavatā: dharmakāyā Buddhā Bhagavantaḥ. mā khalu punar imaṃ bhikṣavaḥ satkāyaṃ kāyaṃ manyadhvam. dharmakāya-pariniṣpattito māṃ bhikṣavo drakṣathaiṣa ca Tathāgatakāyo bhūtakoṭiprabhāvito draṣṭavyo yad uta prajñāpāramitā.* The third quotation is at xi 246. *uktaṃ hidaṃ Bhagavatā: acchaṭāsaṃghātamātrakam apy ahaṃ bhikṣavo bhavābhinirvṛttiṃ na varṇayāmi. sarvaṃ hi saṃskṛtam anityam, sarvaṃ bhayāvagataṃ duḥkham, sarvaṃ traidhātukaṃ śūnyam, sarvadharmā anātmanas tad evaṃ sarvam aśāśvatam anityaṃ duḥkhaṃ vipariṇāmadharmakaṃ viditvā paṇḍitair ihaiva srotaāpattiphalaṃ prāptavyam ... ihaiva-arhattvaṃ prāptavyam. mā no bhūyas tābhiḥ sampattivipattibhir duḥkhabhūyiṣṭhābhiḥ samavadhānaṃ bhūd iti.* The Pali at *AN* i 34–5 (quot. *Mil.* 142,6) is rather different: *appamattakaṃ pi gūtho dugghandaṃ hoti*; *evam eva kho ahaṃ bhikkhave appamattakaṃ pi bhavaṃ na vaṇṇemi antamaso accharāsaṅghātamattaṃ pi-iti.*

In any case, the opponents are personified by Śāriputra, the most outstanding representative of the traditional Abhidharma.[2] The Abhidharma works have, as we know, developed from numerical summaries called *mātṛkā* (Migot 538–9), and in these *mātṛkās* we must, I think, see the forerunners of the lists which figure so prominently in the Prajñāpāramitā Sūtras. First of all, *mātṛkā* means "mother", and Przyluski translates the Chinese equivalent in the *A-yü-wang-ching* as "sagesse-mère". Secondly, both the *Vinaya* of the Mūlasarvāstivādins and the *Aśokāvadāna* give the following definition of the *mātṛkāpiṭaka* (Migot p. 524): It clarifies the distinguishing points of that which ought to be known (*jñeya*). It comprises the four applications of mindfulness, the four right efforts, the four roads to psychic power, the five dominants, the five powers, the seven limbs of enlightenment, the eight limbs of the Path, the four analytical knowledges, the *araṇāsamādhi,* the *praṇidhānasamādhi.*[3]

1 The fourth, at xii 256, refers to *AK-vyākhyā* 23 and *SN* iv 52, but is not distinctive of any school.—There are other quotations at xviii 346–7, xix 356–8, xxii 405, xxviii 445, but they are not much use for historical purposes, and may even refer to other passages in the Prajñāpāramitā itself.

2 A. Migot, "Un grand disciple du Buddha, Śāriputra", *BEFEO,* XLVI (1954), pp. 405–554, Chapter XI.

3 J. Przylusky, *Le concile de Rājagṛha* (1926), p. 45.–This gives 43 items, corresponding to 43 letters in some versions of the Arapacana. It should be remembered that

This is precisely the list which, with many innovations towards the end, takes up so much space in the Prajñāpāramitā Sūtras.

At some time in Buddhist history, probably towards the end of Aśoka's reign (Migot 541), the adherents of a comparatively late concern with *prajñā* (Migot 511–514)[1] composed a literature of *mātṛkās*. Later on the rationalists developed this into works on Abhidharma, the mystics into works on Prajñāpāramitā. Śāriputra was traditionally associated with abhidharmic *prajñā*, or with "analytical knowledge" (*paṭisambhidā, Asl.* 16), and this the Prajñāpāramitā literature regards as both his strength and his limitation. No longer the *dhamma-senāpati,* no longer next to the Buddha himself in his wisdom, he now becomes the representative of an inferior kind of knowledge. His ability to review events impersonally, reducing them into their constituents according to a prescribed method, is a step in the right direction. But it is not sufficient. Śāriputra is thus, in the Mahāyāna literature, addressed by the Buddha as a recipient of the higher wisdom which he has yet failed to grasp. In the *Aṣṭa* he is subordinated to Subhūti, whom he constantly asks for information, whose superiority he repeatedly (e.g. at ii 43–4) acknowledges, who occasionally shows up his utter obtuseness (e.g. at i 20), and who "reproves" him, "although the Ven. Śāriputra has taken hold of the matter correctly as far as the words are concerned" (i 32). His understanding of why the Bodhisattva is a "great being" or a "great hero" is contrasted most unfavourably with that of Subhūti and Pūrṇa (i 18–20), who both had their hearts in the right place. His clear logical mind does not at all feel at home in a doctrine which equates the dream world with the real world (xix 356–61), and he always tries to tie down to neat formulas and precise definitions those spiritual phenomena which transcend them. At viii 187–9 Śāriputra gives the attributes of the perfection of wisdom insofar as they follow from purity, whereas Subhūti understands the absolute purity and the purity of self. Śāriputra, obsessed with his *anattā* doctrine, cannot speak of the self as Subhūti does, Subhūti whose understanding is based on the equivalence of the self and the Absolute, which must seem outrageous to

mātṛkā, according to Monier-Williams, is also an "epithet of certain diagrams written in characters to which a magical power is ascribed".

1 A. K. Warder in his Preface to the P. T. S. edition of Kassapatthera's *Mohavicchedanī* (1961, xix-xxvii) distinguishes six stages in the history of the Pali Mātikās (lists of topics, 'metrics'). He believes that the oldest *mātikā* was the list of 37 *bodhipakkhiyā dhammā,* divided into 7 groups, which the Lord gives as the summary of his teaching in D. N. II 120 (*Mahāparinibbāṇasutta*) and which *Vbh.* 372 simply calls *saddhammo*. The *Nettipakaraṇa* has 43 *bodhipakkhiyā dhammā* (p. 112), adding, according to the cy, 6 *saññās*. The list "gives a consistent and orderly exposition of the striving or *yoga* of the early Buddhists". Many additions were made later on.

Śāriputra. It is greatly conducive to a comprehension of the background of the *prajñāpāramitā* if one notes the formulations of *prajñā* which are put into the mouth of Śāriputra (cf. furthermore iii 77, vii 170–3, 176–7, 181–3, viii 190, x 211–13, xvi 309–20, xxvii 444), and which constitute the agreed starting point of the debate between the Mahāyāna and its Hīnayāna opponents.

Although the rivalry with the Hīnayāna is intense, the term itself is rarely used.[1] The contrast is in the main a fivefold one:

1) The ideals, aims and career of a *Bodhisattva* are opposed to those of the *Arhat* and *Pratyekabuddha.* 2) The *perfection of wisdom* is contrasted with the *wisdom* of the old schools. 3) The Abhidharmists were constantly occupied in "*reviewing*" *dharmas.* By contrast it is said often that one "should not review dharmas". The Abhidharmists were probably too self-conscious of what they were doing, and presumably not without some touch of self-centred pride. 4) The Abhidharmists acquired great skill in reviewing the *rise and fall* of dharmas. Here they are taught that there is no such thing, because of the *non-production* of all dharmas. 5) A *multiplicity* of separate dharmas was considered to constitute the ultimate reality. Here it is taught that a) there is no such multiplicity, because all is one; b) there are no separate dharmas, but what appears to be so are mere words.

As for the new ideas, one must always bear in mind that in these Sūtras we are not dealing with a series of philosophical propositions about the nature of things, but with a set of practices designed to bring about a state of complete detachment by intellectual methods. Among the new ideas one may single out three:

1) The greater interest in the *Absolute* leads to such terms as "Suchness" etc. On the whole, the terminology is , however, that of the Old Wisdom School. 2) The new concept of *skill in means,* through which, in the spiritually advanced, all doings and thoughts become tools of an all-embracing compassion. 3) The concept of the *dedication of merit.* One gives up the merit one has acquired, and transfers it to other beings, so that they may gain full enlightenment.

The thousands of lines of the Prajñāpāramitā can be summed up in the following two sentences: 1) One should become a Bodhisattva (or, Buddha-to-be), i.e. one who is content with nothing less than all-knowledge attained through the perfection of wisdom for the sake of all beings. 2) There is no such thing as a Bodhisattva, or as all-knowledge, or as a 'being', or as the perfection of wisdom, or as an attainment. To accept both these contra-

1 It occurs at xi 238. But other combinations with *hīna* (inferior) are freely used of opponents, e.g. *hīnajātika, hīnaprajña, hīnavīrya, hīnasattva* and *hīnādhimuktika.*

dictory facts is to be perfect.

Not everything that we find in our present text of the *Aṣṭa* belongs to the same period. Like many other Oriental works, the *Aṣṭa* has been subjected to additions and alterations in the course of the centuries, to suit the taste of different generations. The internal evidence of the text itself, a comparison with *Rgs* (no. 5A), with the larger recensions of the *Prajñāpāramitā* (no. 1–4) and with the early Chinese translations make it possible to separate the most obvious accretions from the basic original text which, in its turn, must have grown gradually:

I. Three chapters, XXIX to XXXII, are clearly later than the remainder of the book. They are not found in either *Ś* or *Rgs*. Chapter XXIX is a litany, and chapters XXX to XXXI give the story,—carried on into the first page of chapter XXXII—of how the Bodhisattva Sadāprarudita ('Ever-weeping') went out to seek for perfect wisdom. This story serves the purposes of propaganda and edification. Its authors wished to inspire devotion to the perfection of wisdom, to show that inability to understand it is but due to the unworthiness of people who are unwilling to make the necessary sacrifices, and to indicate the conditions under which it can be attained.

II. A set of four additions (i.e. XIX 365, 7–369; xxvii 449, 12–452, 15; 457–458; xxviii 464a–474) can be inferred from the fact that the name of the Buddha *Akṣobhya* occurs in them. Akṣobhya was very popular at the beginning of the Christian era, and his special connection with the Prajñāpāramitā, in its origin perhaps due to psychological considerations,[1] continued right into the Tantric period (see p. 15). A closer examination of the four passages in question shows that the text was worked over at a time when the cult of Akṣobhya came into vogue, and that a follower of that cult inserted a number of references to him.

Once these later additions are eliminated, chapters XXV to XXVIII (and XXXII) present a fairly coherent argumentation, which at one stage of the development of the text could easily have been a fitting conclusion to the Prajñāpāramitā. The chapters in question would then consist of two different treatises, i.e. 1) the praise of the supreme excellence of perfect wisdom (XXV 424 to XXVIII 460, 14), and 2) the entrusting of the sūtra to Ānanda (XXVIII 460–464a, XXXII 527–529). Such a *parindanā* was

1 Imperturbability is the special result of wisdom, as shown by a passage in Mātṛceṭa's *Śatapañcāśatka*, v. 96:

śīlasampadā śuddhaḥ prasanno dhyānasampadā
tvaṃ prajñāsampadā-akṣobhyo hradaḥ puṇyamaho mahān.

"You are a great lake of merit, pure through your perfect morality, serene (or calm) through your perfect meditation, unperturbed (or 'untroubled', not 'unshakable' as S.B.) through your perfect wisdom."

added to some Mahāyāna Sūtras, as a means of contending for their authenticity as the word of the Buddha himself.[1]

III. A few other suspected additions may be mentioned in passing. Chapters VIII and IX have been worked over by a later hand, and chapter XIII seems to be posterior to *Rgs.* The passage XX 380, 13 to XXI, 395 begins abruptly, the argumentation is fairly incoherent, the style fumbling and clumsy, and the whole is largely an afterthought to chapter XVII. Likewise the bulk of chapters XXII to XXIV seems to be a later insertion.

A verse summary of this text, or at least of its first 28 chapters, is called *Verses on the Accumulation of the Precious Qualities of the Perfection of Wisdom* (no. 5A), in 302 verses in irregular Vasantatilaka metre. Many of the early Mahāyāna Sūtras exist in two forms, in verse and in prose. Usually the verse form is the earlier of the two. The original *Ratnaguṇasaṃcayagāthā* is now lost. All we possess is Haribhadra's revision, which to some extent brings the text in line with the chapter divisions of the *Aṣṭasāhasrikā,* as they existed in the 8th century.

The status of this work is not quite clear. There are three possibilities: 1) The verses formed originally part of the *Aṣṭa,* and were later on separated. 2) The verses are the original form of the *Aṣṭa.* 3) The verses have been made up afterwards. It is very difficult to come to a decision on this, because, whereas in some instances the correspondence between *Rgs* and *A* is nearly literal, in others where the text of *A* is summed up or rewritten, it sometimes appears that the text of *A* is prior to *Rgs,* because *Rgs* is elliptic and unintelligible without reference to *A.*

In chapters 1 to 28, the *Rgs* follows the text of *A* fairly closely. There are, however, even in that section a number of verses, i.e. 31, or 36, one seventh of the total, which have no counterpart in our text of *A.* These are iii 8, v 2 (?), 5–8, vii 7, ix 1, xii 6–9, xiv 1 (?), xix 3–5, xx 5–7, 11, 12 (?), 13, 14 (?), 15, 16 (?), 17–20, xxi 8, xxii 6, xxiii 1, 3, xxiv 2, 6, xxvi 2, 3, xxvii 8. On the other hand, the following passages of *A* are unrepresented in our text of *Rgs*: ii 33–4, 41; iii 50–57, 10; 75–80, 82–92; v. 102–112, 114–122; vi 138, 12–142, 12; 143, 3–150, 11; 161–169; vii 170–1; viii 196–9; ix 200, 201–211, 5; x 221–230; xi 235–238, 240–242, 244–248; xii 257, 20–281, 8; xiii 281–283, xvi 312–321, xix 357–360, 365–369, xxii 405–409, xxiii 410–413, 414–415, xxiv 417–420, 421–423, xxv 428–430, xxvi 434–435, xxvii 444–446, 449, 19–452, 9; xxviii 457–458, 459–466, 471–474, xxix 475–xxxii 529.

1 The *Saddharmapuṇḍarika* is entrusted to a group of great Bodhisattvas (p. 484), the *Tathāgataguhyanirdeśa,* a section of the *Ratnakūṭa,* to the Bodhisattva Guhyaka Vajrapāṇi, the *Vimalakīrtinirdeśa* to Maitreya, the *Sandhinirmocana* to Mañjuśrī (Lamotte, *Asiatica,* p. 383).

These are roughly 240 out of 529 pages, or between one half and one third of the total.

The verses which are given under chapters 29 to 32 of *Rgs* do not at all correspond to the text of *A.* Chapters 29 to 31 describe the five *pāramitās,* beginning with the *dhyānapāramitā* and ending with the *dānapāramitā,* while chapter 32 first of all explains in 5 verses the rewards of practising the six perfections, with verse 6 forming the conclusion of the whole work and giving its title.

2. About the beginning of the Christian era the basic Prajñāpāramitā was *expanded* into a "Large Prajñāpāramitā", as represented today by three different texts—*Perfect Wisdom in 100,000 Lines, Perfect Wisdom in 25,000 Lines,* and *Perfect Wisdom in 18,000 Lines.* These three texts are really one and the same book. They only differ in the extent to which the "repetitions" are copied out. A great deal of traditional Buddhist meditation is a kind of repetitive drill, which applies certain laws or principles to a certain number of fixed categories. If, for instance, you take the statement that "X is emptiness and the very emptiness is X", then the version in 100,000 lines laboriously applies this principle to about 200 items, beginning with form, and ending with the dharmas, or attributes, which are characteristic of a Buddha. Four-fifths of the *Śatasāhasrikā,* or at least 85,000 of its 100,000 lines, are made up by the repetition of formulas, which sometimes (as in ch. 13 and 26) fill hundreds of consecutive leaves. An English translation of the Large Prajñāpāramitā, minus the repetitions, forms a handy volume of about 600 printed pages (see p. 37). The reader of the Sanskrit or Tibetan version must, however, struggle through masses and masses of monotonous repetitions which interrupt and obscure the trend of the argument. The versions in 25,000 and in 18,000 Lines are so much shorter because they give fewer items, sometimes only the first and the last. A version in 125,000 Lines, if it ever existed, is now lost. The version in 25,000 Lines was a favorite with commentators, and the one in 18,000 Lines seems to have been popular in Central Asia.

In addition two short texts, which are more in the nature of specialized treatises, and which show some affinity to the *Ratnakūṭa* collection, belong to the early centuries of the Christian era (see p. 20). The one, a Perfect Wisdom in 500 Lines, also called "The questions of the Bodhisattva Nāgaśrī", (no. 12) applies the basic concepts of the Prajñāpāramitā to the various aspects of begging for alms, of eating, of food, etc. The other, the "Prajñāpāramitā Sūtra explaining how Benevolent Kings may protect their Countries", is mainly concerned with the practical effects of the Prajñāpāramitā on society.

It explains how a ruler's devotion to the Prajñāpāramitā will increase his merit, and will call forth the protection of great and mighty Bodhisattvas, who will ward off all calamities from his country and his people. The greater part of the Sūtra may have been written in China.

3. The huge bulk and chaotic arrangement of the Large Prajñāpāramitā proved an obstacle to later generations (see p. 101). The exuberance and pious ardor of three centuries had produced a huge unwieldy text, invested with a high prestige, but very hard to grasp. The thought, extremely abstract and profound, was not easy to follow. Then there was the huge load of repetitions to cope with. And finally, since the work was a combination of a number of disjointed treatises composed at different times which reflected the interests of succeeding generations of Buddhists, one had to sort out the different arguments, which in a most disconcerting way jumped from one subject to another. The challenge was met in two ways; by new, shorter Sūtras of a philosophical character, and by condensed summaries of the large text.

a. Among the *shorter Sūtras,* the finest are the two earliest, both before A.D. 400, the "Heart Sūtra" in 25, or 14, and the "Diamond Sūtra" in 300 Lines. The "Heart Sūtra", one of the sublimest spiritual documents of mankind, is a restatement of the four Holy Truths, reinterpreted in the light of the dominant idea of emptiness. The "Diamond Sūtra", in spite of its rather chaotic arrangement of great renown in the East, does not pretend to give a systematic survey of the teachings of the Prajñāpāramitā. It confines itself to a few central topics, and appeals directly to a spiritual intuition which has left the conventions of logic far behind. This Sūtra is one of the most profound, sublime and influential of all Mahāyāna Scriptures. It develops the consequences of seeing all things as void of self. Although the term "empty" is not mentioned even once, the doctrine of emptiness is nevertheless established in an *ontological, psychological* and *logical* form.

Ontologically, the selflessness of everything means that there is no dharmas. Even the ultimates of Buddhist analysis do not exist in themselves, nor does the doctrine which contains that analysis. *Psychologically,* we are urged to "raise a thought" which is not fixed, or attached, anywhere, or which does not "stand about anywhere" (ch. 10, 4), or which is supported nowhere, does not lean on anything, does not depend on anything. *Logically,* the Sūtra teaches that each one of the chief Buddhist concepts is equivalent to its contradictory opposite. A special formula is here employed to express this thought, i.e. "A mass of merit, a mass of merit, Subhūti, as a no-mass has that been taught by the Tathāgata. In that sense has He spoken of it as a 'mass of merit' " (ch. 19, 8). The same, or a similar, formula is used for beings (14f, 17f, 21b), the marks of a Tathāgata (5, 13d, 20, 26a), the constituents (dharmas) of a Buddha (8; cf. 17e), the four Fruits (9a-d), Buddhafields (10b, 17g), personalities (10c), particles of dust (13c), true perception (14a), the perfection of patience (14e), the perception, or notion, of beings (14f), endowment with a body (17e), trends of thought (18b), the Tathāgata's perfect material body (20a), the demonstration of Dharma (21a), wholesome dharmas (23), seizing on a self (25), foolish common people (25), the Tathāgata (29), collections of atoms (30a), world systems (30b), seizing on material objects (30b), the view of self (31a), and the notion of dharma (31b).

Sūtras of the same type, probably of the fifth and the early sixth centuries, are the "Perfect Wisdom in 700 Lines" (before A.D. 500) and "Perfect Wisdom in 2,500 Lines" (before A.D. 550), also known as the "Questions of the Bodhisattva Suvikrāntavikrāmin"—and there is also a rather undistinguished "Perfect Wisdom in 50 Lines". The version in 700 Lines deserves to be better known. It tries to give a novel treatment to all the basic teachings of Perfect Wisdom. From the earlier works it differs by its stress on the startling, paradoxical, self-contradictory and nonsensical character of the doctrine of emptiness. Another new feature, observed also in the "Questions of Suvikrāntavikrāmin", is the endeavor to bring out the "hidden meaning" of the sayings of the Buddha. Here we have to see the influence of the Yogācārins.

b. Among the *Versified Summaries* the most outstanding is the *Abhisamaya-alaṅkāra,* "A Treatise explaining the Perfection of Wisdom, or Memorial Verses on the Reunion (with the Absolute)", a work of the fourth century, ascribed by tradition to "Maitreya, the Saviour" (Maitreyanātha). The work is a brilliant versified Table of Contents, which in 273 memorial verses and in nine chapters of unequal length, sums up the contents of the *Pañcaviṃśatisāhasrikā Sūtra,* brings out the logical sequence of its arguments, and at the same time assigns to each section of the text a place on the stages of spiritual progress which Buddhist tradition had mapped out, thus everywhere showing the practical way by which one can become a Buddha. Although a shade too schematic at times, the treatise is invaluable for anyone who wishes to study the Sūtra. In both India and Tibet it has dominated the exegesis of the Large Prajñāpāramitā for centuries to come, whereas in China it remained unknown. The divisions of the *Abhisamayālaṅkāra* were at some later time, probably in the fifth or sixth century, inserted into the text of one of the recensions of the version in 25,000 Lines (no. 2A).

Other Yogācārins also produced versified Summaries of teachings of the Prajñāpāramitā—Asaṅga in the form of a *Śāstra* to the *Vajracchedikā*, and Dignāga (ca. 450) in his *Piṇḍārtha,* which arranges the teaching under 32 subjects, and dwells chiefly on the 16 kinds of emptiness and the antidotes to the ten kinds of false imputation.

4. After A.D. 600, with the spread of *Tantric ideas,* came the desire to adapt the Prajñāpāramitā teachings to the new trend of thought and taste. The new concepts of Vajrayāna philosophy are, however, introduced only in the case of the *Adhyardhaśatikā* (no. 17; cf. 26). The Tantric phase of the Prajñāpāramitā is marked by three distinctive features:

An attempt is made to compress the message of the Prajñāpāramitā into the short, but effective, form of *spells.* In the *Aṣṭasāhasrikā* already the *prajñāpāramitā* had been described as a *vidyā,* and Indra had been advised to use it to defeat the heretics and Asuras (*A* iii pp. 55, 72–74). The *Hṛdaya* (ca. 350) had added a definite *mantra,* and Kumārajīva's translation of the *Mahāmāyūrī* (ca. 400) mentions, at the beginning, a *prajñāpāramitā-dhāraṇī*[1]. The great prestige of the Prajñāpāramitā suggested its use as a source of wonderworking power, and from the 6th century onwards the civil authorities used the Sūtra for penitential services and to work ritual magic,[2] i.e. to produce rain, remove pestilence, etc., and in the 7th century both Harṣavardhana and Hsüan-tsang employed the *Hṛdaya* for purposes of personal protection. "At first, when the Master of the Law was dwelling in Shuh (S.W. China, ca. 618), he saw a diseased man, whose body was covered with ulcers, his garments tattered and filthy. Pitying the man he took him to his convent, and gave him clothing and food; the sick man, moved by a feeling of deep gratitude, gave to the Master of the Law this little Sūtra book (i.e. the *Hṛdaya*), and on this account he was in the habit of reciting it continually. Arriving at the Sha-ho (Sandy Desert), as he passed through it, he encountered all sorts of demon shapes and strange goblins, which seemed to surround him behind and before. Although he invoked the name of Kwan-yin, he could not drive them all away; but when he recited this Sūtra, at the sound of the words they all disappeared in a moment. Whenever he was in danger, it was to this alone that he trusted for his safety and deliverance."[3] In the Tantric literature the prajñāpāramitā has been expressed through the

1 T 988 i, vol. 19, p. 482, col. 3, line 14 just mentions *prajñāpāramitādhāraṇī, Avalokiteśvaradhāraṇī,* and then proceeds to an enumeration of the heavens. The term is not found in the Sanskrit text of the *Mahāmāyūrī.*

2 M. W. de Visser, *Ancient Buddhism in Japan,* I (1928), II (1935).

3 Hwui Li, *The Life of Hiuen-tsiang,* trsl. S. Beal (1914), pp. 21–22.

medium of numerous *bīja-mantras* (usually *Dhīḥ* for the yellow, and *Paṃ* for the white forms), *mantras* and *dhāraṇis* (see p. 89).

By about A.D. 550 the production of Sūtras in the old style seems to have come to an end. Between A.D. 600 and 1200 a number of Tantric abbreviations of the Prajñāpāramitā were then composed, all very short. The most interesting is the "Perfection of Wisdom in a Few Words" (no. 18), which is designed as a counterpart to the "Heart Sūtra". While the *Hṛdaya* is addressed to the spiritual elite, this Sūtra appeals to the less endowed, to beings who have "but little capacity to act", who "have little merit", who are "dull and stupefied". Ten other Tantric Prajñāpāramitā texts are found in the Tibetan Kanjur (no. 17, 19–26, 32). One of these, "Perfect Wisdom in One Letter", deserves mention for its brevity, the one letter "A" being said to contain and represent the Perfection of Wisdom. Another text gives the 108 "names" or "epithets" of Perfect Wisdom, and another the 25 "Doors" by which it may be approached. A Tantric text which is in a class by itself is the "Perfection of Wisdom in 150 Lines" (no. 17), before A.D. 650, which, although called a Prajñāpāramitā, expounds the new ideas of Tantric Buddhism.

Finally, personified as a deity, the Prajñāpāramitā is inserted into the pantheon of *mythological figures,* becomes the object of a cult, and a number of Ritual Texts describe the methods by which her spiritual power can be evoked. The personification of the Prajñāpāramitā goes back to the fourth century. Statues of the Prajñāpāramitā are attested in India as early as 400 A.D. by Fa-hsien's account (cf. S. Beal, *Si-yu-ki,* I, p. xxxix). All the early representations of the Prajñāpāramitā are now lost. No surviving example seems to be older than ca. A.D. 800. The earliest literary documents are preserved only in Chinese. The oldest is the *Dhāraṇisamuccaya* (no. 33), translated before 625. A.D. In its section on the Bodhisattvas it gives a long chapter on the Prajñāpāramitā, which begins with a *prajñāpāramitāmahāhṛdaya-sūtra.* It then proceeds to make remarks on the figure of the prajñāpāramitā (see p. 88), its mudrās, mantras, maṇḍala and ritual. Here we have (p. 805b) our earliest description of a Tantric two-armed P. P. (1Cd). Our second document is a Commentary to the *Ninnō* (no. 34), which was translated into Chinese about 750 A.D. There the Prajñāpāramitā is said to sit cross-legged on a white lotus. The body is golden yellow, grave and majestic, with a precious necklace and a crown, from which silken bands hang down on both sides. Her left hand, near her heart, carries the book. Her right hand, near her breasts, makes the gesture of argumentation.[1] A statue

1 *Seppō-in.* Cf. de Visser, *Ancient Buddhism in Japan,* p. 173.–In this case, the ring finger touches the thumb. In others, it is the forefinger (e. g. a Buddha in Tun-

in the Lama temple in Peking is the one surviving work of art which corresponds to this description.[1]

In the *Mi-tsung* form of Tantrism the Prajñāpāramitā occurs twice in the *garbhadhātumaṇḍala.* The Prajñāpāramitā is, however, not among the 110 persons mentioned in the *Vairocana-sūtra,* nor among the 164 of Śubhākarasiṃha's commentary. It is found only in the *genzus* (see p. 27), which go back to about 800 A.D. In the commentary to the *Vairocana Sūtra* (T 1796; IV, 623a, 12–15) we read that the officiant, in order to contemplate Vairocana, "stood between the two *vidyārājā* (i.e. Acalanātha and Trailokyavijaya)". This place, where he identified himself with Vairocana, was called the "chamber of the Buddha". When the officiant left it, his place should be taken either by his *svādhidevatā,* or by the *prajñāpāramitāsūtra.* Originally, so the Japanese assume,[2] the Maṇḍala was a real structure on the ground, in which the officiant stood in person. When he left the Maṇḍala, the Sūtra was placed on the spot where he had stood. Later on, when the Maṇḍala became a painting, the place of the officiant was unoccupied, and the image of the Prajñāpāramitā was inserted in his stead. Several very early rituals (*vidhi, vidhāna*) relating to the *Vairocana Sūtra* already mention all the five persons of the Vidyādharavṛti. T 851, which is attributed to Śubhākarasiṃha himself (A.D. 716–735) describes the four *vidyārājā* as placed underneath Vairocana (p. 100 b-c) and, a bit further on (p. 106b 16–25), the *prajñāpāramitā vidyārājñi* as placed in front of Vairocana. She has six arms: the first left hand carried the *poṭhi* on the palm, the first right hand is in the *mudrā* of protection; the second left hand is raised to the navel, the second right hangs down in *varada*; the third right and left hands are in the "basic *mudrā*" (i.e. the dharmacakra?). She carries armor and headdress, and is called the "mother of the Buddha".

The *Mañjuśrīmūlakalpa* describes at least two maṇḍalas in which the Prajñāpāramitā occurs as a subordinate figure. One of them is a very elaborate maṇḍala of Śākyamuni in which she figures twice,[3] another has Mañjuśrī for its central figure.[4]

The developed Vajrayāna places the Prajñāpāramitā with Akṣobhya, Vajrapāṇi and others into the *dveṣa* family. The connection, which began very early (see p. 8), continued to be maintained by psychological links.

huang and Tibet), in others again the middle finger (some Chinese Buddhas).

1 1Cc Cf. E. Conze, *TYBS* 247–8, 264–5.

2 *Mikkyō Daijiten,* II (Kyoto, 1932), p. 1029. Toganoo Shōun, *Mandara no Kenkyū* (Koyasan, 1927), p. 144.

3 Il, p. 40, trsl. *BEFEO,* XXIII, 313–4.

4 xxviii, p. 318. M. Lalou. *Iconographie des étoffes peintes* (1930), pp. 64–5, Planche VII.

The Prajñāpāramitā would appeal to those who are dominated by hate, since aggressiveness aims at "smashing the offence", and a more thorough annihilation of the world than by the analysis of the Prajñāpāramitā is not easily conceived. How different from the attitude of those who are dominated by greed, and who find their outlet in *bhakti*![1] A number of *sādhanas* of the Prajñāpāramitā are preserved in the *Sādhanamālā* (see no. 35). All the yellow forms are documented in works of art, in Java, India, Nepal or Tibet (see *Oriental Art,* 1949 = *TYBS* 263sq.). The drawing of the white Prajñāpāramitā in the "Five hundred gods of Narthang", section *Rin-'byuṅ* 67a corresponds to *sādhana* 154. In addition to the visual appearance of the Prajñāpāramitā, each *sādhana* gives the germ syllable and the mantra which correspond to each form (see p. 89). The mantra for no. 153 is *oṃ dhīḥ śruti-smṛti-vijaye svāhā.* The mantra of the six-armed Mi-tsung form is *oṃ dhī śrī śruta vijaye svāhā,* and the *Kauśika* (no. 19) has under no. XIV, *oṃ dhī śrī śruti smṛti mati gati vijaye svāhā. Dhī is* usually explained as *dharmadhātu.* Otherwise *dhīḥ* is an abbreviation for *prajñā,* often used in verses for metrical reasons, e.g. *AK* i pp. 81, 291. It means "thought, conception", etc. Others say that (as *dī*) it means "splendor". *Śrī,* "splendor, beauty, prosperity, glory, majesty", is used of Lakṣmī. *Śruti* alludes to the threefold division of *prajñā* into *śrutamayi cintāmayi bhāvanāmayi,* i.e. the wisdom which consists in hearing, or learning from others, in reflection, and in meditational development. *Vijaya,* "victory" or "victorious" is personified in Shingon maṇḍalas (cf. Hôbôgirin s.v. *Bijaya*).

5. After A.D. 1200 there are no more works on Prajñāpāramitā in India. Buddhism itself disappeared from that country. But before that happened, the Prajñāpāramitā had experienced a resounding success under the Pāla dyansty, which between 750 and 1200 ruled over Magadha and Bengal, and patronized a Buddhism which combined Prajñāpāramitā and Tantra. Tāranātha (pp. 217–8) reports that Dharmapāla (A.D. 770–815) "made Haribhadra and Buddhajñānapāda his priests, filled all regions with Prajñāpāramitā and Guhyasamājatantra, and ordered that the scholars who knew Guhyasamāja and the Pāramitās should occupy the place of honor. Immediately on ascending the throne, he invited all those who explained the Prajñāpāramitā, but he chiefly honored the Ācārya Haribhadra. This king founded a total of 50 religious schools, of which 35 were devoted to the exposition of the Prajñāpāramitā. Beginning with this king, the Prajñāpāramitā spread more and more". The work of interpretation increased in

1 See E. Conze, *Hate, love and perfect wisdom,* The Mahabodhi Journal 62, 1954, pp. 3–8.—TYBS, 1967, pp. 185–190

momentum under the Pāla dynasty, and about 20 Pāla commentaries are still extant, mostly in Tibetan translations.

The Pāla commentators were, however, unaware of the long historical development of the Prajñāpāramitā literature which we have outlined so far. To them all the Sūtras were not only contemporary with each other, but also with the Buddha Śākyamuni himself. Their classification of the texts is therefore different from that adopted here. Dharmamitra, for instance, in AA-cy 5–2, according to Bu-ston (II 49) classified the extant Prajñāpāramitā texts as follows: Their subject-matter may be either (1) the essence of the doctrine, or (2) the process of intuition of the truth (*abhisamaya*). The first is expounded in the *Hṛdaya* etc., in discourses which demonstrate the absolute truth, i.e. the emptiness of all the elements of existence and the three doors to deliverance. The second is expounded in *Ś*, the most detailed of all; P, the most detailed of the discourses of the intermediate compass; *Ad*, the intermediate of the intermediate; *Da*, the most abridged of the intermediate; *A*, the most detailed of the abridged; and *Rgs*, the most abridged of the abridged. These all have the same subject matter, which is the teaching about the eight forms of the intuition of the Path. They differ only in being either more diffused or more abridged. Tsoṅ-kha-pa, in AA-cy 15, objects, however, that the *Saṃcaya*, as forming chapter 84 of *Ad*, cannot be regarded as an independent Sūtra.

Another Tibetan division is as follows:

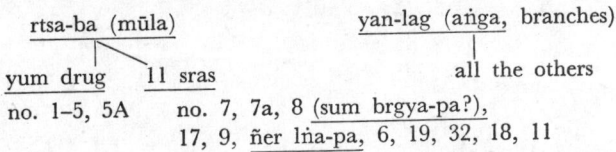

rtsa-ba (mūla) — yan-lag (aṅga, branches)

rtsa-ba (mūla):
- yum drug: no. 1–5, 5A
- 11 sras: no. 7, 7a, 8 (sum brgya-pa?), 17, 9, ñer lṅa-pa, 6, 19, 32, 18, 11

yan-lag (aṅga, branches):
- all the others

The teachers of this period regarded the Prajñāpāramitā as the Buddha's "second turning of the wheel of Dharma" (as already *A* ix 203 had done), the Hīnayāna being the first, and the Yogācāra the third. Bu-ston (I 48–51) remarks on this subject that the teaching of this period is that of emptiness, and aims at causing all those who had adhered to false views to abstain from them, and at directing them to the unique vehicle to salvation, to the doctrine of emptiness and of monism (*ekanaya*). The place where it was delivered was the Gṛdhrakūṭa mountain. "The duration of time was, according to Ṭho-lo 30 years, according to Chim-pa 27 years, according to Chag 31 years, and according to others 12 years." In the larger Sūtras, from 100,000 to 8,000 Lines, the enquirers are always the same i.e. Subhūti, Śāriputra, Ānanda, etc., and so is the prophecy granted to the Goddess of the Ganges. They were therefore delivered at the same time, although they were expounded differently, in conformity with the faculties of the listeners. According to whether that is weak, intermediate or keen, one is made to understand the doctrine in three ways, i.e. as detailed, intermediate or abridged. The Prajñāpāramitā in its full extent is not to be found among men, but only among superhuman beings.[1]

1 Bu-ston II 170: "The detailed Prajñāpāramitā containing 1,000,000,000 *ślokas* is preserved in the abode of the king of the Gandharvas, the intermediate (of the detailed), of 10,000,000 *ślokas,* in the realm of the king of the Gods, and the abridged (of the detailed), that is the *Śatasāhasrikā,* exists in its complete form in the region of the Nāgas."

B. THE DEVELOPMENTS OUTSIDE INDIA

1. In *China* translations of *Prajñāpāramitā* texts had a decisive influence on the development of Buddhist thought. Their basic ideas had a close affinity with the indigenous tradition of the neo-Taoist "Dark Learning", and in consequence they enjoyed a quite extraordinary vogue in the third and fourth centuries of our era. For that early period only a knowledge of the versions in 8,000 and 25,000 *ślokas* is attested with any degree of certainty.

The *Aṣṭasāhasrikā* was first made accessible in 179–180 A.D. by Lokakṣema (Chih-lu-chia-ch'an), an Indo-Scythian from Kushāṇa. The translation in 10 fasc. is called the *Tao-hsing Sūtra,* the "Sūtra of the Practice of the Way"[1] (T 224). Lokakṣema collaborated with Chu Shuo-fo, an Indian, and with several Chinese laymen (Z 35). His version is described as "crude and sometimes hardly intelligible" (Z 61). When we compare it with our present Sanskrit text we find many omissions, and much seems abbreviated (e.g. ix 205–7, xxviii 462 sq.), also there are a few transpositions (e.g. iv 98–99 comes before page 96; also the hymn at vii 170–1 is rearranged). On some occasions the text is nearer to that of the Large Prajñāpāramitā than to the *Aṣṭa* (e.g. at i 3, 17, 30), and on others there are great differences which cannot always be explained by Lokakṣema's incomprehension (e.g. at i 26–7, 29, 32, viii 185, 192, viii 199–ix 200, 202–3). About half a century later, ca. 225, Chih Ch'ien, an Indo-Scythian who went from Lo-yang to Chien-yeh, made another translation of *A* (T 225; B 289; cf. 117–9). This is more polished than Lokakṣema's, but rather free, and guided by the desire "to present the doctrine to the literate public in a more palatable form". The first chapter contains many anonymous commentarial additions (Z 54) and probably belongs to a later period[2]. Although it was a "highly polished and very 'Chinese' version", it lost its influence soon after "the first half of the third century" (Z 65). In 382, Dharmapriya, a Hindu *śramaṇa,* together with Chu Fo-nien, translated an extract, only 13 chapters of *A* (T 226; B 156, Z 202, 204, 394).

The *Pañcaviṃśatisāhasrikā* was first translated in 286 by Dharmarakṣa, an Indo-Scythian from Tun-huang, from an Ms brought from Khotan. Dharmarakṣa worked together with Gītamitra. Only a part of his version,

1 B 39–40 —The earliest catalogues also mention another Han version of *A* (or of part of it), in one *chüan,* ascribed to Chu Shuo-fo or to Lokakṣema, Z 332.
2 *A* was translated a century later by Wei Shih-tu (B 134). This translation is lost. But see Z 78. – cf. Z 53 for what might be another lost translation of *A.*

up to chapter 27, has come down to us (T 222; cf. B 86, Z 65–70, 197). Another translation of *P* followed in 291, when the Khotanese Mokṣala translated at Ts'ang-yüan, together with the sinicised *upāsaka* Chu Shu-lan, a birch bark text of *P,* brought from Khotan (T 221). It is called "The Scripture of the Emission of Rays", in view of the first chapter of *P* which describes the miracles performed by the Buddha as a prelude to the preaching of the Sūtra. This work "perhaps more than any other scripture would come to play a dominant role in the formation of Chinese Buddhist thought" (Z 63). All the "indigenous schools of speculative thought" in the 4th century "were primarily based upon different interpretations of the older versions of the *Prajñāpāramitā*", notably that of Mokṣala and Lokakṣema Z 65).[1] In 304 the text was once more revised, and "the redactors divided the text into twenty *chüan* and added section headings" (Z 64).

Any translations of other texts that may have been made in this period are now lost, and we cannot be sure that they ever existed. Yen Fo-t'iao of Southern China is credited with a translation of the version in 500 Lines, under the title *Ta-pan-jo-na-chia-shih-li-fên* (made under the Han according to *Chêng-yüan hsin-ting shih-chiao mu-lu* II, T 2157, p. 780 a-b. And Dharmarakṣa may have, between 307 and 313, translated the *Ninnō* (B 96, 192).

A new development starts with Kumārajīva, who was born in A.D. 344 as a native of Kuchā, and came to China in 385, where from 401 to 413 he worked at Ch'ang-an. He translated the versions in 25,000 and 8,000 Lines (T 223 and 227), the "Diamond Sūtra" (T 235), Nāgārjuna's large commentary to the version in 25,000 Lines (T 1509), and perhaps (see Hikata p. xxiii) the *Ninnō* (T 245, which is said to be quite similar to that of Dharmarakṣa (Bagchi 193)). His pupils translated the *Hṛdaya* (T 250). The *Hṛdaya* was first attributed to Kumārajīva in the *K'ai-yüan-shih-chiao-lu* in 730. The table in *JAs* 1931, p. 155 reveals a tendency to multiply Kumārajīva's works as time went on.

Between 420 and 479 Shih Hsiang-kung, a Chinese monk, produced the second translation of the *Pañcaśatikā* (T 234; Bagchi 404). Shortly after 500 the *Saptaśatikā* was twice translated, first by Mandrasena (T 232) and then by Saṅghabhara (T 233), both from Fu-nan in Cambodia. Mandrasena worked for a time with Saṅghabhara in Nanking, then the capital of Liang. He knew little Chinese, and his translation is obscure (Bagchi 414–7). A little later, in 509, Bodhiruci, of Northern India, translated the "Diamond Sūtra" for the second time (T 236), as well as some of its commentaries (T 1511 and 1512, ascribed to Vasubandhu). A lost trans-

1 L. Hurvitz, "Chih Tun's Notions of Prajñā," *JAOS* 88, 1968, pp. 243–261.

lation of a *Ninnō* i belongs to the same century, although the information about it seems to be conflicting. It was done either by Chên-ti in the Chiang-hsi province (ca. 535–546), or it is ascribed to Chên-ti (Paramārtha) who wrote it in 554 (Bagchi 193, 422–3). Paramārtha's *Jên-wang pan-jo-shu,* (6 fasc.) of 549 (Bagchi 424), is of course, a different, though related, work. In 565 Upaśūnya from Central India translates the Questions of the Deva-king Pravara (T 231; Bagchi 266, 431). About the same time, in 562, Paramārtha of Ujjayinī in West India, produced the third translation of the "Diamond Sūtra" (T 237; Bagchi 425), while about 600 Dharmagupta from South India, who worked between 591 and 619 in China, produces the fourth (T 238; Bagchi 467), a very literal one, and also translates one commentary to it (T 1510).

Hsüan-tsang, who returned from India in 645, worked between 659 and 663 on his translation of the "Great Prajñāpāramitā" (T 220; vol. V, 1–1074; VI, 1–1073; VII, 1–1110), in 600 fascicles. It consists of the "16 meetings in 4 places", i.e. of 16 sermons held respectively on Vulture Peak (1–6, 15), in Anāthapiṇḍada's Park at Śrāvastī (7–9, 11–14), in the Abode of the Paranirmitavaśavartin Gods (10), and at the Snowy Heron Pond in the Bamboo Park near Rājagṛha (16; the Sanskrit gives: *Rājagṛhe... Veṇuvane Kalandakanivāpe*). This translation comprises the following texts[1]:

1.	no. 1	(Ś)	400 fasc.	
2.	no. 2	(P)	f. 401–478	
3.	no. 3	(Ad)	f. 479–537	The *Fa-yüan chu-lin* (T 2122), ch. 100, says that the original was in 18,000 verses.
4.	no. 5	(A)	f. 538–555	Corresponds closely to Sanskrit *A,* though less than the Sung translation (T 228).
5.	no. 5	(A)	f. 556–565	The *Fa-yüan chu-lin,* ch. 100, says that the original was in 4,000 verses. A great deal of it, though not all, corresponds to part 4. It represents a primitive state of the text, comparable to the one translated in the 2nd century A.D.
6.	no. 12a		f. 566–573	
7.	no. 7	(Sa)	f. 574–575	
8.	no. 12	(Na)	f. 576	
9.	no. 8	(V)	f. 577. A.D. 648	
10.	no. 17	(150)	f. 578	

1 For the first five items see also Yamada's Table (*Bongo Butten no Shobunken,* 1959) and Hikata's Table II.

11.–15. no. 14 f. 579–592
16. no. 6 (Su) f. 593–600.

In addition, Hsüan-tsang in 649 translated the *Hṛdaya* (T 251). His translation is practically identical with that of Kumārajīva. It uses (at no. 7) a different character for 'skandha', omits the two additions which Kumārajīva had inserted after no. 9 and no. 21, and omits the words *mahāmantro* at no. 52 where also 5 Nepalese manuscripts and the Tibetan translations have only *mantro*. (The numbers refer to *JRAS* 1948, pp. 34–7 = *TYBS* 149–153).

Divākara, a monk from Central India, greatly interested in magic, translated no. 8-cy 3 in 683. Bodhiruci, from Southern India, in 693, and Śikṣānanda from Khotan, who lived in China between 695–705, and 708–10, translated the *Hṛdaya*. Both translations are now lost, and we know of them only through a Catalogue (T 2154 of A.D. 730). Then I-ching, the famous Chinese traveller, in 703 translates the *Vajracchedikā* for the fifth and last time (T 239), as well as 8 cy-1, and 1–1 and 1–1–3 in 711. In 693 Bodhiruci of South India and about 725 Vajrabodhi, who had studied at Nālandā, made the second and third translation of the *Adhyardhaśatikā* (T 240 and 241). Then in 741 Dharmacandra (?) from East India for the first time translates the long text of the *Hṛdaya* (T 252). The body of the Sūtra here agrees literally with Kumārajīva's translation.

Amoghavajra, born in Ceylon, came to China, with Vajrabodhi, his teacher, in 724, and his work of translating extended from 746 to 771. He translated the *Adhyardhaśatikā* (T 243), and the *Ninnō* (T 246), adding 36 *dhāraṇis* at the end of the 7th chapter. The emperor T'ai-tsung wrote in 765 a preface to the latter work, in which he says that he ordered Amoghavajra to "complete" this text (Matsumoto p. 21). Amoghavajra also translated a number of texts interpreting the *Ninnō* (no. 27–8, 33–4).

About 790 Prajñā, of Kafiristan, who had studied in Kashmir and Nālandā, translates the *Hṛdaya* once more (T 253). His translation agrees with that of Kumārajīva after line 9. Between 800 and 1000 there was a long pause in the work of translation, which was only then resumed by a group of translators. There was just one translation of the *Hṛdaya*, i.e. that of Prajñācakra, in 861 (from Central Asia, T 254).

The version in 150 Lines was once again translated, in a very enlarged form (T 244), by Dharmadeva (?), Fa-t'ien, a monk from Nālandā, who came to China in 973. Devaśānti (?), T'ien-hsi-tsai, also known as Dharmabhadra (Fa-hsien), from Kashmir, arrived in China in 980 and died in 1001. He translated for the first time the *Ratnaguṇasaṃcayagāthā* (T 229) in 991, the *Svalpākṣarā* (T 258) in 982, and two small Tantric texts (no. 38 and 39). Dānapāla (?) (Shih-hu), from Oḍḍiyāna, started work in China in 982. He translated three Sūtras once again, i.e. the *Aṣṭasāhasrikā* as *Daśasāhasrikā-prajñāpāramitā* (T 228), the *Adhyardhaśatikā* (T 242) and the *Hṛdaya* (T 257). Other texts he translated for the first time, i.e. the *Aṣṭaśatikā* (T 230), *Nitārtha, Ardhaśatikā, Kauśikā* (T 247–249) and no. 40, as well as cy 5 and 5–1 to no. 5. Dharmarakṣa (Fa-hu) from Western India came to China in 1004 and worked there until 1054. He translated 5-cy 6 together with Wei-ching, a Chinese *śrāmaṇa,* who began work about 981, and to whom we also owe no. 15 (T 260).

The writing of commentaries began about 580, and some information about the commentators can be found in Index 4.

No iconographical data are available for China outside the sphere of Lamaist influence. Statues of the Prajñāpāramitā have been found only in Lama temples, for instance in the one of 1653 in Peking (cf. W. E. Clark, *Two Lamaist Pantheons,* 1937, 4A 17 and 6 A 61) and in the 18th century Yung-ho-kung in Hall X (Lessing I, 1942, p. 75). No indigenous Chinese representations of the Prajñāpāramitā, either Mi-tsung or Ch'an, seem to be extant.

2. Most of our Prajñāpāramitā manuscripts come from *Nepal,* where they continued to be copied out for nine centuries with steadily diminishing accuracy. The *Aṣṭasāhasrikā* was regarded as one of the "nine great dharmas". In iconography we must mention the trinities composed of the Buddha, the four-armed Prajñāpāramitā and the four-armed Avalokiteśvara—in *namaskāraḥ* and with rosary and lotus, or book—representing Buddha, Dharma and Saṃgha respectively, which were very popular in Nepal, and are often found in temples and on house altars (see E. Conze, *OA,* III, pp. 106–7). The Prajñāpāramitā is here considered as the quintessence of the doctrine, just as the compassionate activity of Avalokiteśvara is the model for the duties of the monastic community.

The same trinity occurs frequently in *Khmer* sculpture and inscriptions of the 10th and 11th centuries, on many votive tablets (Brah Bimb) of the same period, in *Siam,* and sometimes perhaps in Tibet. The votive tablets show the Buddha in meditation on a Nāga, on his right a four-armed Avalokiteśvara, and on his left a two-armed Prajñāpāramitā. The four-faced monolithic *caityas* of *Cambodia* often show Prajñāpāramitā together with Lokeśvara. Sometimes the Buddha on a Nāga is added as a third, and Vajrapāṇi, or Hayagrīva, as a fourth (E. Conze, *OA,* III, p. 107). Inscriptions between 950 and 1000 likewise link the Prajñādevī, or Divyadevī, with

Lokeśvara, and also in some cases with Vajrapāṇi and the Buddha. In Cambodia Buddhist theology was strongly influenced by Śivaism. Lokeśvara corresponded to Maheśvara, just as the Prajñādevī to the Śivaite devī. At the end of the 12th century, King Jayavarman VII consecrated statues of his mother as prajñāpāramitā, mother of the Buddhas.

3. In *Tibet* the ideas of the Prajñāpāramitā were first introduced by Śāntarakṣita and Kamalaśīla about A.D. 750. They played a great part in the controversies which took place about 794 between Kamalaśīla and the Chinese Ch'an monk, the Hva-śaṅ Mahāyāna, and both sides are fond of quoting the Prajñāpāramitā, either the large text or the *Vajracchedikā*, in support of their views.[1] The Ch'an followers claimed to expound nothing but the "true principles of wisdom",[2] and to achieve a state of "thoughtlessness in perfect wisdom",[3] quite in the spirit of the 8th century Ch'an, which had given the subtitle of *Mahāprajñāpāramitāsūtra* to Hui-nêng's *Platform Sūtra* (T 2007), and which had placed the *Vajracchedikā* above all other Sūtras (Shen-hui, in Gernet pp. 99–105). It is curious to note that the Prajñāpāramitā doctrine which had in India led by natural stages to the scholasticism of the *Abhisamayālaṅkāra,* should on Chinese soil have brought forth the diametrically opposite quietism of the followers of the "sudden enlightenment".

Translations of the texts and commentaries were made between 790 and 840, and in them Ye-śes-sde took a prominent part. About 800 we have the first translation of the *AA*, by sKa-pa dPal-brtsegs, or dPal-brtsegs Rakshita of the sKabs clan, who lived under the kings Khri-sroṅ lde-btsan (755–797), Sad-na-legs (798–817) and Ral-pa-can (817–836). He was one of the redactors of the *'Phaṅ-thaṅ-ma* and the *lDan-dkar-ma* catalogue.[4]

After the eclipse of 840 to 1000, the ideas were reintroduced by such men as Dīpaṅkarasrījñāna (Atīśa)[5], Abhayākaragupta, etc. Further translations were executed between 1000 and 1150. The *Abhisamayālaṅkāra* maintained its importance for the teaching of Prajñāpāramitā. It was translated a second time by Rṅog blo-ldan śes-rab (1059–1109), who also wrote a commentary to it (AA-cy 12). For other commentaries see pages 112–120, which give some slight idea at least of the "enormous literature of manuals for the study of this subject in monastic schools" of which Obermiller (p. IX) speaks.

1 Cf. P. Demiéville, *Le Concile de Lhasa,* I (1952).
2 Ibid., p. 111.
3 p. 100; cf. also p. 102 n., 162 n. 3, 335.
4 Cf. *Blue Annals,* I, 102, 331, 344. M. Lalou, *JAs,* 1953, pp. 313sq.
5 His instructors in Prajñāpāramitā on p. 243 of *Blue Annals.*

The 13th century saw the final codification of the *Kanjur*. The Prajñāpāramitā Sūtras comprise in the Peking edition 30 texts in 24 volumes, in the Narthang and Derge editions 23 texts in 21 volumes. In the Kanjur of Lhasa, Derge and Peking, the Berlin Ms of the Kanjur and the Mongolian Kanjur (Ligeti vol. 47, no. 779–791), thirteen texts are added at the end of *Śer-phyin,* which are to be found in the last volume of *mdo* in the edition of Narthang, and in the British Museum Kanjur Ms. They are sometimes said to be translated from the Pali, but they differ too much from the Pali text, and on closer investigation they turn out to represent Hīnayāna Sūtras from the Canon of the Sarvāstivādins and other Hīnayāna sects in contact with Tibet. They were jointly translated by Ānandaśrī and Ñi-ma rgyal-mtshan dpal bzaṅ-po, and a number of them have been translated into French by L. Feer in his *Fragments extraits du Kandjour* (1883). They are listed in To 31–43 (=0 747), and they are: 1. *Dharmacakrapravartanasūtra,* fol. 183b–187a (Feer 111–123); 2. *Jātaka-nidāna,* fol. 187a–264b; 3. *Āṭānāṭiya-sūtra,* f. 264b–274b; 4. *Mahāsamaya-sūtra,* f. 275a–278b; 5. *Maitri-sūtra,* f. 278b–286a; 6. *Maitrī-bhāvanā-sūtra,* f. 286a–287a (Feer 221–3); 7. *Pañca-śikṣyānuśaṃsā-sūtra,* f. 287a–292b (Feer 230–243); 8. *Giri-Ānanda-sūtra,* f. 293a–295b (Feer 145–50); 9. *Nandopananda-nāgarāja-damana-sūtra,* f. 295b–298a (Feer 415–419); 10. *Mahākāśyapa-sūtra,* f. 298a–299a (Feer 150–2); 11. *Sūrya-sūtra,* f. 299b–300a; 12. *Candra-sūtra,* f. 300-ab (Feer 411–13), and 13. *Mahāmaṅgala-sūtra,* f. 300b–301b (Feer 224–227).

Bu-ston's (1290–1364) "History of Buddhism" (*Chos-'byuṅ,* trsl. by E. Obermiller, 2 vols, 1931–2) contains a great wealth of information about the history of the Prajñāpāramitā. One would also have to compare the genealogies which Bu-ston gives in volume MA of his "Collected Works", i.e. of the transmission of *AA* (9B–10A, no. 34) and of the *Śatasāhasrikā* (10B, no. 36). A great deal of information about the Prajñāpāramitā is also contained in the "Blue Annals" (*Deb-ther sṅon-po*) of 'Gos lo-tsā-ba gshon-nu-dpal (1476–8) (trsl. G. Roerich, 1949, 1953).

He mentions (pp. 69–70, 206–7, 209, 249, 265, 1107) several translations made in the 11th and 12th centuries, chiefly of works connected with the *AA* and also numerous commentaries (pp. 94, 330–1,336) up to the 15th century. The Prajñāpāramitā was greatly esteemed, copied out, studied, and valued as a precious gift and for the magical powers believed to be inherent in it. The great importance attached to the Prajñāpāramitā and its place in the scheme of studies is shown by the advice 'Brog-mi took to India around 1010, "Listen to the Vinaya, for it is the Basis of the Doctrine. Listen to the Prajñāpāramitā, for it is the Essence of the Doctrine. Listen to the Vajrayāna, for it is the Spirit of the Doctrine"

(p. 206). Don-grub rin-chen, Tsoṅ-kha-pa's teacher, had given him the following instruction: "You will first study earnestly the *Abhisamayālaṅkāra* which is the ornament of the three "Mothers" (the large, middle and abridged versions of the Prajñāpāramitā). If you become learned in it, you will be able to master all the Scriptures" (p. 1074).

Three lines of transmission and interpretation of the Prajñāpāramitā should be distinguished (pp. 330–1):

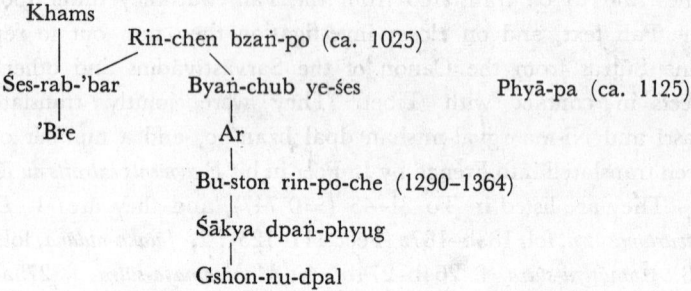

Khams
Rin-chen bzaṅ-po (ca. 1025)
Śes-rab-'bar — Byaṅ-chub ye-śes — Phyā-pa (ca. 1125)
'Bre — Ar
Bu-ston rin-po-che (1290–1364)
Śākya dpaṅ-phyug
Gshon-nu-dpal

Much attention was naturally paid to the relations between Prajñāpāramitā and Tantra, and attempts were made to combine the practices of the two (cf. pp. 724–5 on the bKa'-brgyud-pa discussions about Mahāmudrā and Prajñāpāramitā; cf. also pp. 910, 913–4, 921–2, 924, 938, 977–9). Of great interest is the account of the "*Precepts of the Prajñāpāramitā*", a term frequently used to indicate the *Shi-byed* system and the *gCod* rites.

The first is called *sDug-bsṅal Shi-byed* for the following reason: "Most of the secret precepts and instructions which reached Tibet helped to protect disciples from sinful actions and purified the defilements of their minds. This doctrine brings a speedy alleviation of the sufferings of those who, by the influence of their former lives, are afflicted in body, tormented by diseases, poverty-stricken, tormented by devils, and enables them to practise Yoga" (p. 986). "It was also so named after the Mantra which alleviates all sufferings" uttered by the Buddha in the *Prajñāpāramitāhṛdaya*. (*sDug-bsṅal thams-cad rab-tu shi-bar byed-pa'i sṅags, sarvaduḥkha-praśamanamantraḥ*). (More information about this pp. 896–911.)

The system called "The Prajñāpāramitā cutting (the influence of) the demons" (*pha-rol-tu phyin-pa bDud-kyi gCod-yul*) seems to go back to Maitrī-pa. It is based on a verse of the *Ratnaguṇasaṃcayagāthā* (XXVII 3): "A Bodhisattva endowed with the powers of learning (*mkhas stobs ldan*; *balavān vidu*) cannot be overcome by the four Māras, on account of four reasons: 1) because he abides in the Void, 2) because he has not abandoned living beings, 3) because he acts as he speaks, 4) and because he is sustained by the Sugata's blessing."

The followers of the *gCod-yul* system observe the above four religious injunctions as the foundation of their religious training (p. 981). (1) To abide in the Void means first to abandon the view which maintains the substantiality of the aggregates which constitute the individual stream or continuity, and secondly the non-acceptance of the notion of the reality and substantiality of other living beings. (2) "The non-abandoning of living beings means a practice characterised by the great compassion, and abstention from doing harm to demons (*mi ma-yin*) and others, by which one becomes free from any sort of illwill towards living beings, and makes them enter on the path to enlightenment." (3) To observe the moral rule of the Bodhisattvas of acting as one speaks "means to abstain from harsh actions (*tho-co ma yin*), and to abstain from breaking the vows which were taken at the time of the manifestation of the Mental Creative Effort towards Enlightenment". (4) To strive for the blessing of the Sugata means to take one's refuge with the Teacher and the spiritual Lineage, and to offer prayers to them.

4. In *Japan,* the texts were used on a large scale ceremoniously, to give peace to the empire, and to avert calamities. De Visser (*Ancient Buddhism in Japan*) has collected a great many details on the history of these ceremonies. The *Dai-hannyà-kyō* had its greatest vogue in the 9th century. The "reading" of the large Prajñāpāramitā by revolving the rolls on which it is written is still a feature of Zen monasteries. Several commentaries to the *Ninnō* were composed between 700 and 1700 (no. 13 cy. 5–15). Iconographically important are the *genzu* (current images) (see p. 15) of the *Mahāvairocana Sūtra* which developed in the Shingon sect. The oldest representation of the *garbhadhātumaṇḍala* is that of the Takao-san near Kyōto, which is said to have been executed by Kūkai between 824 and 833. This painting, without colours, in gold and silver on purple silk, has now become rather indistinct. Generally, a copy made by Kenni in 1034 is the model for reproductions. In 1869 wood cuts were made after this copy, which are preserved in the Ninnaji of Kyōto. They are reproduced in *Taishō Issaikyō, Zuzō,* vol. I, p. 700 and 725. In Japan other paintings of this maṇḍala exist, some in colours, which are said to go back to the Japanese pilgrims who visited China in the 9th century.

Most of these have 444 figures. The Prajñāpāramitā occurs: 1) in the centre of the *Vidyādhara-vṛti,* flanked by four angry *vidyārājās,* and 2) among the ten *pāramitās* of the *Ākāśagarbha-vṛti.* The actual representation of these two prajñāpāramitās varies greatly. Of the first we have at least two descriptions. The one is by Toganoo Shōun (in *Mandara no kenkyū,* p. 145), to which corresponds the Prajñāpāramitā from the lid of the Sūtra box from Nanatsudera, Nagoya (1175), with two Bodhisattvas, two Disciples, and the 16 Guardians, as well as the illustration of the *Taishō Issaikyō* (see E. Conze, *Oriental Art,* II, 1949, pp. 49–50). A different one is given by Shunnyū (890–927) in *Taizōkai-shichishū* (in *Dainihon Bukkyōzensho,* XLIV, p. 230). Of the second we have at least three differing descriptions, one in the *Taizōkai-shichishū* (quoted *Dnbz,* XLIV, p. 266), the second in T 853, a 9th century ritual for T 848 by a Chinese, and a third one is adduced from other sources in *Mikkyō Daijiten,* p. 1839.

A *Ninnōkyō Mandara,* in colours on silk, was painted in the early part of the 12th century, traditionally by Jōkai (1075–1149), who copied the Chinese originals brought home by Kōbō Daishi (in A.D. 806; cf. *Kokkwa* no. 363 iii). It is preserved in the Daigoji at Kyōto. There are also drawings of deities of the *Ninnōkyō,* after Kōbō Daishi's designs (*Kokkwa* no. 363 iv and v).

The coming of European influence has led to editions of Sanskrit texts by Wogihara, Matsumoto, Masuda, Toganoo and others, in the thirties of the 20th century. In 1932 Tokumyō Matsumoto published, in German, a survey of the Prajñāpāramitā literature after Chinese sources. In addition we have two important essays written by D.T. Suzuki, one dealing with the "significance of the Hṛdaya in Zen Buddhism" (*Essays in Zen Buddhism,* III, 1934, pp. 187–206), and another with the "philosophy and religion of the Prajñāpāramitā" (*ibid.,* pp. 207–288). The last 40 years have seen about one hundred short articles on problems connected with the literature on P. P., some in English, but most in Japanese. In 1944 K. Kajiyoshi's monograph of more than 1,000 pages on the early P. P. Sūtras concluded that the original *Prajñāpāramitā* is roughly identical with the first chapter of *A,* as extant in Lokakṣema's translation of A. D. 179. His suggestion is much nearer the mark than the later ones of M. Suzuki and R. Hikata (*FBS* p. 170). His only difficulty is that, alas, by 1944 Obermiller's *Ratnaguṇa* had not yet travelled from Leningrad to Japan. Since Kajiyoshi only knew its Chinese translation of A. D. 991 it was natural that, unaware of its archaic diction, he mistook it for a late *śāstra.* In his fine edition of no. 6 R. Hikata in 1958 included a valuable essay on the P. P. literature (see *FBS* pp. 169–171). Recently interest has returned to the *Abhisamayālaṅkāra,* and we may mention H. Amano's well-produced "Study on the Abhisamaya-alaṃkāra-kārikā-śāstra-vṛtti" (1975) as a first step towards the much-needed edition and translation of Haribhadra's *Sphuṭārtha* (see p. 113). For the rest there is a vast expository literature on Zen, which incidentally cannot fail to come to grips with some aspects of P. P. thought.

5. For *Europe,* the Sanskrit Prajñāpāramitā was first discovered by B.H. Hodgson in Nepal between 1830 and 1840. The manuscripts arrived in 1837 in Paris. There is in the Bodleian an earlier attempt by a Spaniard to translate parts of the Chinese Prajñāpāramitā, but he desisted fairly soon. In 1837 I.J. Schmidt published the first Tibetan version of a Prajñāpāramitā, i.e. the "Diamond Sūtra". Isaak Jacob Schmidt (1779–1847), of whom we have a biography by F. Babinger (*Festschrift F. Hirth,* Berlin 1920, *O.Z.* vol. 8, pp. 7–21), was born in Amsterdam, went in 1800 to Russia, and was all his life a faithful member of the Herrnhuter Brüdergemeinde. He translated the New Testament into Mongol and Kalmuk. In 1828 he published a booklet called "Über die Verwandtschaft der gnostisch-theosophischen Lehren mit den Religionssystemen des Orients, vorzüglich dem Buddhismus". In the *Mémoires* of the Academy of St. Petersburg further articles of his appeared on Buddhism in 1834 and 1835. E. Burnouf made a translation of the first 28 chapters of the *Aṣṭa,* which is preserved in manuscript in the Bibliothèque Nationale, and in 1844 he published in his *Introduction à l'histoire du Buddhisme Indien* the first chapter of his translation as a "fragment bizarre".

When we consider the work done during the last century by Europeans, or under the influence of European philological methods, we find that during the first 60 years attention was almost entirely confined to the Diamond Sūtra and *Hṛdaya.* The larger Prajñāpāramitās have only very gradually appeared on the horizon, first through editions made by Hindus (i.e. by Mitra in 1888, Ghosha from 1888 to 1913, and N. Dutt in 1934), then by a partial German translation by Walleser (1914), and then, after 1930, the interest was stimulated by publications about the *Abhisamayālaṅkāra.* After 1940 the bulk of the work has been done by two men, Edward Conze and Etienne Lamotte. In an appendix, on pp. 127 to 137, Dr. Akira Yuyama has listed Prof. Conze's 62 contributions to P. P. studies. From his fastness in Louvain Prof. Lamotte, his exact contemporary from across the German border, has done no less,—not only by his superb annotated rendering of the *Ta-chih-tu-lun,* but also by introducing new standards of precision and comprehension into the treatment of kindred texts such as the *Vimalakīrtinirdeśa* (1962). These two were not alone, of course, and other scholars have made valuable contributions. Apart from G. Tucci, C. Pensa, J. W. de Jong, L. Schmithausen, L. Lancaster, etc. there are the numerous publications about the Mādhyamikas who restated P. P. thought in more philosophical terms. Even the non-academic public has increasingly responded by buying this literature, motivated partly by the vogue of Zen which D. T. Suzuki initiated 40 years ago, and partly by the impasse which Western thinking has reached in recent years.

ANNOTATED BIBLIOGRAPHY

A. ORDINARY PRAJÑĀPĀRAMITĀ SŪTRAS

AA. The large Sūtra

1. THE PERFECTION OF WISDOM IN 100,000 LINES.

S: *Śatasāhasrikā prajñāpāramitā-sūtra.*

S: Manuscripts in Calcutta, Cambridge, New Delhi, Paris, and Tokyo.

s: ed. P. Ghosha, *Bibl Ind.*, I, 146–148 (1902–1913). ch. 1–12.

Ch: T 220, 1–400. Hsüan-tsang, A.D. 659–663.

S. Lévi, Un fragment chinois de la S. P. In: A. F. R. Hoernle, *Manuscript Remains*, I, 1916, 390–395.

Ti: *Śes-rab-kyi pha-rol-tu phyin-pa stoṅ-phrag brgya-pa.* 300 bampos. 0 740. -To 8. —Cf. also To 5574 (11). 5275 (122).

ti: *Sher-phyin*, ed. P. Ghosha, 3 vols, *Bibl. Ind.* (Calcutta, 1888, 1890, 1891). pp. 511, 252, 565. Up to *bampo* 78=Skr. vol. II p. 39, 14=middle of ch. 12. —Fragments IOSC no. 107–109.

M. Lalou, Les manuscrits tibétains des grandes Prajñāpāramitās trouvés à Touen-houang, *Silver Jubilee Volume of the Zinbun-Kagaku-Kenkyūsho Kyōto University*, 1954, pp. 257–261. —Les plus anciens rouleaux tibétains trouvées à Touen-houang, *Rocznik Orientalistyczny* xxi, 1957, pp. 149–152. —Manuscrits tibétains de la Ś.P. cachés à Touen-houang, *JAs* 252, 1964, pp. 479–486. —*Inventaire des manuscrits tibétains de Touen-houang conservés à la Bibliothèque Nationale* (*Fonds Pelliot Tibétain*), vol. III, 1961, xix, 220 pp.

Mo: Ligeti no. 746–757. vol. 26–37. —trsl. Siregetü güüsi chorji (ca. 1600).

e: SS no. 11, 44–5, 49, 55, 66, 85, 91, 96, 105, 125, 127.

For ch. IX, pp. 1450–1453, cf. S. Lévi, *Ysa* (1929), in *Mémorial Sylvain Lévi* 1937, pp. 355–363. —Sten Konow, "The Arapacana Alphabet and the Sakas", *Acta Orientalia*, XII (1934), pp. 13–24. —F. W. Thomas, "A Kharoshṭhi document and the Arapacana alphabet",

Miscellanea Academica Berolinensia, 1950, pp. 194–207.

This Sūtra falls into three somewhat unequal parts:

Part I is an expansion of chapter I of the *Aṣṭa.* It covers chapters 1 to 13, or 638 of the Cambridge Mss Add 1633 and 1630. There is much expansion, and also seven new items are added, i.e. 1. Cosmic miracles, which precede the teaching (i 3–55, 17). 2. The aims and desires of a Bodhisattva which are fulfilled by the practice of perfect wisdom (i 55, 17–118, 7). 3. Preliminary Instructions to a Bodhisattva (i 118, 27–308, 19). 4. An interlude (i 308, 22–323). 5. A classified list of dharmas (vii 1257, 15–1263, 8. 6. Lists enumerating 20 kinds of emptiness, 112 concentrations, 17 practices, 43 *dhāraṇi*-doors, and 10 stages (vii 1407–1473, 18). 7. An explanation of the difference between worldly and supramundane perfections (xiii f. 137b–139b).

Part II follows *A* ch. ii to xxviii fairly closely, usually expanding the text, but often, especially in the later parts, abbreviating it. It covers chapters 14 to 51, or 1,021 leaves of the Cambridge Mss Add 1630, 1631, 1632. In this part almost no new matter is added to the *Aṣṭa* except quite at the beginning. Quantitatively the expansion, which was greatest in the first part, in some sections up to 80 times the length of the *Aṣṭa,* diminishes as we get to the end of *A,* particularly in chapters 40 to 51, which correspond to *A* ch. 18–28. Chapter 26 of *Ś* occupies an anomalous position. It is abnormally long, but contains only a part of ch. 8 of *A,* the bulk of it consisting merely of repetitions.

Part III is an independent treatise. It can be said to begin with chapter 52 of *Ś,* and covers 413 leaves. This part is throughout concerned with the obvious conflict that exists between an ontology which proclaims the emptiness of everything, and the practical needs of the struggle for enlightenment. It also gives a number of useful definitions, e.g. of the three kinds of omniscience, of the Buddha, of enlightenment, of perfect wisdom, of *prapañca,* of the major and minor marks of a Buddha's body, and so on. Part III does not begin abruptly. One might rather say that the text of *A* slowly peters out. The turning point is a long discourse on the six perfections, which Haribhadra calls *ṣaṭ-pāramitā-niṣpatti* (ch. 51, 194b–208a) and which develops a sentence in *A* xxviii 472, i.e. *prajñāpāramitāyāṃ hi Subhūte carato bodhisattvasya mahāsattvasya dānapāramitā bhāvanāparipūriṃ gacchati, evaṃ śīlapāramitā,* etc. The remaining sentences of *A* xxviii 472–3 occur then scattered about in *Ś* ch. 53, 263b and 264. From then onwards the text follows entirely its own logic, if one can speak of logic in this context. This independent development is perhaps indicated in *Ś* ch. 53, 274a 3 by a restatement by Subhūti of the basic question with which Śāriputra had opened the discussion in the beginning (*Ś* i 55 and 118), i.e. *katham Bhagavan prajñāpāramitāyāṃ caritavyam? kathaṃ prajñāpāramitābhinirhartavyā? kathaṃ prajñāpāramitā bhāvayitavyā?*

In substance *Ś* is the same as *P* and *Ad*, and there is no reason to believe that it is later than they. The additional 75,000 or 82,000 *ślokas* are due to nothing but the copying out in extenso of the repetitions for the purpose of acquiring merit. *Ś* was composed in an age which loved long books, as witness the *Mahāvibhāṣā*, the *Mahābhārata*, etc.

There is some evidence that *Ś* was either composed, or worked over at different times. The repetitions give usually 18 kinds of emptiness, the special treatise on emptiness (VII pp. 1407–1411) 20, but in such a way that it is obvious that originally there were only 16, the last four being added rather abruptly. Occasionally we also hear of lists of 7 (*Ś* i 137, though the corresponding passage of Gilgit *P* gives 10), and 14 (Gilgit *Ad* LXIII, 248 b).

Bu-ston (II 50) points out that in *Ś*, as distinct from the other long versions, four chapters are absent, and he says that they "have not been brought by Nāgārjuna from the realm of the Nāgas". They are 1. The Questions of Maitreya (*Ad.* ch. 83, *P* ch. 72). They contain the Yogācāra teaching on the three aspects of reality (*parikalpita, paratantra, pariniṣpanna*). Tsoṅ-kha-pa has discussed this problem in detail in his *Legs-bśad sñiṅ-po*. 2.3. The chapters on Sadāprarudita and Dharmodgata (*Ad* 85–86, *P* 73–75). 4. The summary at the end (*parindanā, Ad* 87, *P* 76) (see p. 45).

Commentaries:

Cy 1: Dharmaśrī (?), *-vivaraṇa* (*vyākhyā?*)
Ti: *rnam-par bśad-pa.* mdo-'grel XI 256a–331b. —To 3802

Cy 2: Daṃṣṭrasena, *-bṛhaṭṭikā*
Ti: *rgya-cher bśad-pa.* mod-'grel XII, 1–392a, le'u 1–23; XIII 1–308, le'u 24–52. —To 3807. trsl. Surendrabodhi, Ye-śes-sde.

Cy 3: Smṛtijñānakīrti, *-traya-samāna-artha-aṣṭa-abhisamaya-śāsanā.*
Ti: *'bum daṅ ñi-khri lṅa stoṅ-pa daṅ khri-brgyad stoṅ-pa gsum don mthun-par mṅon-rtogs brgyad-du bstan-pa.* mdo-'grel II 207a–275a. —To 3789.
According to Tsoṅ-kha-pa's AA-cy 15, p. 105 feeble, and full of mistakes.

Cy 4: Daṃṣṭrasena, *Ārya-śatasāhasrikā-pañcaviṃśatisāhasrikā-aṣṭādaśasāhasrikā-*

prajñāpāramitā-bṛhaṭṭikā.

Ti: *rgya-cher bśad-pa.* mdo-'grel XIV 1–333a.—To 3808. trsl. Surendrabodhi, Ye-śes-sde.

According to Tāranātha (212 n.) the Tibetan king Khri-sroṅ lde-btsan added a *Ṭīkā* to this commentary. Its standpoint is Yogācāra, and according to Bu-ston (I 52–3) it proceeds by way of three "media" and eleven "instructions". The subject is opened up by means of an introduction (*Ś* i 4–55). Then comes (1) "the medium of teaching in abridged form", as, "O Śāriputra, the Bodhisattvas and Mahāsattvas who wish to attain complete enlightenment with regard to all the elements of existence, in all their forms, must be keen upon (the study of) the perfection of wisdom" (*Ś* i 55), where the individual, the cause, the subject and the way (of studying) is briefly indicated. Next comes (2) "the medium of moderate teaching", up to the close of the first chapter (of *AA*,=*Ś* ch. 13), and finally (3) "the medium of teaching in detail", ch. 14 up to the end.

The 11 instructions are: 1.–3. the precepts delivered to Śāriputra (as above), 4. the speech of Subhūti (?), 5.–6. the two instructions delivered to Indra (?), 7.–10. the four to Subhūti, 11. one to Ānanda (ch. 50 ?).

Cy 5: *Śatasāhasrikāprajñāpāramitā.*

Ti: *śes-rab-kyi pha-rol-lu phyin-pa stoṅ-phrag brgya-pa'i don ma nor-bar bsdus-pa.* (*'bum chuṅ*). mdo-maṅ no. 102, f. 322b–328a.

Colophon: *Jo-bo-rjes Bal-po a-su-la gnaṅ/Bal-pos śo-lo-kar dkor-pa rdzogs so/Jo-bo-rje dpal-ldan A-ti-śas lo bcu-gñis-kyis bar-du gsuṅs rab-rnams gzigs-pas/'bum chuṅ 'di kho-na phan-yon śin-tu che-bar 'dug-pas/phyi rabs-kyi gaṅ-zag rnams-kyis kyaṅ 'di-la klog 'don byed-pa gal che gsuṅs so.*

Cy 6: Kloṅ-rdol bla-ma ṅag-dbaṅ blo-bzaṅ, *'bum-gyi 'grel-rkaṅ brgya-rtsa-brgyad ṅos-'dzin.*

Ti: To 6542, Da 1–16 (a brief explanation of the 108 topics of Ś).

2. THE PERFECTION OF WISDOM IN 25,000 LINES.

S: *Pañcaviṃśatisāhasrikā prajñāpāramitā-sūtra.* Lost.

s: The New Delhi Collection of Gilgit Mss contains folios 1 to 187 of *P*. At folio 150, although the pagination is continuous, the text breaks off in the middle of chapter 21 (=*P*, Add 1629, f. 156 b) and is resumed again in chapter 30 (=*P* 301). About 30 folios have thus inadvertently dropped out. At folio 188 (=*P* 361) the text changes without any warning into that of *Ad* (see no. 3).

A facsimile of the entire P. P. Gilgit Ms (no. 2 and 3) in: R. Vira and L. Chandra, *Gilgit Buddhist Manuscripts,* New Delhi, Śatapiṭaka Series, volume 10, parts 3 and 4, 1966; part 5, 1970.

s: 91 very short fragments from this, or another recension shorter than *Ś*, are preserved in the Indikutaśaya Copper Plaques in Sinhalese script of the 8th or 9th century. The majority belong to *P*, ed. Dutt, pp. 5–14. *Epigraphica Zeylanica,* iii (1928–1933), L 1933, pp. 200–212. For the Mss and some illustrations see B. Bhattacharya, in *Bulletin of the Baroda State Museum and Picture Gallery* I 1, 1943–4, pp. 17–36.

Ch: T 221 xx. 76 ch. Mokṣala, A.D. 291. T viii, 1–146. *The Prajñāpāramitā-sūtra which emits light.*

ch: T 222 x. Dharmarakṣa, A.D. 286. —T viii 147–216. —Incomplete, only up to ch. 27, i.e. the end of *A* ch. 2.

Ch: T 223 xxvii (or xL). Kumārajīva, A.D. 403–4. —T viii 216–424 (*Mahāprajñāpāramitāsūtra*).

T 220, pp. 401–478. 85 ch. Hsüan-tsang, A.D. 659–663. —T vii 1–426.

Ti: *śes-rab-kyi pha-rol-tu phyin-pa stoṅ-phrag ñi-śu lṅa-pa.* 76 ch. trsl. Ye-śes-sde? 0 731. —To 9. —Cf. To 5574 (7).

Mo: Ligeti no. 758–761. vol. 38–41.

This Sūtra must have existed in a variety of recensions. The recension of *P* which forms the basis of the Tibetan translation is practically identical with *Ś*, except for some minor stylistic variations, though naturally it omits most of the repetitions of *Ś*. The version of Kumārajīva shows greater differences from *Ś*.

Commentaries:

Cy 1: (Nāgārjuna), *Mahāprajñāpāramitopadeśa.*

ch: *Ta-chih-tu-lun.* T 1509 C. trsl. Kumārajīva, A.D. 405 (cy to T 223). —See pp. 93–94.

f: E. Lamotte, *Le traité de la grande vertu de sagesse,* I (1944), ch. 1–15; II (1949), ch. 16–30; III (1970), ch. 31–42; IV (1976), ch. 42–48.

j: Yamakami, Sōgen, *Kokuyaku Daichidoron,* I–IV (1919–20). Mano, Shōjun, *Daichidoron,* I–Vb (1935–6).
Cf. *HJAS,* X 2, (Sept. 1947). —*Muséon,* VII (1906), pp. 34–35, on Pali quotations in this cy. —*Bibl. Bouddhique,* I, (1930), no. 105; IV–V (1934), no. 307 on Mpp-ś in Tun-huang and Khara-khoto. —P. Demiéville, in *JAs,* 1950, pp. 375–395. —Other reviews of Lamotte: see *Bibliographie Bouddhique,* XXI-XXIII (1952), p. 17. Also Conze, *OA,* 1950, pp. 167–8, Baruch, *AM,* 1949.-K. Venkata Ramanan, *Nāgārjuna's Philosophy as presented in the Mahā-Prajñāpāramitā-Śāstra,* 1966, 1975. -M. Saigusa, *Studien zum Mahāprajñāpāramitā (upadeśa)śāstra,* 1969.

Cy 2: Chi-tsang. Ch: T 1696 i.

Cy 3: Yüan-hsiao. Ch: T 1697 i.

2A. A RECAST VERSION OF NO. 2.

S: *Ārya-pañcaviṃśatisāhasrikā bhagavatī prajñāpāramitā Abhisamayālaṅkāra-anusāreṇa saṃśodhitā.*

S: Nepalese manuscripts in Cambridge (Add. 1628, 1629; 18th and 19th century), Paris (Bibl. Nat. Sanscrit 68–70, 71–73, 19th cent.; good); Tōkyō Un. Library, Matsunami, no. 234 (good), 476 fols. Also no. 235. Fragments in Kajiyoshi.

s: ed. N. Dutt, *Calcutta Oriental Series,* no. 28 (1934), 269 pp. (lst *abhisamaya*).

s: E. Conze, "The Buddha's lakṣaṇas in the Prajñāpāramitā", *Journal of the Oriental Institute* (Baroda) XIV, 1965, pp. 225–9.

s: E. Conze, "Maitreya's Questions' in the Prajñāpāramitā", *Mélanges d'Indianisme à la mémoire de Louis Renou,* 1968, pp. 229–242.

s: Takayasu Kimura, Pañcaviṃśatisāhasrikā Prajñāpāramitā (II. 1), *Taishō Daigaku Kenkyūkiyō,* no. 56 (1971) 164–29; P. P. (II 2), *TDK* no. 57 (1972) 524–503; P. P. (II 3), *TDK* no. 58 (1973) 270–238; P. P. (II 4), *TDK* no. 61 (1975) 668–665. (Based on Mss Tōkyō no. 234, 235; Cambridge Add 1628, 1629).

Ti: mdo-'grel III-V. —To 3790. 3 vols. trsl. Śāntibhadra, Tshul-khrims rgyal-ba.
Attributed to Haribhadra. This constitutes a different version which departs in some ways from the Sanskrit text of the Nepalese manuscipts,

and is obviously later than it.

Mo: Xylographs (*T'oung Pao,* 27, 1930).

E: E. Conze. *The Large Sūtra on Perfect Wisdom,* with the divisions of the Abhisamayālaṅkāra. Part I. 1961. Parts II and III, 1964, repr. 1966. —xviii, 679 pp. UCP, Berkeley, Cal. 1975. (see p. 41) -Rev.: G. Schopen IIJ 19, 1977, pp. 135–152.

N. Hakamaya, A consideration on the *Byams shus-kyi le'u* from the historical point of view. *Journal of Indian and Buddhist Studies* XXIV 1, 1975, pp. 499–489.

This version may possibly belong to the 5th century, if we can believe Tāranātha's account which says that the doubts of Ārya-Vimuktisena, who had found discrepancies between *P* and *AA,* had been removed by a copy of *P* in eight sections which the Upāsaka Śāntivarman had brought to Benares from the South (pp. 139, 144–5). It follows the text of the other large Prajñāpāramitās usually quite closely, but superimposes on it the framework of the *AA,* and after each section the appropriate heading from *AA* is added. The chief particularities of the revision are:

1. A few *additions*: At the end of *Ś* ch. 5 one page (*P* 149, 14–150, 17) is inserted to complete the "fourfold discrimination" (*AA* I 3 t-u). At the beginning of *Ś* ch. 63 about one half of a leaf is added (*P* 523a–b), in order to gain a textual basis for the first three items of the 8th abhisamaya i.e. the *svābhāvika-kāyaḥ,* the *sāṃbhogika-kāyaḥ,* and the *nairmāṇika-kāyaḥ.* -which in all probability were alien to the text of the Prajñāpāramitā as it stood.

2. Actual *omissions* are very rare. One can, however, notice some desire to abbreviate ch. 2–20 of *A,* while at the same time adding lists and cliches.

3. *Transpositions* are fairly frequent. The chapters on the varieties of the thought of enlightenment (*AA* I 2) and on the different kinds of Bodhisattvas (*AA* I 2, 3c) are completely rearranged. Later on, 50 leaves of *Ś* ch. 53 (fol. 209–254) are transferred to follow on ch. 48 of *Ś.* In these three cases the rearrangement seems to have been due to a desire to fit the text into the scheme of the *AA.* At the end of the first *abhisamaya,* two passages on the worldly and supramundane perfection of wisdom (*P* 265–6) are absent in the corresponding part of *Ś,* where they are found elsewhere. It may also have been a wish for greater logic and lucidity which dictated the rearrangements, compared with *Ś,* of the very difficult argument at *P* 261–2.

4. *Minor alterations* are very numerous, and mostly terminological. They often aim at greater conciseness, but in most cases no principle can be discovered behind them.

In its lowest subdivisions the *AA* directly contacts the text of the Prajñāpāramitā, and can be checked against it. In many instances the text on which the *AA* is based differs materially from all the nine recensions of the Large Prajñāpāramitā that have survived. We have no means of deciding whether the countless minor variations of the scheme from the other texts are innovations on the part of the author of *AA,* or whether they are based on a special form of *P,* which may have been popular in Yogācāra circles. For instance, in agreement with *AA* VIII v. 38 (*bodher aṅgeṣu*) no. 2A has at P 574a 3 the question: *katamāni Bhagavan bodhisattvasya mahāsattvasya bodhyaṅgāni*? Ś 68, fol. 578a 11 has, however, *mārgāṇi* in the place of *bodhyaṅgāni.*

In the *bhūmi* chapter a few interesting divergences may be commented upon. In the first *bhūmi,* the first list of *Ś-S, P-Ti, Ad-Ti* and no. 2A gives *hitavastutāparikarman* as a separate item. It occurs in the second list only in no. 2A, which here follows *AA* I v. 48, and which drops the 9th item of the first list, i.e. *mānastambhanirghātana,* whereas *Ad-Ti* drops *adhyāśayaparikarman* in the first list, but gives it in the second. *Hitavastutāparikarman* was probably originally a gloss, which developed the *-ādi* following *adhyāśaya,* and we know from the *Mahāyānasūtrālaṅkāra* X 20 (ed. Lévi p. 16) that the expressions *adhyāśaya* and *hitavastutā* were closely associated in the current descriptions of the first stage.

A great diversity exists only on the fifth stage. There is no agreement even on the number of items. *P-Dh* (List 1) and *P-Mo* (list I) give 8; no. 2A, *Ś-Hs, Ad-Hs, P-Hs* and the *AA* give 10: *P-Dh* (list II), *P-Mo* (list II), *P-Ku* give 12; *P-Ti* gives 6 plus 8, *Ś-S* and *Ś-Ti* 6 plus 18. Within the same text there is often no agreement between the first and the second enumeration. The oldest documents, *P-Dh* (list I) and *P-Mo* (list I) count only eight dharmas "which should be avoided". In their second lists they increase this number to 12. The later recensions essentially adhere to this figure, although by subdivisions, etc., they seem to arrive at a different result.[1] The case of *vicikitsā* throws a certain light on the interdependence of the various recensions. It is absent in the oldest Chinese versions (*P-Dh, P-Mo, P-Ku*), in the second list of *Ś-S,* and in the three Tibetan versions (*Ś, P, Ad*). It appears, on the other hand, in the first list of the latter, in the two lists of no. 2A, and in all the versions of Hsüan-tsang (*Ś-Hs, P-Hs, Ad-Hs*). Under the synonym of

1 This, and other problems connected with the *bhūmi* chapter have been discussed by Prof. E. Lamotte and myself in our edition of that chapter, which has so far remained unpublished.

vimati it occurs also in the *AA*. As for *vyāpādacitta,* on the other hand, it appears in the majority of the recensions, but is absent in no. 2A and in all the versions of Hsüan-tsang. In the original Sanskrit of *Ś* it was equally missing, and its insertion in the second list is, as the displacement of a sentence shows, due to a later hand. This observation, together with the preceding one, indicates a certain affinity between the first list of Sanskrit *Ś,* no. 2A and the versions of Hsüan-tsang.

These details could be pursued indefinitely, but little that is definite could at present be gained thereby.

Commentaries:

Cy 1: (Maitreyanātha), *Abhisamaya-alaṅkāra-nāma-prajñāpāramitā-upadeśa-śāstra* (or: *-kārikā*)

S: ed. Th. Stcherbatsky and E. Obermiller, *Bibl. Buddh,* 23 (Leningrad 1929), vol. I, (xii) 40 pp. Repr. 1970.
ed: G. Tucci, *Abhisamayālaṅkārālokā* (Baroda, GOS, 1932),
ed: U. Wogihara, *Abhisamayālaṅkārālokā* (Tokyo, 1932–35),
ed. K. Kajiyoshi, *Genshi Hannya-kyō no kenkyū* (1944), pp. 274–320.

Ti: (Byams-pa mgoṅ-po), *śes-rab-kyi pha-rol-tu phyin-pa'i man ṅag-gi bstan-bcos mṅon-par rtogs-pa'i rgyan shes bya-ba'i tshig.* trsl. Go-mi 'chi-med, Blo-ldan śes-rab (1059–1109 A.D.). mdo-'grel I, 1–15b. —To 3786. —Ed. Stcherbatsky, as S. 72 pp. —To 6787, 1–16 ('bras-spuṅs pho-braṅ edition), To 6793, 1–13 (Se-ra edition), To 6805, 1–46 (Mongolian edition), To 6804, 1–55 (an old Ms.).

E: E. Conze, "Abhisamayālaṅkāra", *SOR,* VI (1954) (Translation pp. 4–106, Vocabulary pp. 107–178, Tibetan-Sanskrit Index pp. 179–223).
Review: de Jong, *Le Muséon,* LXVIII, 3–4 (1955), pp. 394–7.

j: K. Kajiyoshi, As S (4). —Also *ibid.,* pp. 663–980: Detailed survey of divisions of AA.

f: viii 1–12, 33–40, *JAs,* 1913, pp. 605–608.
Cf. E. Obermiller, "The doctrine of the Prajñāpāramitā as exposed in AA of M," *Acta Orientalia,* XI (Leiden 1933), pp. 1–133; 334–54. —*Analysis of the AA,* I (1933), 106 pp.;

II (1936), to p. 275 (end of ch. II); III (1943), to p. 404 (to AA IV 5, 3=A xv 292); no part IV. —G. Tucci, *Some aspects of the doctrines of Maitreyanātha and Asaṅga* (Calcutta, 1930). —E. Conze, "Maitreya's Abhisamayālaṅkāra", *East and West* (Rome), V 3 (1954), pp. 192–7, —"Marginal Notes of the Abhisamayālaṅkāra", *Liebenthal Festschrift, Sino-Indian Studies,* V 3 (1957), pp. 21–35. —N. R. Lethcoe, "Some notes on the Relationship between the AA, The Revised P and the Chinese Translation of the Unrevised P", *JAOS* 96, 1976, pp. 499–511.

There are more than 40 sub-commentaries to the *AA,* which will be listed on pages 112 to 120.

3. THE PERFECTION OF WISDOM IN 18,000 LINES.

S: *Aṣṭādaśasāhasrikā prajñāpāramitā-sūtra.* Lost.

s: One Gilgit Ms of this version in New Delhi extends from folio 188r (ch. 48, *P* 363a) to the end, i.e. folio 308r, end of ch. 82. Folios 211r to 218r are lost. Folios 218v to 263v (ch. 55–69) are now in Rome, and have been edited in the S. O. R. —The New Delhi Collection of Gilgit Mss also contains another fragmentary Ms of *Ad,* of which 64 scattered leaves are preserved.

s: ed. E. Conze, *The Gilgit Manuscript of the Aṣṭādaśasāhasrikā Prajñāpāramitā.* Chapters 55 to 70, corresponding to the 5th abhisamaya. Edition and translation, xxvi+390 pp., SOR xxvi, 1962. —Chapters 70 to 82, corresponding to the 6th, 7th and 8th abhisamayas, xxiii+254 pp., SOR XLVI, 1974.

s: ed. Sten Konow, "Central Asian fragments of the *Ad* and of an unidentified text", *Mem. Arch. Survey of India,* 69 (1942).

s: ed. Bidyabinod, *Mem. Arch. Survey of India,* 32 (1927).

s: Ms Stein Ch 0079a, palm leaf, ca A. D. 600. 69 fols. —Described in E. Conze, "Preliminary Note on a Prajñāpāramitā manuscript", *JRAS,* 1950, pp. 32–36.

Ch: T 220, 479–537. Hsüan-tsang 659–663 (see p. 21).

Ti: *śes-rab-kyi pha-rol-lu phyin-pa khri-brgyad stoṅ-pa.* 87 ch. trsl. Ye-śes-sde? 0 732. 3 vols. —To 10.

The translator of no. 3 must have been different from the translators of no. 1–2, because many of the technical terms are rendered by different Tibetan equivalents.

Mo: Ligeti no. 762–764. vols 42–44.

e: E. Conze SOR XXVI, 1962 (ch. 55–70).—SOR XLVI, 1974 (ch. 70–82).

Both reprinted in E. Conze, *The Large Sūtra on Perfect Wisdom,* 1975 (see p. 37), pp. 431–652.

e: SS no. 83, 116, 119.

A useful guide to the large Sūtra is provided by the chapter headings of *Ad* in correspondence with other divisions. In the following Table the chapter headings in the first column are retranslated into Sanskrit from the Tibetan. Where there is any doubt I have added the Tibetan in a footnote. The second column gives the pages of the Narthang edition of *Ad*; the third, first the pages of the *Śatasāhasrikā* after Ghosha, and then the folios after Ms Cambridge Add 1630, 1627, 1632; the fourth, the pages of *A* after Mitra; the fifth, sixth and seventh the chapters of *P* after Mokṣala, Dharmarakṣa and Kumārajīva; the eighth, the pages of *P* after Dutt and then according to the Ms Cambridge Add 1628; the ninth, the divisions of *AA* according to my translation. (See also Hikata's Tables III and IV).

Ad	Ad-N	Ś, page	A, page	P-Mo	P-Dh	P-Ku	P	AA
1. Nidānam[1]	1	i 4	i 3, 12	1	1	1	4	—
2. Cittotpāda[2]	16b	i 55, 17	i 3, 17	2	2	2	17	I 1
3. Upaparīkṣā[3]	34a	i 118, 9	i 4, 18	3–6	3	3–4	37	I 2, 1
4. Asamasama	83b	i 311	—	7	4	5	93	—
5. Jihvendriya	86b	i 316	—	8	5	6	95	—
6. Subhūti	89a	ii 324	i 5	9	6	7	98	I 2, 9
7. Nyāmāvakrānti	107a	iii 474	—	10	7	8	115, 10	I 2, 10
8. Śreṇika parivrājaka	116a	iv 504	i 7, 9	11	8	9	123	I 3f
9. Nimitta[4]	136a	v 683	i 11,12	12	9	10	138	I 3n
10. Māyopama	151a	vi 886	i 16, 2	13	10	11	150	I 3v
11. Apatrāpya[5]	173a	vii 1209	i 17, 21	14	11	12	160	I 4
12. Dṛṣṭiprahāṇa	188a	vii 1270, 3	i 18, 4	15	12	14	172	I 6, 2
13. Ṣaṭpāramitā	192a	vii 1298,12	i 20, 9	16–17	13–14	15–16	175	I 7
14. Abaddham-amuktam	209a	vii 1342,16	i 20, 13	18	15	17	185	I 9, 1
15. Samādhi	225a	vii 1412	—	19	16	18	198	I 9, 13
16. Dhāraṇīmukha-praveśa	244a	ix 1427	—	20	17	19	203	I 9, 14
17. Bhūmiparikarma	262b	x 1454	i 23, 13	21	18	20	214	I 9, 16
18. Mahāyāna-bhūmi-niryāṇa-nirdeśa	280a	x 1473, 19	i 23, 16	22	19	21	225	I 9, 17
19. Abhibhavana	295b	xi 1530	i 24, 5	23–24	20–21	22–23	231	I 10, 1
20. Advaya	325a	xii 1636	i 25, 4	25–26	22–23	24–25	242	I 10, 6a
21. Sthavira Subhūti[6]	353b	xiii f. 1	i 26, 15	27	24	26	256–269	I 10, 6b
22. Śakraparivarto prathamaḥ	374a	xiv 144b	ii 33	28	25	27	f. 200b	II 1
23. Durvigāhyaṃ[7] nāma	391a	xv 170b	ii 39	29	26	28	208a	II 3, 1, 2
24. Ananta	397a	xvi 195b	ii 41	30	27	29	211	II 3, 1, 3
25. Śakra-parivarto nāma dvitīyaḥ[8]	414a	?	ii 48	31	—	30	219b	II 4, 6
26. Parigraha	420b	xvii 273a	iii 51	32	—	31	223a	II 4, 10
27. Caitya[9]	434a	xviii 279	iii 54	33	—	32	230a	II 5, 3
28. Bodhicittaguṇa-parikīrtana	449a	xix 291a	iii 70	34–35	—	33–34	239	II 6, 2, 1
29. Anya-tīrthika	457a	xx 296b	iii 76	36	—	35	241a	II 6, 2, 2

1 So also P-Ti 1, Ś-Ti 1.
2 P-Ti2: Ś-Ti 2 *Śāriputra.*
3 *ñe-bar brtag-pa. brtag-pa=parīkṣā.* —But Mhyv 7469: *upalakṣaṇam.*
4 *mtshan-ma: lakṣaṇa?*
5 Central Asian Ms Konow: *aupamya* (later corrupted into *auttapya*?).
6 P-Ti 13, Ś-Ti 14: *Subhūti.* Gilgit *P* 13: *Subhūtiparivartaḥ.*
7 *rtogs-par dka'-ba shes bya-ba.* So Mhvy. 2927.
8 So also in Sanskrit Ad., Sten Konow pp. 33–34.
9 *mchod-rten; or: stūpa?*

Ad	Ad-N	Ś	A, page	P-Mo	P-Ku	P	AA
30. Dhāraṇa-mānanā-anuśaṃsā	460b	xxi 298b	iii 80	37	36	242b	II 6, 2, 3
31. Śarīra	471b	xxii 312b	iv 94	38	37	244	II 6, 3, 2
32. Puṇya-viśeṣa[1]	499b	xxiii 325b	v 104	39	38	249b	II 7, 1, 3
33. Anumodana-pariṇāmanā[2]	510a	xxiv 382b	vi 135	40	39	258a	II 8
34. Abhinirhāra-guṇapraśaṃsā	II 23b	xxv 410a	vii 170	41	40	270a	II 10
35. Sattvaniraya[3]	34a	xxvi 1	vii 176	42	41	273b	II 11
36. Sarvadharma-viśuddhi-nirdeśa[4]	47b	xxvii 252a	viii 187	43	42	282	II 11, 5
37. Vihāra[5]	61b	xxviii	viii 193	44	43	286b	III 7
38. Anupalambha[6]	80b	xxix 293a	ix 204	45	44	297a	IV 1
39. Uttara-diśitantrī[7]	90b	xxx 295b	x 208	46	45	299b	IV 2
40. Māra	122b	xxxi 353a	xi 232	47	46	315a	IV 4
41. Māragaṇa-visaṃyukta[8]	132b	xxxii 358b	xi 243	48	47	319B	IV 4, 21
42. Lokasaṃdarśana[9]	146a	?	xii 254	49	48	328a	IV 5
43. Acintya	158b	xxxiii 380a	xii 272	50	49	333a	IV 5, 1b
44. Sabhā[10]	170b	xxxiv 413b	xiii 281, 1	51	50	338b	IV 5, 2, 5
45. Nau	179b	xxxv 432b	xiv 286	52	51	343a	IV 5, 2, 12
46. Sarvadharma-svabhāvanirdeśa[11]	187b	xxxvi 442a	xv 292	53	52	348a	IV 5, 2, 16
47. Rāgavinaya	199a	xxxvii 472	xv 299	54	53	356a	IV, 5, 4
48. Bodhisattva-śikṣā-avasthā	206a	xxxviii 1	xv 303	55	54	361a	IV 5, 4, 10
49. Avaivartika	231a	xxxix 60b	xvii 323	56	55	377a	IV 8
50. Avinivartanīya-liṅga-nirdeśa[12]	243a	xL 72b	xvii 331, 25	57	56	383b	IV 8, 2, 2
51. Upāyakauśalya-nirdeśa	255a	xLi 78b	xviii 341	58	57	390a	IV 8, 3
52. Ṣaṭpāramitānām upāya-paripūri[13]	272b	xLii 96b	xix 356	59	58	398b	IV 9

1 Ś-Ti 24: *Śakra*. Ad-Gilgit ND 27/18b: *Śakraparivarto dvātṛṃśatimaḥ.*

2 Ś-Ti 25: *Pariṇāma(na)*.

3 *sems-can dmyal-ba* So also P-Ti 26.

4 So also P-Ti 27, without *-nirdeśa*.

5 *gnas-pa*. Or: *gnas-pa med-pa?*

6 *dmigs-su med-pa*; or: *anārambaṇa?*

7 *byaṅ phyogs-kyi rgyud.*

8 *bdud-kyi tshogs-pa mi ldan-pa.*

9 Gilgit P 32: *Tathatāparivartaḥ.*

10 *dus-pa*. Or: *saṃnipāta*, or *samāgama?*

11 Gilgit P 36: *Agatikaparivartaḥ.*

12 S 40: *avinivartanīya*. P-Ti 40: *phyir mi ldog-pa*. Gilgit Ad 50: *avaivartyākāraliṅga-parivartaḥ*. S-Ti 41: *phyir mi ldog-pa'i rnam-pa daṅ tshul.*

13 *pha-rol-tu phyin-pa drug-gi thabs yoṅs-su rdzogs-pa.*

Ad	Ad-N	S, fol.	A, page	P-Mo	P-Ku	P	AA
53. Gaṅgādevī-vyākaraṇa[1]	287b	xLiii 102a	xix 365	60	59	404b	(IV 10)
54. Upāyakauśalya-bhāvanā-nirdeśa	291a	xLiv 103b	xx 370	61	60	406a	IV 11
55. Vikalpa-prahāṇa-nirdeśa	301b	xLV 111b	xx 380	62	61	412a	V 1
56. Śikṣāsamatā	324b	xLvi 132b	xxiii 410	63	62	421a	V, 2, 5
57. Caryā	335a	xLvii 137a	xxv 424	64	63	425a	V 2, 9
58. Avikalpa-nirdeśasya dṛṣṭa-anta-vyapadeśa[2]	343a	xLviii 159a	xxvi 434	65	64	428b	V 3
59. Asaṅga[3]	354b	xLix 167b	xxvii 444	66	65	430b	V 5b
60. Parīndanā	364a	L 175a	xxvii 454	67	66	445a	V 5g
61. Akṣaya	378b	LI 184a	xxviii 468	68–69	67–68	451b	V 5i
62. Vyutkrāntaka-samāpatti[4]	385b	LII 196a	—	70	69	455a	V 5k
63. Advaya-dharmasya bahuparipṛcchā	403a	LIII 209b 254a	—		70	436b-445a 465b	V 5d V 6b
64. Samyaknirdeśa	445b	LIV 300a	—	71	71	479b	V 7
65. Kalyāṇamitra-śuśrūṣā-sevanā-paryupāsanā-upāya	455b	LV 313b	—	72	72	484b	V 8, 5

Ad	Ad-N	S, fol.	P-Mo	P-Ku	P	AA
66. Upāyakauśalyanirdeśa[5]	460b	LVI 320a	73	73	487b	V 8, 8
67. Śīla	462b	LVII 320b	74		488a	V 8, 9
68. Vivṛddhi	462b	LVIII 321a			488b	V 8, 9
69. Mārgabhāvanānirdeśa	463b	LIX 322a		74	490a	V 8, 9
70. Anupūrvacaryāśikṣā-nirhāranirdeśa	482b	LX 355a	75	75	501b	V 8, 16
71. Alakṣaṇa-anupalambha-dharmatā	496a	LXI 369a	76	76	508b	VI 13
72. Alakṣaṇatā-nirdeśa	514b	LXII 401b	77	77	517a	VII 3
73. Lakṣaṇa-anuvyañjana-akṣara-abhinirhāra-nirdeśa[6]	528a	LXIII414b	78	78	523b	VIII 4
74. Sarvadharmasamatā-nirdeśa[7]	III 25a	LXIV 454a	79	79	540b	VIII 5, 3

1 Ś 44: *Gaṅgādevībhaginyā-parivarto*. P-Ti 43: *Gaṅgādevī*.
2 *rnam-par mi rtog-pa bstan-pa'i dpe brjod-pa.*
3 *chags-pa med-pa; nirupalepa?*
4 *thod-rgyal-du sñoms-par 'jug-pa*. AA: *avaskanda-*, Ad: *avaskandaka-*.
5 So skr. Ś 56. Gilgit Ad 66.
6 So Ś-Ti 63, P-Ti 62. Ś 63 skr., but-*abhinirhāra-pāramitā.*
7 *Samatānirdeśa* in Ś-skr. 64, Ś-Ti 64, P-Ti 63.

Ad	Ad-N	S, fol.	P-Mo	P-Ku	P	AA
75. Akopya-nirdeśa[1]	41a	LXV 470	80	80	548b	VIII 5, 7
76. Sattvaparipācanasannāha	61b	LXVI 509a	81	81	558a	VIII 5,10
77. Buddhakṣetrapariśuddhi-nirdeśa	78a	LXVII 553a	82	82	565a	VIII 5,12
78. Buddhakṣetrapariśodhana-upāyakauśalyanirdeśa nāma	90b	LXVIII 564a	83	83	570b	VIII 5,15
79. Abhāvasvabhāvanirdeśa	102a	LXIX 583a	84	84	574b	VIII 5,20
80. Asaṃkleśa-avyavadānam	108b	LXX 585a	85	85	583b	VIII 5,22

Ad	Ad-N	S, fol.	A	P-Mo	P-Ku	P-Ti	P	AA
81. Paramārthayoga	115a	LXXI 590b	—	86	86	70	586a	VIII 5,24
82. Akopyadharma-tā-nirdeśa[2]	127b	LXXII 604b-607a	—	87	87	71	592a-594b	VIII 5,26
83. Bodhisattvaśik-ṣā-prabhāvanā[3]	130a	—	—	—	—	72	—	—
84. Saṃcayagāthā	147a	—	—	—	—	—	—	—
85. Sadāprarudita[4]	175a	—	xxx	88	88	73	—	—
86. Dharmodgata	199b	—	xxxi	89	89	74–75	—	—
87. Parīndanā	210b -213	—	xxxii	90	90	76	—	—

4. THE PERFECTION OF WISDOM IN 10,000 LINES.

S: *Daśasāhasrikā prajñāpāramitā-sūtra.* Lost.

s: ch. 1–2 (restored): Sten Konow, "The first two chapters of the *Da*", *Avhandlinger utgift av det norske Videnskap-Akademi i Oslo,* II, Hist. Filos. Klasse, 1941, no. 1, Oslo.

Ti: *śes-rab-kyi pha-rol-tu phyin-pa khri-ba stoṅ-pa.* 33 ch. trsl. Jinamitra, Prajñāvarman, Ye-śes-sde. O 733.—To 11.

Mo: Ligeti no. 765. vol. 45.—trsl. Siregetü güüsi (ca. A.D. 1600).

e: SS no. 106.

The special feature of this Sūtra lies in that the definitions of the terms, which are scattered through the other versions of the Large Prajñāpāramitā, have all been gathered together into the first two chapters, in 57 groups. They are introduced by the question: "Which are the all-dharmas in which the Bodhisattvas, the great beings do not settle down?" Most of the items are common to both Hīnayāna and Mahāyāna.

1 *mi 'khrugs-pa bstan-pa; akṣobhya-?*
2 So Gilgit *Ad* 82. *Ś* skr. 72–S-Ti 72, P-Ti 71: *chos ñid mi 'gyur-pa bstan-pa.*
3 P-Ti 72: *byaṅ-chub sems-dpa'i bslab-pa-la rab-tu phye(dbye)-ba.*
4 Ti-P 73: *Bodhisattvasya Sadāpraruditasya samādhimukhāni labdhāni.*

The remaining 31 chapters are a somewhat erratic contraction of the Large Prajñāpāramitā (see Hikata pp. xiv and xxxxviii-ix), which awaits further elucidation. For instance, chapters 3 to 14 correspond roughly to ch. 3 to 21 of *Ad,* ch. 15–16 to *Ad* 22–23, then at ch. 18–20 there is a jump to *Ad* 35–38, ch. 21–24 cover portions of *Ad* 44–48, and so on. It is not impossible that this version was composed in Tibet.

5. THE PERFECTION OF WISDOM IN 8,000 LINES.

S: *Aṣṭasāhasrikā prajñāpāramita-sūtra.*

ed. R.Mitra, Calcutta, 1888, *Bibl. Ind.* 110. xxvi, 530 pp.

ed. U. Wogihara, Tōkyō, 1932–35 (With Haribhadra's commentary, i.e. 5–cy 1).

ed. P.L. Vaidya, Darbhanga, 1960.

For the text see J. W. de Jong, "Notes on Prajñāpāramitā Texts", *Indologica Taurinensia* II, 1974, pp. 107–119. E. Conze, *JRAS* 1978, pp. 14–18.

The palmleaf missing between Mitra pp. 464 and 465 in E. Conze, *BSOAS,* XIV, (1952), pp. 261–2. For some Mss see: A. Ghose in *Rūpam* 38–39, pp. 78–82; H.C. Hollis in *Bulletin of the Cleveland Museum of Art* 26, 1939, pp. 30–33; H. Sastri, *Proceedings of the Asiatic Society of Bengal* 1899, pp. 39–40.

Ch: T 224 x. Lokakṣema, A.D. 179–180. —*Prajñāpāramitā-sūtra of the practice of the Way.*

L.R. Lancaster, "The oldest Mahāyāna Sūtra: Its significance for the study of Buddhist development", *The Eastern Buddhist* N. S. VIII, 1975, pp. 30–41.

T 225 vi (or iv). Chih-ch'ien, ca. A.D. 225. *Sūtra of unlimited great-brightness-crossing.*

L.R. Lancaster, "The Chinese translation of the Aṣṭasāhasrikā-Prajñāpāramitā-Sūtra attributed to Chieh Ch'ien", *Monumenta Serica* xxviii, 1969, pp. 246–257.

ch: T 226 v. Dharmapriya, A.D. 382. Only 13 ch. (cr. to ch. 1–8 and 16–23 of Sanskrit). Extract. (*Mahāprajñāpāramitā-sūtra*).

Ch: T 227 x. Kumārajīva, A.D. 408. T viii pp. 536–586. (*Mahāprajñāpāramitā-sūtra*).

T 220, 4–5. Hsüan-tsang, ca. A.D. 660.

T 228 xxv. Dānapāla, A.D. 985. T viii pp. 587–676 (with chapters in Sanskrit). (*The Prajñāpāramitā-sūtra, mother of the Buddha, who gives birth to the triple Dharmapiṭaka*).

L. Lancaster, *An Analysis of the Aṣṭasāhasrikā-prajñāpāramitā-sūtra from the Chinese Translations.* pp. 406, Dissertation, Wisconsin Univ. 1968 (unpubl.)

Ti: *śes-rab-kyi pha-rol-tu phyin-pa brgyad stoṅ-pa.*

O 734 (enumerates many translators & revisors), (colophon trsl. in Beckh pp. 8–9). —To 12 (Ka 1b–286a). —To 6758, Ka 1–428 (Tshe mchog gliṅ edition).

Mo: Ligeti no. 766. vol. 46.

Also: Ms Royal Library Copenhagen, 159 fol., between 1593–1603. —Another translation by Bsam dan seṅ-ge, ca. A.D. 1620, Block-prints Peking 1707, 1727, cf. W. Heissig, *Ural-altaische Jahrbücher,* XXVI (1954), p. 112.

E: E. Conze, Bibl. Ind. 284, Calcutta 1958, 225 pp., 1970. —*The Perfection of Wisdom in eight thousand Lines and its Verse Summary,* xxii 325 pp., 1973. —Reprinted, with corrections 1975.

e: Hari Prasad Shastri, BTS of India, *Journal* etc., 1894, II, part 2, pp. 7–11 (=xi 232–240); 3, pp. 10–15 (parts of xviii).

Bendall-Rouse, *Śikṣāsamuccaya* (1922), pp. 37–41, 495 sq., 315 sq.

E. J. Thomas, *The Perfection of Wisdom* (1952), pp. 34–42 (from ch. xxx-xxxi).

E. Conze, ed. *Buddhist Texts* (1954), no. 124–5, 128, 136–7, 141, 143–4, 165, 167.—*SS* no. 5, 7–10, 13–22, 24–31, 34–39, 43, 51–53, 64, 69, 74, 78–81, 86–7, 93, 101–4, 109-11, 114, 117, 126.

g: M. Walleser, *Prajñāpāramitā, Die Vollkommenheit der Erkenntnis* (Göttingen, 1914), pp. 34–139 (ch. 1, 2, 8, 9, 13, 15, 16, 18, 19, 22, 27). Cf. *Ost. Ztschr.,* IV, 207, sq. —*DLZ,* XXXVI, Sp. 1932–7, and no. 44–46. M. Winternitz, *Der Mahāyāna Buddhismus* (1930) (A i 3–6, 20 sq., 23 sq., ii 39 sq., xi, 321 sq., xviii 341 sq., 347 sq., xxii 396–8).

E. Frauwallner, *Die Philosophie des Buddhismus* (1956), pp. 151-163 (i 3–6, 20–21, ii 45–7, viii 190–2, xxii 399–400.

f: ch. 1, to p. 27, in: E. Burnouf, *Introduction à l'histoire du Buddhisme Indien* (1844), pp. 465–483; 2nd ed. pp. 414–430.

ch. 1–28, trad. E. Burnouf, Ms in Bibliothèque Nationale, Fonds Burnouf. no. 64, 430 pages in 4°.

cf. E. Conze, "The composition of the Aṣṭasāhasrikā Prajñāpāramitā", *BSOAS*, XIV (1952), pp. 251–262. Reprinted in *TYBS* 1967, pp. 168–184.

The contents of this Sūtra are not easily summarized. One can, nevertheless, indicate roughly the sequence of its themes. The first two chapters expound the *elusiveness of perfect wisdom,* and they contain all the essential doctrines of the book. Chapters 3 to 5 are then devoted to the *advantages* derived from the practice of perfect wisdom, and chapter 6 is a treatise on the metaphysical problems connected with the process of *dedicating* all merit to the full enlightenment of all beings. Chapters 7 to 10 touch on a *variety of topics,* such as the attributes of perfect wisdom, its relation to the other *pāramitās,* the reasons why some believe in it and others do not, its depth and purity, its relation to attachment and non-attachment, to reality and illusion, and its effects on the believer. Chapter 11 then describes the obstacles which *Māra* puts in the way of the study of the Prajñāpāramitā, chapter 12 proceeds to analyse the kind of *knowledge* which the *Tathāgata* has of the world, and chapter 13 discusses the attributes of the *Absolute.* In chapter 14 the *Disciples and Pratyekabuddhas* are unfavourably compared with the Bodhisattvas, and chapter 15 first outlines the *help* which Bodhisattvas give to others, and then describes the *perfection of wisdom.* This is followed in chapter 16 by a rhapsody on *Suchness* and the Tathāgata, which constitutes the culminating point of the Sūtra, and is followed by an earthquake.

Chapter 17 is a monograph on the attributes and tokens of *irreversibility.* Chapter 18 then deals with the *ontology* of perfect wisdom, i.e. with emptiness, etc. This topic is further pursued in the first part of chapter 19. In its second part, chapter 19 describes how the *six perfections* should be practised in relation to other beings, and this is followed by a description of the *prediction* to Buddhahood of the *Ganges Goddess.* The first part of chapter 20 treats of *skill in means,* and then the discussion swerves back to *irreversibility* (xx 380–4), and proceeds from there to the evils of *pride* (ch. 21).

Chapters 22 to 28 again range over a wide variety of topics, such as the importance of good friends, the meaning of emptiness, the value of perfect wisdom, the conditions which lay open to the influence of Māra, the marks of perfect training, the nature of illusion, the praise of the life of a Bodhisattva, and the prediction to Buddhahood of many thousands of monks. In the course of chapter 28 this Sūtra is *entrusted to Ānanda,* the miraculous appearance of *Akṣobhya's Buddhafield* is described, followed by a meditation on extinction, non-extinction and *conditioned co-production.* In chapter 29 we have another *litany,* in chapters 30 and 31 a story about the Bodhisattva *Sadāprarudita* and his search for perfect wisdom,[1] and in chapter 32 once more the *transmission* of the Sūtra to *Ānanda.*

The chapter divisions present a number of difficult problems:

a) Often the chapters are linked together. In many cases the argument simply goes on, — as between 3–4–5, 7–8–9 –, 11–12, 15–16, 25–26, and 30–31. Similarly, 18, 19 and 20, up to p. 380, once formed one continuous argument, which was then interrupted by the insertion of the episode of the Ganges Goddess (xix 365–9). Where there may be any doubt about the continuity, sometimes a special reference is made back to the preceding chapter, e.g. at vii 177 to vi 158–9, after a break through the insertion of a litany; or at xi, which deals with the *doṣā,* which at the beginning are contrasted with the *guṇā* that had been treated in ch. 10. At the beginning of ch. 17, the first answer to the question about the marks of an irreversible Bodhisattva is that "he does not prattle away", etc., and the passage about Suchness which precedes it is inserted to form a link with the subject of Suchness discussed in ch.16. At ch. 18, there is at the beginning a special reference to the subject of ch.17, i.e. to the marks of an irreversible Bodhisattva. Lokakṣema, as a matter of fact, abbreviates the connecting link, omits the first two sentences, and begins his ch. 16 straight away with *A* 341, *pratibalo,* etc. These efforts to preserve the impression of a continuous argument are probably due to a later hand.

At 10, 13, 14, 15, 23, 24, 25, 28, 29, however, the chapter division coincides with a clear break in the argument. In two cases, at ch. 21 and 23, the chapter division cuts through the argument in an illogical and arbitrary manner, and it would have been more suitable to begin ch. 21 at *A* xx 380, and chapter 32 after the conclusion of the story of Sadāprarudita. At *A* xx 380 in fact Lokakṣema and also the large Prajñāpāramitās begin a new chapter. Lokakṣema has no new chapter at *A* ch. 21, nor any of the large *Prajñāpāramitās.*

b) The present division into chapters may be later than the earliest Chinese translations. I add here the division of Lokakṣema, T 224, ca. 180, underlining those headings which differ from the Sanskrit. (See also Hikata's Table I).

Sanskrit *A*	Lokakṣema
1. sarvākārajñatācaryā	1. *mārgacaryāparivartaḥ*
2. Śakra	2. (Śakra) paripṛcchā
2. p. 48	3. guṇa

1 See L. Lancaster, "The Story of a Buddhist Hero", *The Tsing Hua Journal of Chinese Studies,* N.S. X 2, 1974, 83–89

3. aprameya-guṇa-dhāraṇa-pāramitā-stūpa-satkāra	
4. guṇa-parikīrtana	
5. puṇya-paryāya	
6. anumodanā-pariṇāmanā	4. *upāyakauśalya*
7. niraya	5. niraya
8. viśuddhi	6. viśuddhi
8. p. 199	7. stuti
9. stuti	
10. dhāraṇa-guṇa-parikīrtana	8. (aprameyaguṇa)dhāraṇa
11. Mārakarma	9. (*sarvākāra-*)*abhisaṃbodha*
12. lokasaṃdarśana	10. (loka)saṃdarśana
13. acintya	11. acintya
14. aupamya	12. aupamya
15. deva	13. *vikalpa*
16. tathatā	14. anādibhāva (or: tathatā?)
17. avinivartanīya-ākāra-liṅga-nimitta	15. avinivartanīya
18. śūnyatā, p. 341	16. Gaṅgā-upāsikā
19. Gaṅgādevībhaginī	
20. upāyakauśalya-mīmāṃsā	17. *śūnyatā*
20. p. 380	18. *viveka*
21. Mārakarma	
22. kalyāṇamitra	19. kalyāṇamitra
23. Śakra	20. Śakra devendra
24. abhimāna	21. abhimāna
25. śikṣā	22. śikṣā
26. māyopama	23. *caryā*
27. sāra	24. sāra-asāra
28. p. 459 Avakīrṇakusuma	25. *parīndanā*
p. 468	26. *akṣaya*
29. anugama	27. anugama
30. Sadāprarudita	28. Sadāprarudita bodhisattvo
31. Dharmodgata	29. Dharmodgata bodhisattvo
32. parindanā	30. parīndanā

The titles given to some of the chapters in the Sanskrit text are fairly late. Chapter 28, for instance, is named after a later addition, and also the title of chapter 1 is unlikely to be the original one. *Sarvākārajñatā* is mentioned in *A* only at xxx 507, a passage which belongs to one of the most recent strata of the Sūtra. Its distinction from the Disciples' *sarvajñatā* is a later scholastic refinement, present in the Large Prajñāpāramitā, but quite absent in *A*, where *sarvajñatā* is clearly and constantly used from chapter 1 to 28 for the omniscience of the Buddha.

Commentaries:

Cy 1: Haribhadra, *Abhisamayālaṅkārālokā*

S: ed. U. Wogihara (Tōkyō, 1932–35), 995 pp. (with text of *A*), repr. 1973.

ed. G. Tucci, *GOS*, 62 (Baroda, 1932).

Ti: *rgyan-gyi snaṅ-ba*. mdo-'grel VI, 1–426 a. vol. III, p. 277 many translators and revisors. —To 7391. *'grel-chen.*

e: G. H. Sasaki and G. W. F. Flygare, *The Doctrine of Nonsubstantiality*, Otani University, Kyōto, 1953 (part of ch. 18).

cf. MCB, III, pp. 383–9. R. Mano, "'*Tathāgata*' in Haribhadra's Commentary", *JIBS* 16, 1968, pp. 975–69.

It is stated at the end of this very important work (p. 994) that it was written in the monastery of Trikaṭuka, and that king Dharmapāla patronized it. The explanation of the Sūtra is here based on "the four great commentaries" (Bu-ston II 159), and follows (*AAA* p. 1) Asaṅga's *Tattvaviniścaya*, Vasubandhu's *Paddhati*, Ārya Vimuktisena's *Vṛtti* (quoted 15 times) and Bhadanta Vimuktisena's *Vārttika* (quoted twice).

Cy 1–1: Dbyaṅs-can dga'-ba'i blo-gros, *'phags-pa brgyad stoṅ-pa'i 'grel-chen rgyan snaṅ-las btus-pa'i ñer mkho mdo-don, Lta-ba'i mig-'byed.* To 6578, Ka 1–63. —This is an explanation of terms in the *AAA*.

Cy 2: Ratnākaraśānti, *-pañjikā Sāratamā nāma.*

S: *Sāratamā*. To be edited by P. S. Jaini in the Tibetan Sanskrit Works Series, Patna.

cf. P. S. Jaini, "The Āloka of Haribhadra and the Sāratamā of Ratnākaraśānti. A comparative study of the two commentaries of the Aṣṭasāhasrikā", *BSOAS* 35, 1972, 271–284.

Ti: mdo-'grel X, 1–253a. —To 3803. trsl. Subhūtiśānti, Śākya blo-gros.

Cy 3: Abhayākaragupta, *-vṛtti Marmakaumudī nāma.*

Ti: mdo-'grel XI, 1–256a. —To 3805. trsl. Abhayākaragupta, Śes-rab dpal.

Cy 4: Jagaddalanivāsin, *-āmnāyānusāriṇi nāma vyākhyā.*

Ti: *man-ṅag-gi rjes-su 'braṅ-ba shes bya-ba'i rnam-par bśad-pa.* mdo-'grel XV, 1–371a. —To 3811. trsl. Alaṅk(ār)adeva, Ga-rod tshul-khrims 'byuṅ-gnas.

The next three items are only loosely connected with no. 5, and they are not properly commentaries to it, although they represent themselves as such.

Cy 5: Dignāga, *Prajñāpāramitā-piṇḍārtha.*

S: ed. G. Tucci, *JRAS,* 1947, pp. 56–59.

ed. E. Frauwallner, *Wiener Ztschr. f. d. Kunde Süd- und Ostasiens,* III (1959), pp. 140–4; cf. pp. 116–20.

Ch: T 1518 i. Dānapāla, A.D. 982.

Ti: *bsdus-pa'i tshig-le'ur byas-pa* (*saṃgrahakārikā*). mdo-'grel XIV 333a–336a, and CXXVIII no. 7.—To 3809, trsl. Tilaka-kalaśa, Blo-ldan śes-rab. —Ed. *JRAS,* pp. 68–75.

E: G. Tucci, *JRAS,* 1947, pp. 59–65 (Notes 65–68).

Cy 5–1: Triratnadāsa, *-vṛtti. Prajñāpāramitā-saṃgraha(-kārikā)-vivaraṇa.*

Ch: T 1517 iv, Dānapāla, A.D. 982.

Ti: *bsdus-pa'i tshig-le'ur byas-pa'i rnam-par 'grel-pa.* mdo-'grel XIV 336a–362a. —To 3810. trsl. Thig-le bum-pa, Blo-ldan śes-rab.

Cy 6: Kambarāmbara(pāda), *Āryāṣṭasāhasrikāyāḥ prajñāpāramitāyāḥ piṇḍārtha.*

S: ed. G. Tucci, *MBT,* I (1956), pp. 216–217.

Ch: T 1516 ii. Dharmarakṣa, A.D. 1004. —Ed. in Tucci, pp. 223–4.

Ti: *Bhagavatī prajñāpāramitā navaślokapiṇḍārtha: bcom-ldan 'das-ma śes-rab-kyi pha-rol-tu phyin-pa don bsdus-pa'i tshigs-su bcad-pa dgu-pa.*

a) trsl. Śraddhākaravarman, Rin-chen bzaṅ-po: mdo-'grel XVI, 3b–4a. —To 3812 (=4462). —Ed. in Tucci, *MBT,* I, pp. 218–220.

b) trsl. Sumanaḥśrī, Rin-chen grub. mdo-'grel XVI 1–3a. —Ed. in Tucci, *MBT,* I, pp. 223–4.

E: G. Tucci, *MBT,* I, pp. 225–231.

Cy 6–1: *-piṇḍārthaṭīkā.*

Ti: *rgya-cher bśad-pa.* mdo-'grel XVI 4b–9a. —To 3813(=4463). trsl. Kamalagupta, Rin-chen bzaṅ-po.

Included in S, Ti and Ch as running commentary. A few excerpts in Tucci, *MBT,* I, pp. 226–230.

Cy 7: Ṅag-dbaṅ byams-pa, *Yum śes-rab-kyi pha-rol-tu phyin-pa brgyad stoṅ-pa'i don slob-dpon seṅ-bzaṅ daṅ, phyogs glaṅ gñis-kyi 'chad-tshul mdor-bsdus, Sgron-gsal.*

Ti: To 6155, Cha 1–7. Explanation of differences between cy 1 and cy 5.

5A. VERSES ON THE ACCUMULATION OF PRECIOUS QUALITIES.

S: *Prajñāpāramitā-ratnaguṇasaṃcayagāthā.*

S: (1) Recension A (=Calcutta Ms, A.D. 1174), ed. A. Yuyama, Cambridge, 1976. —cf. E. Conze *IIJ* iv, 1960, pp. 37–58. —F. Edgerton *IIJ* v, 1961, pp. 1–18.

(2) Recension B (=Chinese blockprint, 18th century), ed. E. Obermiller, Leningrad, 1937 (BB xxix); Reprint Osnabrück, 1970. Reissue, with corrections and a Sanskrit-Tibetan-English index by E. Conze, 1960 (*IIR* v).

(3) Recension C (other late Mss from Nepal), ed. P. L. Vaidya, *MSS* I, 1961, pp. 352–404.

cf. R. O. Meisezahl, *Oriens* xvii, 1964, pp. 289–301 (review of Conze, 1960=*IIR* v)

Ch: T 229 iii. Dharmabhadra, A.D. 991. *The Prajñāpāramitā Sūtra which is the storehouse of the precious virtues of the Mother of the Buddhas.* —Bibliography: A. Yuyama pp. xxxix-xliii.

Ti: *śes-rab-kyi pha-rol-tu phyin-pa sdud-pa tshigs-su bcad-pa.*

(1) Recension A. Tun-huang Mss (ch. 84 of no. 1 (S), as also the Calcutta Ms), ed. A. Yuyama, 1976, pp. 156–191.

(2) Recension B.

a. trsl. Vidyākarasiṃha, Dpal-brtsegs. O 735. —To 13, Ka 1b–19b. ca A.D. 825.

b. 84th chapter of no. 3 (*Ad*). Narthang III f. 147b–175a

c. Bilingual Xylograph, ed. Obermiller, as S: (2).

Agrees largely with (b), but there are minor differences of which the more important have been noted in my Index in *IIR* v.

Bibliography: A. Yuyama, pp. xxx-xxxviii.

Mo: Ligeti no. 767, vol. 47, 1–27v. —A. Yuyama pp. xliv-xlv.

Hsi-hsia: A. Yuyama p. xlvi.

E: (Recension B) E. Conze, "The Accumulation of Precious Qualities", in *Indo-Asian Studies,* Part 1, ed. Raghu Vira, 1962, pp. 126–178. —Repr. in *The Perfection of Wisdom in Eight Thousand Lines and its Verse Summary*, 1973 (repr. 1975), pp. 3–73.

The historical value of this document is greatly reduced by the fact that the existing version is not the original one. At the end we have two verses in Śārdūlavikrīḍita metre, which indicate that the text was reviewed by Haribhadra, and brought into line with the chapters of *A* as they existed at the time. After that the colophon runs in the Xylograph: *Āryāṣṭasāhasrikāyāḥ Bhagavatyāḥ Prajñāpāramitāyāḥ parivarta-anusāreṇa Bhagavatī Ratnaguṇasaṃcaya-gāthā samāptā.* In the Tibetan translation of *Ad* these two verses and the colophon are omitted.

The work is written in mixed Sanskrit. It contains many Prakritisms, and has hardly been Sanskritized at all. At the beginning of the *Subodhinī* it is said to have been first delivered in the dialect of Central India; according to Bu-ṣton (II p. 51) in the dialect of Magadha. The language does not attain the grammatical precision of Sanskrit, but is full of ambiguities, and without the help of the Tibetan translation it would often be nearly impossible to make out the meaning. It is very similar to Edgerton's "Buddhist Hybrid Sanskrit". Collation with the Calcutta Ms (=A) has now revealed many of the deviations from ordinary Sanskrit usage in Obermiller's edition as mere errors of transmission, and also made it probable that the discretion of individual scribes had something to do with the retention or rejection of non-Sanskritic forms. The linguistic detail of this important text has now been studied by A. Yuyama.

The distinction between *-a* and *ā,* and between short and long vowels in general, is often not observed. This also accounts for the apparent elision of the initial letter of a word, when it follows a vowel, e.g. *pratibhāna (a)neka* xi 2, *yujyatu (u)pāya-yukta xvi* 3, *manyanu (u)papadyati xxi* 1, *atikrānta (a)nāgata* xxviii 2; *vidhamitva vidya* stands for *vidhamitvā avidyā* at xxviii 7; we further have *bhonti (i)ha* at xxv 4, *puna (ā)khyāyati* at xviii 6, *sarveṣu (u)-pādu* at i 27, and *na ca (a)saṃskṛte,* according to the Tibetan, at xx 18. There are also other contractions, like *tatha mi* (or A: *tathimi*) for *tathā ime* xxv 4, *emeva* for *evam eva,* and *atha* for *yathā.*

The final *-ā* and *-am* of the Nominative often appears as *-u,* and sometimes as *-i.* Instead of the Accusative the Nominative is often given. The gen. sing. of *sāgara* appears as *sāgari* at xviii 1. The gen. plur. is often *-āna* instead of *-ānām.* At v 3 *sattvi* (A: *a*) is Dative, at i 11 *puramakehi* (A: *puremakehi*) is given for *pūrvakaiḥ* of *A,* and at ii 13 *adhvanasmin* (A: *adhvakasmin*) for *adhvani.* At xx 7 we have *antare,* but at vi 3 *antari* for *antare.* In some cases I have not understood the declension, e.g. at ii 9 *rūpe* is nom. plur. (*gzugs*) and *rūpi* Locative (*gzugs-la*)?

Ahu is given for *aham, aya* and *ayu* for *ayam, imu* at xxv 2 for *imām, ubhi* and *ubhayo* for *ubhaya, eti* for *ete, tatu* for *tadā, sa ci* for *sacet, yadyāpi* for *kiṃ cāpi, kutu* for *kuto* (xxvi 4). *Ahu-mahya* is *ahaṃ-mama,* an abbreviation for *ahaṃkāramamakārau.*

A number of words differ from the Sanskrit form, e.g. *raha* for *arhat, pratyaya* for *pratyekabuddha, istri* for *strī,* etc. In some cases the order of words seems reversed, e.g. *āvaraṇa-kleśa* for *kleśa-āvaraṇa, kāmārtha* for *artha-kāma.*

Sometimes the language of this work resembles Pali, as when it gives *daka* for *udaka, geha* for *gṛha, parikhinna* for *parikṣiṇa, lena for layana, saṃkileśo* for *saṃkleśa, vuccati* for *ucyate.* The treatment of the verb also shows many similarities to Pali: *o-* often takes the place of *ava-*. *Bhavanti* occurs as *bhonti,* and so we have *prabhoti* and *abhibhoti. Bhaviṣyati* occurs as *bheṣyati,* the present form in *-ayati* often as *-ayi,* and the Causative in *-eti* is frequent. At iv 5 *dadantu* stands for the *dadataḥ* of *A. Pari-eṣati* stands for *paryeṣati, khipitva* for *kṣipitvā, sthihate* for *tiṣṭhati,* and *sthihitva* for *sthitvā.*

See: A. Yuyama, *A Grammar of the Rgs,* xxxii, 190 pp., Canberra 1973. —"Some Glossarial Notes on the Rgs", *Proceedings and Papers of the 14th Congress of the Australasian Universities Language and Literature Association (19–26. 1. 72),* ed. K. I. D. Maslen, 1972, pp. 30–37. —"Remarks on the metre of the Rgs", *Studies in Indo Asian Art and Culture,* vol. 2 (*Āchārya Raghu Vira Commemoration Volume*) (*Śatapiṭaka Series,* 96), 1973, pp. 243–253.

Commentaries:

Cy 1: Haribhadra (?), *-pañjikā. Subodhinī.*

Ti: *rtogs-par sla-ba.* trsl. Jetahaṅṅu Śāntibhadra, 'bro Seṅ-dkar Śakya 'od. —mdo-'grel VII, pp. 1–93. —To 3792, *dka'-'grel shes bya-ba.*

Cy 2: Buddhaśrījñāna, *-pañjikā.*

Ti: *dka'-'grel.* mdo-'grel VIII, pp. 135–223. —To 3798, trsl. Vidyākarasiṃha, Dpal-brtsegs.

Cy 3: Dharmaśrī, *prajñāpāramitā-kośa-tāla-nāma.*

Ti: *mdzod-kyi lde-mig ces bya-ba.* mdo-'grel XI, pp. 331–340. —To 3806. trsl. Ba-rig. (Peking 5204: Ba-reg).

These three commentaries relate the contents of *Rgs* to *AA.*

AB. Abbreviations

6. THE QUESTIONS OF SUVIKRĀNTAVIKRĀMIN.

S: *Suvikrāntavikrāmi-paripṛcchā prajñāpāramitā(-nirdeśa-)sūtra.* Or: *Sārddha-dvisāhasrikā prajñāpāramitā-sūtra.*
ed. T. Mastumoto (Tōkyō 1956), 99 pp..
ed. R. Hikata (Fukuoka 1958), 129 pp.
(Reviews: *IIJ* ii, 1958, pp. 316–8, iii, 1959, pp. 232–4; repr. *FBS*).
ed. P. L. Vaidya, *MSS* I, 1961, pp. 1–74.

Ch: T 220, 593–600. Hsüan-tsang. no. 16, T vii 1065c–1110a.
Ch. 1 and 2 ed. also in T. Matsumoto's ed. of ch. 1 and 2 in *Die Prajñāpāramitā Literatur* (1932), pp. 4–29, and *Festschrift Kahle* (1935), pp. 181–188.
The chapter division is different from that of the Sanskrit and Tibetan. The chapters begin at the following folios of the Sanskrit text: I 2b, II 16b, III 26b, IV 31a, V 52b, VI 70b, VII 84a, VIII 100b.

Ti: *('phags-pa) rab-kyi rtsal-gyis rnam-par gnon-pas shus-pa śes-rab-kyi pha-rol-tu phyin-pa bstan-pa.* 7 ch. trsl. Śīlendrabodhi, Jinamitra, Ye-śes-sde. 0 736.—To 14, Ka 20a–103b.

Mo: Ligeti no. 768, vol. 47, 27v–136r.

E: E. Conze, *SPT* pp. 1–78.

The book is divided into seven chapters. The first chapter (*Nidāna*) shows considerable affinities to the first chapter of the *Aṣṭa.* The list of the attributes of an Arhat at the beginning of *A* is worked up into a more detailed description of the attributes of those for whom this discourse is intended (4a–6b). The remainder of the chapter is devoted to definitions of the basic terms, i.e. perfection of wisdom (6b–13a), Bodhisattva and great being (13a–18b), and great vehicle (18a–19b). The explanation is, however, much more inclined than *A* to strain after paradoxes, to rely on the ambiguities of words, to go into the details of the Abhidharma, and to dwell on the hidden meaning of the Lord's sayings. The sequence of the argument in chapter 1 can be seen from the following Table:

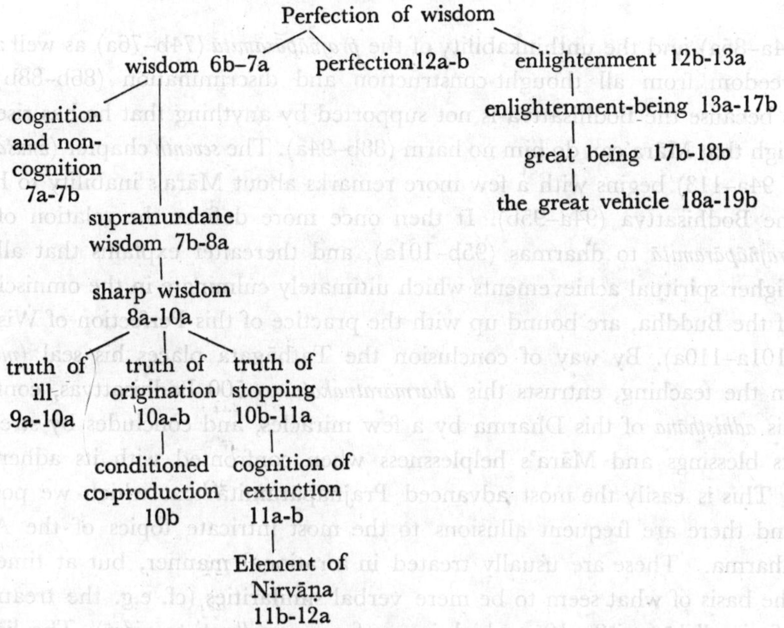

The *second* chapter (*Ānanda,* fol. 19b–24b) praises the qualities of those who are assembled to hear the perfection of wisdom, and describes those who are excluded from its understanding. The *third* chapter (*tathatā,* f. 24b–37), in which the Lord addresses Suvikrāntavikrāmin, expounds the well-known ontological doctrines of these Sūtras, concerning emptiness, Suchness etc. In the *fourth* chapter (*aupamya,* f. 37b–60a), both dharmas and *prajñāpāramitā* are compared to a dream, a mockshow, a reflected image, a mirage, an echo, the pith of a banana tree, or a bubble, and there are in all 12 comparisons of this kind. They are followed (40b–52b) by lengthy reflections on the *prajñāpāramitā* as being *apariniṣpannā,* inaccessible and without own-being, without relation to any dharma, but deep, perfectly pure and infinite. The Sūtra then describes in some detail the persons who can understand the *prajñāpāramitā* and those who cannot. Śāradvatīputra then, in the *fifth* chapter (*Subhūti,* f. 60a–64b) urges Subhūti to break his silence and to explain the Dharma to this pure assembly, but Subhūti replies that there is nothing in particular that can be explained and that needs explaining, and that therefore he does not feel called upon to explain the Dharma. In the *sixth* chapter (*caryā,* f. 64b–94a) the Lord explains the implications of "coursing" in perfect wisdom, and of "developing" perfect wisdom, paying particular attention to the discussion of "perverted views" (*viparyāsa*) (64b–67a, 76a–78a, 81a, 88a), and constantly emphasising the absence of a basis (*ārambaṇa* 67a–74b,

84a–85a) and the unthinkability of the *prajñāpāramitā* (74b–76a) as well as its freedom from all thought-construction and discrimination (86b–88b). It is because the Bodhisattva is not supported by anything that he has risen so high that Māra can do him no harm (88b–94a). The *seventh* chapter (*anuśaṃsā*, f. 94a–113) begins with a few more remarks about Māra's inability to harm the Bodhisattva (94a–95b). It then once more defines the relation of the *prajñāpāramitā* to dharmas (95b–101a), and thereafter explains that all the higher spiritual achievements which ultimately culminate in the omniscience of the Buddha, are bound up with the practice of this Perfection of Wisdom (101a–110a). By way of conclusion the Tathāgata places his seal (*mudrā*) on the teaching, entrusts this *dharmaratnakośa* to 500 Bodhisattvas, confirms his *adhiṣṭhāna* of this Dharma by a few miracles, and concludes by stressing its blessings and Māra's helplessness when confronted with its adherents.

This is easily the most advanced Prajñāpāramitā text which we possess, and there are frequent allusions to the most intricate topics of the Abhidharma. These are usually treated in a rational manner, but at times on the basis of what seem to be mere verbal similarities (cf. e.g. the treatment of *nirvedhikā* at i 8a–10a, which jumps from *nirvidhyati* to *vidyā*). The lists to which the various propositions are applied differ considerably from the standard lists of the large Prajñāpāramitā, and many of the pages of this Sūtra are similar to the litanies of chapters 29 to 31 of the *Aṣṭasāhasrikā*. There are many other echoes of the *Aṣṭasāhasrikā*, and large stretches of the *Suvikrāntavikrāmiparipṛcchā* appear to be variations on the themes of the first two chapters of the *Aṣṭa*.

7. THE PERFECTION OF WISDOM IN 700 LINES.

S: *Saptaśatikā prajñāpāramitā-sūtra.*

ed. G. Tucci, *Memorie della R. accad. dei Lincei, Classe di scienze morali etc.*, ser. 5a, vol. 17 (Roma, 1923) (uses only Ms Cambridge Add 868, 17th or 18th century).

s: ed. J. Masuda, *Journal of the Taisho University,* vols 6–7 (tome 7) (Tōkyō, 1930), part 2, pp. 185–241 (first half only, fol. 1–23a) (uses also Kawaguchi Ms from Nepal, and Kyōto Ms (Imp. Un.)). —Reprinted in P.L. Vaidya, *MSS* I, 1961, pp. 340–351.

Ch: T 232 ii. Mandra(sena). A.D. ca. 502–557. —T viii pp. 726–732. *The Prajñāpāramitā as taught by Mañjuśrī.* —Also at T 310 as 46th Sūtra of *Mahāratnakūṭa.*

T 233 i. Sanghabhara (Sanghapala), A.D. ca. 506–520. —T viii pp.

732–739. Title as T 232.

T 220 (7), no. 574–5. trsl. Hsüan-tsang, A.D. 660–663.

ed: First half also in Masuda.

Ti: (*'phags-pa*) *śes-rab-kyi pha-rol-tu phyin-pa bdun brgya-pa* (*śhes bya ba theg-pa chen-po'i mdo*).

0 737; 760(46) in *Ratnakūṭa,* trsl. Surendrabodhi, Ye-śes-sde. —To 24, Ka 148a–174a; 90 (*Ratnakūṭa*).

Mo: Ligeti no. 769, vol. 47, 136r–171v. —Also no. 838 in *Ratnakūṭa.*

E: E. Conze *SPT* pp. 79–107.

(e: *SS* no. 4, 56, 68, 94, 98–100, 118, 122–3.)

(e: First part in E. Conze *TYBS*, 1967, pp. 191–206.)

The interlocutors are the Buddha, Mañjuśrī, Maitreya, Śāradvatīputra, Ānanda and Nirālambā Bhaginī. This text contains fewer repetitions than the others, and little space is devoted to its praise. It may have been composed about A.D. 450.

The Sūtra falls roughly into five parts: 1. *Nidāna,* 1a–3a. —2. Dialogue, 3a–22b. The problems covered here are: The Suchness of the Tathāgata, development of perfect wisdom (6b–9a), reasons for not trembling (9a–13b), the non-existence of enlightenment, and of all the stages preceding it (M 219–241). —3. Cosmic phenomena, and Ānanda's question, 22b–23a. This first half may originally have been entitled *puṇyakṣetranirdeśa* (23b). 4. Discussion continued, 23b–41b: The unthinkable concentration and cognition (23b–26b), qualifications of the believers (27a–34a), the concentration on one single array (34a–36b), full enlightenment and its conditions (37a–38b), qualities of the sermon and of the listeners worthy of it (38b–41b). —5. End. Śakra and miracles, 41b–43a.

Like the *Vajracchedikā,* this Sūtra also endeavours to bring out the startling and paradoxical character of the teaching. Again and again it returns to the identity of seemingly contradictory opposites, such as reality-limit and individuality (M 213), self and Buddha (M 221), enlightenment and the five deadly sins (M 231–2). The "hidden meaning" (*saṃdhā*), mentioned once in the *Vajracchedikā* (ch. 7), but never in the large Prajñāpāramitā Sūtras, plays a big part (e.g. M 214, 227–9, 240), and pseudo-etymological derivations abound. In this way, *aṇu* is connected with *anuttara* at M 231, and with *anutpanna* at M 228, or *agrā* with *agrāhyatvād* at M 204, etc. There are some echoes of the previous Sūtras (e.g. 31a–32b, and 40–41a are echoes of P 17 sq.), but in general the old problems are subjected to a novel treatment. The concentration on "one single array" (*eka-vyūho samādhi*) occurs also in

Ś and *P* in the list of concentrations (as no. 83). It is there explained as "the reviewing of the duality of no dharma whatsoever" (P 202: *yatra samādhau sthitvā na kasyacid dharmasya dvayatāṃ samanupaśyati*).

Commentaries:

Cy 1: Vimalamitra, *-ṭikā.*
Ti: *rgya-cher 'grel-pa.* mdo-'grel XVI, 9a–105a. —To 3814.

Cy 2: Kamalaśīla, *-ṭikā.*
Ti: *rgya-cher bśad-pa.* mdo-'grel XVI, 105a–209b. —To 3815. trsl. Vimalamitra, Surendrākaraprabha, Nam-mkha' skyoṅ.

7a. PERFECT WISDOM IN 500 LINES.

S: *Pañcaśatikā prajñāpāramitā-sūtra.* Lost.

Ti: *śes-rab-kyi pha-rol-lu phyin-pa lṅa brgya-pa,* trsl. Śīlendrabodhi, Jinamitra, Ye-śes-sde. 0 738. —To. 15, Ka 104a–120b.

Mo: Ligeti no. 770, vol. 47, 171r–197v.

E. E. Conze, *SPT* pp. 108–121.

This is a straightforward account of the ontology of the Prajñāpāramitā.

8. THE "DIAMOND SŪTRA" (THE PERFECTION OF WISDOM WHICH CUTS LIKE A THUNDERBOLT).

S: *Vajracchedikā prajñāpāramitā-sūtra.*

ed. E. Conze, *SOR*, XIII (1957), pp. 27–63. —1974, 2nd edition, with corrections and additions.

ed. M. Mueller, *Anecdota Oxoniensia, Aryan Series,* vol. 1, part 1, (1881), pp. 19–46. Repr. 1972.

ed. N. Dutt, *Gilgit Manuscripts,* IV, 1959, pp. 141–170.

ed. P. L. Vaidya, *MSS* I, 1961, pp. 75–89.

s: ed. F. E. Pargiter, "V. in the original Sanskrit", in: A. F. R. Hoernle, *Manuscript Remains of Buddhist literature found in Eastern Turkestan* (1916), pp. 176–195.—Missing: ch. 1—middle of 2; ch. 4 middle—ch. 10; ch. 16c–17b.

ed. N. P. Chakravarti, "The Gilgit Ms of the V.", in: G. Tucci, *MBT*, I (1956), pp. 182–192 .—Missing ch. 1–13c, 14e–15b.

Ch: T 235, Kumārajiva, A.D. 402. T viii pp. 748–752.—Also in Hashimoto, see J.

cf. F. W. Thomas, "A Buddhist Chinese Text in Brāhmī Script", *ZDMG* (1937), pp. 1–48.—H. W. Bailey, "Vajraprajñāpāramitā", *ZDMG*, 92 (1938), pp. 579–593; with F.W. Thomas' reply at pp. 594–610.—E. Conze, "The frontispiece to the Tun-huang print of 868 A.D.", *The Middle Way*, XXX, 1 (1955), pp. 1–2.—Cf. E. Conze's edition pp. 1–3.

T 236, Bodhiruci, A.D. 509. T viii pp. 752–61.

T 237, Paramārtha, A.D. 562. T viii pp. 762–66.

T 238, Dharmagupta, A.D. 605. T viii pp. 766–772.—This translation sets out to reproduce the Sanskrit original in Chinese with great literal fidelity.

T 220, (9), Hsüan-tsang, A.D. 648. T vii pp. 980–985.

T 239, I-ching, A.D. 703. T viii pp. 772–75.

Ti: *śes-rab-kyi pha-rol-tu phyin-pa rdo-rje gcod-pa.*

trsl. Śīlendrabodhi, Ye-śes-sde. —0 739. —To 16, Ka 121a–132b. —ed. I. J. Schmidt, *Mém. Ac. Imp. des Sciences de St. Pétersbourg*, IV (1837), "Über das Mahāyāna und Pradschnā-Pāramitā der Bauddhen".—mdo-maṅ no. 109. —To 6763 (old Ms), 6762 (Lhasa blockprint), LSOAS 82827 (Peking blockprint). —Hashimoto (see J) reproduces very legibly "by the offset method" a Ms "on dark blue paper with silver lettering", given to him in Mongolia. —Peking blockprint, with S, 74 ff.: To 6773, LSOAS 34849. —Dam-pa's translation, see Heissig, p. 145, n. 2—Central Asian: IOSC no. 170. 32ff, KHA fol. 58–90; frgs. no. 100, 171–176 617, 707. —Tun-huang, Lalou no. 10, 34, 99–100, 116, 118, 577, 578–9, 587.

khotanese: ed. Sten Konow, "The V. in the old Khotanese version of Eastern Turkestan", in Hoernle, etc., I, 1916, pp. 214–356.

cf. Sten Konow in *Norsk Tidsskrift for Sprogvidenskap*, XI (1938), pp. 25 sq. —cf. E. Leumann, *Zur nordarischen Sprache und Literatur*, 1912, pp. 77–82.

The Khotanese version, of the 8th to 10th century, is shorter than the Sanskrit text. It omits chapters 13c, 15b, 16c, most of 17d, 18b–25, 27, 28, 30a, 30b (except the last three sentences). In addition it shows variations from the Sanskrit at 6 and 7, and at 9 and 32a it has what appear to be commentarial additions.

sogdian: ch. 3, 4. ed. H. Reichelt, *Die soghdischen Handschriftenreste des Britischen Museums*, vol. II, (1931) pp. 72–5. —ch. 32, ed. *Stzb. Berl. Ak. d. Wiss.*, 1934, pp. 644–57; cf. 571.

cf. F. Weller, "Bemerkungen zur soghdischen V.", *Acta Orientalia*, XIV (1936), pp. 112–146 (shows that the translation was made from T 235).

uigur: G. Hazai & P. Zieme, Fragmente der uigurischen Version des Jin 'gangjing mit den Gāthās des Meisters Fu, Schriften zur Geschichte und Kultur des alten Orients 3, Berliner Turfantexte I, 1971.

Mo: Kanjur. Ligeti no. 771, vol. 47, 192v–209v.

Other translations: Heissig no. (171). —LSOAS 41650. —For prints and manuscripts see p. 18 of my edition.

N. Poppe, *The Diamond Sūtra.* Three Mongolian Versions of the Vajracchedikā Prajñāpāramitā, Text, Translations, Notes, and Glossaries. Asiatische Forschungen 35. 1971. 230 pp.

trsl. Toyin Guisi (ca 1640): A. Sárközi, "Toyin Guisi's Mongol Vajracchedikā", *AOH* 27, 1, 1973, pp. 43–102.

Manchu: Kanjur.

de Harlez' bilingual Chinese-Manchu Ms of 1837 (from T 235), ed. Ch. de Harlez, *WZKM*, 11 (1897), pp. 209–230.

Kalmuk: cf. *Central Asiatic Journal* 2, 1956, pp. 155–157.

N. Poppe: "An Oyrat Vajracchedikā fragment from Turfan", *Central Asiatic Journal* VII 3, 1962, 170–8 (ch. 25–28).

E: S. Beal, in *JRAS*, N. S, I, pp. 1–24 (1864–5). From T 235.

F. M. Müller, in "Buddhist Mahāyāna Sūtras", *SBE*, 49, 2, (1894), pp. 111–144 (from S). Repr. 1968.

W. Gemmel, *The Diamond Sūtra*, (1912), xxxii, 117. From T 235.

e: Sten Konow, 1916, in Hoernle, etc., I, pp. 276–288. From Khotanese.

e: D. T. Suzuki, in *Manual of Zen Buddhism* (1934), pp. 43–56 (ch. 1–16, 18, 23, 26, 29, 32). From T 235.

E: Wai-tao, in *Buddhist Bible*, ed. D. Goddard (1935), pp. 87–107. From T 235, but the sections are said to be arranged "according to the original order" (p. 661), quite arbitarily in fact.

Shao Chang Lee, *Popular Buddhism in China,* (1940), pp. 27–52 (from T 235).

A. F. Price, *The Jewel of Transcendental Wisdom* (1947); reprinted in 1955 as *The Diamond Sūtra.* From T 235.

E. Conze, *Vajracchedikā Prajñāpāramitā* (1957), pp. 65–92 (from S). — *SPT* pp. 122–139.

Hsüan Hua, 1974 (see Cy 16) (From T 235).

F: Ch. de Harlez, *JAs,* 8ième série, tome 18 (1891), pp. 440–509. From S. *WZKM,* 11, (1897), pp. 331–356. From Manchu.

f: A. David-Neel, *La connaissance transcendante,* 1958, pp. 150–171 (from Ti).

G: I. J. Schmidt, *Mém. Ac. de St. Pétersbourg,* IV (1837). From Ti. M. Walleser, *Prajñāpāramitā. Die Vollkommenheit der Erkenntnis* (1914), pp. 140–158. From S.

J: *Mō-zō Bon-kan-wa Gappeki, Kongō Hannya Haramitsu-kyō,* ed. Hashimoto Kōhō and Shimizu Ryōshō (Tōkyō, 1941).

In addition to a J translation (pp. 173–200) made from the Mongol, this work gives M. Müller's S, the Ch of T 235, and a Ti and Mo text.

H. Nakamura and K. Kino, Tōkyō. 1960. —G. Nagao, Tōkyō 1967.

Estonian: L. Mäll, Teemantsuutra, "Pronksnaeratus", Tallinn 1975, pp. 243–261.

This Sūtra is a short text of 32 chapters, in the form of a dialogue between Subhūti and the Buddha. The Sanskrit original does not, however, give any chapter division, and the one adopted by Max Müller and subsequent scholars dates back to ca. A.D. 530, when it was introduced into Kumāra jīva's translation in China. The first part, which ends at ch. 13b with *tenocyate prajñāpāramiteti,* is fairly coherent. This cannot be said of the second part. Even Asaṅga, Vasubandhu and Kamalaśīla have failed to find a plausible logical sequence behind its repetitions and abrupt transitions, and it may well be that it is no more than a chance medley of stray sayings. Glosses may have in the course of copying become mixed up with the text itself, and at some time the palm leaves appear to have been displaced, and so the sequence of the existing text seems to have been determined by a series of mechanical accidents.

Information about the title of this Sūtra, its transmission, and its philosophical message can be found in the Introduction (pp. 1–15) to E. Conze's edition, and the chief technical terms are explained there in the Glossary (pp. 93–113).

Commentaries:

Cy 1: Asaṅga, *Triśatikāyāḥ prajñāpāramitāyāḥ kārikāsaptati.* 77 vv.
S: ed. G. Tucci, *MBT,* I (1956), pp. 54–92.
Ch: In T 1511, trsl. Bodhiruci, A.D. 509. —Ed. with S in Tucci.
T 1514 i, trsl. I-ching, A.D. 711. —ed. with S in Tucci.
Ti: *śes-rab-kyi pha-rab-rol-tu phyin-pa rdo-rje gcod-pa bśad-pa'i bśad sbyar-gyi tshig-le'ur byas-pa.*
Tanjur ño CXXVIII no. 1 (not in Bu-ston's Catalogue, nor in the Derge edition, or in To). —Cf. from Tun-huang, Lalou no. 605: 2f. end of *V. -rnam-par bśad-pa tshig-le'ur byas-pa* (*V-vibhāṣā-kārikā*), attributed to Dbyig gñen.
E: trsl. G. Tucci, *MBT,* I (1956), pp. 93–128.

Cy 1–1: Subcommentary by Vasubandhu.
S: Lost.
Ch: T 1511 iii, trsl. Bodhiruci, A.D. 509.
T 1513 iii, trsl. Yi-ching, A.D. 711.

Cy 1–1–1: Subcommentary by Vajrarṣi.
Ch: T 1512 x. trsl. Bodhiruci (cf. Bagchi 253).

Cy 1–1–2: K'uei-chi: Ch: T 1816 iii (to T 1511).

Cy 1–1–3: I-ching: Ch: T 1817 i (to T 1511).

Cy 2. Vasubandhu (Asaṅga).
S: (*Saptārth(ik)aṭikā?*). Lost.
Ch: T 1510 ii, trsl. Dharmagupta, ca. A.D. 600.
For two recensions see G. Tucci, *MBT,* I (1956), pp. 18–9, 41–50.
Ti: *don bdun-gyi rgya-cher 'grel-pa.* To 3816. attr. to Dbyig gñen. trsl Gshon dpal, A.D. 1450.
e: Summary in G. Tucci, *MBT,* I (1956), pp. 131–171.

Cy 3: Śrīdatta (Guṇāda?): Ch: T 1515 ii. trsl. Divākāra, A.D. 683.

Cy 4: Kamalaśīla, *-ṭikā.*

Ti: *rgya-cher 'grel-pa.* mdo-'grel XVI, 209b–285b. —To 3817, trsl. Mañjuśrī, Jinamitra, Ye-śes-sde. —Fragments (12 ff) in IOSC no. 177 and no. 178 (?), 4ff.

This cy generally follows the arrangements of cy 2. It tries (250a–266a) to find a unifying link between chapters 17 to 29 by regarding them as an account of the seven accomplishments of a Buddha.

Cy 5: Chih-i Ch: T 1698 i

Cy 6: Chi-tsang. Ch: T 1699 iv.

Cy 7: K'uei-chi. Ch: T 1700 ii.

Cy 8: Tsung-mi. Ch: T 1701 ii.

Cy 9: Tzŭ-hsüan. Ch: T 1702 i.

Cy 10: Tsung-lei and Ju-ch'i. Ch: T 1703 i.

Cy 11: Chih-yen. Ch: T 1704 ii.

Cy 12: Lü-tsu.
f: de Harlez, *JAs*, 1891, pp. 499–509.

Cy 13: Han-shan. *Chin Kang Chüeh I* 1616.
E: Ch. Luk, "The Diamond Cutter of Doubts", in *Ch'an and Zen Teaching,* First Series, 1960, pp. 149–206.
f: Ch. Luk, *La Pensée Bouddhique,* VI, 5 (1958), pp. 16–18.

This is a very fine commentary which concentrates on the spiritual meaning as seen by a Ch'an master. Han-shan maintains that the Sūtra does not aim at revealing the Wisdom which removes the defilements of beings, but only sets out to cut off peoples' doubts and awaken their faith. The doubts concern (1) the nature of the true Buddha, (2) the Dharma, which had been expounded in apparently selfcontradictory terms, and (3) the student who may well wonder whether he is really qualified for this sublime teaching, and whether he can actually observe it. Han-shan regards the commentary of Vasubandhu, the 21st Patriarch of the Ch'an sect, as the only one which is really authoritative. If the Sūtra is interpreted as a Remover of Doubts, one must first discover the hidden doubts which Subhūti had in his mind. Because these were not expressed in words, Ānanda did not record them, but only the Buddha's replies. Han-shan lists 35 such doubts, as against Vasubandhu's 27. Part I of the Sūtra (ch. 1–16) is held to deal with 17 coarse errors, part II (ch. 17–32) with 18 subtle ones. It was thus a continuous string of the Disciple's wrong conceptions, from the coarsest to the finest, which the Buddha broke up successfully in His teaching of Prajñā. When all the erroneous views were completely eliminated, the original nature of all living beings, including Subhūti and the Tathāgata, was fully revealed. The translator, Charles Luk (Lu K'uan Yü) is a disciple of the Ven. Hsü Yün, a Ch'an abbot in the Fu Chien province, who lived from 1840 to 1959.

Cy 14: Ye-śes rgyal-mtshan, blo-bzaṅ.
Ti: *Rdo-rje gcod-pa'i phan-yon* (On the benefits of the V.). To 6811. 36ff.

Cy 15: E. Conze, *Buddhist Wisdom Books* (1958), pp. 21–74 (Reprinted from: *The Middle Way,* 1956 and 1957). Repr. 1966, 1970, 1972, 1975 (with corrections). The cy to ch. 13 to 19 in: "Some more comments on the Diamond Sūtra", *Vajra* 3, 1976, pp. 3–14.

Cy 16: Dhyāna Master Hsüan Hua, *A General Explanation of the Vajra Prajñā Pāramitā Sūtra,* 1974.

Cf. also Lalou 606, frgs of a cy to V, 52ff. —cf. G. Hazai and P. Zuene, "Ein uigurisches Blockdruck-fragment einer Einleitung zum Vajracchedikāsūtra", *Acta Orientalia* 21, 1968, 1–14. —G. Schopen, The phrase 'sa pṛthivīpradesaś caityabhūto bhavet' in the Vajracchedikā: Notes on the cult of the book in Mahāyāna. *IIJ* 17, 1975, pp. 147–181. —K. Kino, On the influence of V upon the SaPu.-sūtra, *JIBS* 10, 1962, pp. 380–376.

9. THE PERFECTION OF WISDOM IN 50 LINES.

S: *Prajñāpāramitā-ardhaśatikā*; or: *pañcāśikā?*. Nepalese Ms, S. Matsunami, *Catalogue,* 1965, p. 187 (*Advaya-śatikā*)

Ch: T 248 i. Dānapāla, ca. A.D. 1000. —T viii pp. 845–6.

Ti: (*'phags-pa*) *bcom-ldan-'das-ma śes-rab-kyi pha-rol-tu phyin-pa lṅa bcu-pa.* O 740. —To 18, Ka 139b–142a. —Narthang, Sna-tshogs 252a–255b.

Mo: Ligeti no. 772, vol. 47, pp 209v–212v.

E: E. Conze, *SPT* pp. 154–6.

This Sūtra is a compilation of three or four stock phrases from the larger Sūtras, and may have originated at any time after the completion of the Large Pajñāpāramitā. It begins with an exhortation to practise the perfection of wisdom, and similar passages occur at *A* i 6–7=*Ś* 502=*P* 123. Then it proceeds to give the list of the wholesome dharmas embodied in the perfection of wisdom, i.e. the list of items which is constantly repeated in the large Sūtra. It then considers the difficulties of fathoming the prajñāpāramitā in a way very close to *A* viii 185=*Ś* xxvi f. 6a, sq., and ends up with an assurance that the constant practice of perfect wisdom shall lead to full enlightenment.

10. THE SŪTRA WHICH GIVES THE DIRECT MEANING OF PERFECT WISDOM.

Ch: T 247 i. trsl. Dānapāla, A.D. 980–1000. —T viii p. 845. —*Buddha-bhāṣita-nita-artha-prajñāpāramitā-sūtra.*

With a few variations this Sūtra gives two extracts from the Large Prajñāpāramitā (*P* 17—21, and *P* 37—38), interrupted by an enumeration of the 10 *vikalpas* of Yogācāra tradition (see pp. 99–101).

11. THE HEART SŪTRA.

This exists in two versions, a long (L) and a short (Sh) one. They agree in the body of the Sūtra, but the longer recension has, both at the beginning and the end, an account of the circumstances of its preaching.

S: *Prajñāpāramitā-hṛdaya-sūtra.*

ed. E. Conze, *JRAS,* 1948, pp. 34–47 (L)=*TYBS* pp. 149–154.

ed. F. M. Müller, "Buddhist Texts from Japan", *Anecdota Oxoniensia, Aryan Series,* vol. 1, part iii. *The ancient palm-leaves containing the Prajñāpāramitā-hṛdaya-sūtra and the Uṣṇiṣa-vijaya-dhāraṇī,* ed. F. M. Müller and B. Nanjio (1884); (L, S), Repr. 1972.

ed. Shaku Hannya, "The prajñāpāramitāhṛdayasūtra", Sanskrit and Tibetan texts (+some notes), *The Eastern Buddhist,* 2, (1922–3), pp. 163–175 (L).

ed. D. T. Suzuki, *Essays in Zen Buddhism,* III (1934), p. 190 (Sh); *Manual of Zen Buddhism* (1935), p. 27 (Sh).

ed. P. L. Vaidya, *MSS* I, 1961, pp. 97–9 (inaccurate).

Ch: T 250. Kumārajīva, ca. A.D. 400 (or one of his disciples) (Sh). —T viii p. 847. —*Great-perfection-of-wisdom great-knowledge-divine-Sūtra.* —

Text from Kuchā.

T 251. Hsüan-tsang, A.D. 649. (Sh) *Prajñāpāramitāhṛdayasūtra.* In T printed with 1. Imperial preface of Ming dynasty, by T'ai-tsu (1368–98); 2. Preface by priest Hui-chung of T'ang. -Stein collection S 4216, the only dated edition, A.D. 749. BSOS IX p. 11.—ed. in D. T. Suzuki, *EZB*, III, p. 191. —Ch. edition, Bodl. Chin. 505f/2 ser. d. 353, 7 pp. in large letters. —Jap. edition, with transliteration into Hiragana, *Zō-ho sho-da-ra-ni,* Nanjio Cat. Bodl. no. 3.

For the differences between T 250 and T 251 see E. Conze, *JRAS,* 1948, p. 50.

T 252. Dharmacandra, A.D. 741 (L.) —*The Prajñāpāramitāhṛdayasūtra which is the Storehouse of Omniscience.* —Text from Eastern India. Agrees closely with T 251.

T 253. Prajñā. A.D. 790 (L). Text from Kashmir. The bulk agrees verbally with T 251.

T 254. Prajñācakra, A.D. 861 (L). Text from Central Asia.

T 255. Fa-ch'êng, A. D. 856 (L). Text from Tibet; found in Tun-huang; agrees with Ti.

T 257. Dānapāla, ca. A.D. 1000 (L). —*Prajñāpāramitā Sūtra of the holy mother of the Buddha, spoken by the Buddha.* —Text from Udyāna.

cf. Ch. Willemen, "The Chinese Prajñāpāramitāhṛdayasūtra", *Samādhi* VI, 1972, pp. 14–22 (T 251); pp. 52–65 (T 250); pp. 102–15 (T 253–4); pp. 152–66 (T 255, 257).

In addition five translations are now lost; the first apparently goes back to A.D. 223. See the list on p. 2 of W. Fuchs, *Hsin-ching,* 1970, where a few of the dates differ from mine.

Ti: *bcom-ldan-'das-ma śes-rab-kyi pha-rol-tu phyin-pa'i sñiṅ-po.* trsl. Vimalamitra (L) Rin-chen sde. Revised by Dge-blo, Nam-mkha'. 0 no. 160, —To 21, Ka 144b–146a. Also 531 (Rgyud). —Narthang, Sna-tshogs no. 13, f. 262b–264a; Rgyud DA, xi, no. 13, pp. 92a–94. —ed. Eastern Buddhist II, 1922. —mdo-maṅ no. 101. —To 6760, 8ff (Lhasa edition); 6761, 8ff (Kun-bde gliṅ edition); IOSC 117; 118, 2; 119–121. Central Asia, Lalou, (ca. A.D. 800–1035) no. 22.3–87.4–101.2 (end missing). —449 trsl. from Ch., 450, 457–8, 460, 462. —448 phonetic transcription of

Chinese version–463. 464. —Fragments 451, 456, 461. —Total, or fragments, 465–493, 494. 1264–1277.

The Tun-huang version in D. Ueyama *JIBS* 26, 1965, pp. 783–779.

Another translation, which differs in details:

ed. L. Feer, *Tableau de la grammaire mongole* (Paris, 1866), Appendix.

Sogdian: E. Benveniste, *Textes sogdiens,* 1940, 142–4.

Mo: Ligeti no. 162; vol. 12, 44r–45v (Dandr-a).

Collection of Schilling von Canstadt. Bibl. de l'Institut de France; cf. *T'oung Pao,* XVII (1930), no. 3543–no. 3588, LI, fol. 224r–225v.

Polyglots.

Manchu: Ms of 1837. ed. Ch. de Harlez, *WZKM,* 11 (1897), pp. 212–3.

J. L. Mish, The Manchu version of the HS, *Etudes Mongoles* 5, 1974, pp. 87–90.

Polyglots: In the 18th century the Hṛdaya was printed in polyglots at the instigation of the Manchu Court where the Sūtra was greatly esteemed. Occasionally, as in the Ch'ien-lung print of ca. 1770, the Sanskrit text is given in Lantsa characters. (See Ce on p. 154 of TYBS). Others give translations into Chinese (similar to T 253 and 254), Manchu, Mongol and Tibetan. L. Feer, in *L'essence de la science transcendante,* 1866, prints Ti, Skr, Mo. Now we have the beautiful reproduction of the 1724 print in W. Fuchs, *Die mandschurischen Druckausgaben des Hsin-ching* (*Hṛdayasūtra*), 1970, who also gives the pentaglott of the Ch'ien-lung period. cf. also L. Hurvitz, Two polyglot recensions of the Heart Scripture, *Journal of Indian Philosophy* 3, 1975, pp. 17–66.

E: S. Beal, *JRAS,* N. S., I (1865), pp. 25–29; *Catena of Buddhist Scriptures from the Chinese* (1871), pp. 282–284 (from T 251).

F. M. Müller; as at S; and *SBE,* 49, 2 (1894), pp. 153–4 (from S). Repr. 1968

Shaku Hannya, *EB,* II, 3–4, (1923), pp. 165–6 (from Ch).

K. Saunders, *Lotuses of the Mahayana* (1924), pp. 42–4 (from Ch?).

Lee Shao-Chang, *J. North China Branch, RAS,* LXV (1934), pp. 150–1 (from T 251).

D. T. Suzuki: *EZB,* III (1934), pp. 192–4; *Manual* (1935), pp. 27–32.

W. Y. Evans-Wentz, *Tibetan Yoga and Secret Doctrines* (1935), pp. 355

-9 (from Ti).

T. Richard, in Ashvaghosha, *The awakening of faith,* 1961, pp. 95–6 (grotesque).

D. Goddard, in: *A Buddhist Bible,* 2nd ed. (1938), pp. 85–6; "made from various English translations".

Lee Shao-Chang, *Popular Buddhism in China* (1939), pp. 23–26 (from T 251) —Also in: C. H. Hamilton, *Buddhism* (1952), pp. 113–115.

J. Tyberg, *Sanskrit keys to the Wisdom Religion* (1940), p. 147.

E. Conze, *The Middle Way,* XX, 5, (1946), p. 105 (from S); —Also *Buddhist Texts* (1954), no. 146. —Also *SS* no. 54. *SPT* pp. 140–143.

E. J. Thomas, *The Perfection of Wisdom* (1952), pp. 79–80 (from S).

Alex Wayman, *Berkeley Bussei* (1957) pp. 12–13 (from S). —*PhEW* xi, 1961, pp. 109–113 (with comments).

Lu K'uan-yu in *Fo-hsüeh ts'ung-shu,* Bilingual Series I, Taipei 1962, pp. 134–136.

Thong-pa Lama, *The Middle Way* XL 1, 1965, pp. 29–30.

Ph. Kapleau, *The Wheel of Death,* 1971, pp. 82–84.

F: L. Feer, "Fragments Extraits du Kandjour", *AMG,* V (1883), pp. 177–9 (from Ti).

P. Regnaud et M. Ymaizoumi, *Actes du 6ième Congrès International des Orientalistes,* III (1885), pp. 189–190 (from S).

Ch. de Harlez, *JAs,* 18 (1891), pp. 445–6 (from Manchu). Also: *WZKM,* 11 (1897), pp. 331–3.

La Pensée Bouddhique, 1941, pp. 12–14 (after Vai-Tae et D. Goddard).

J. Bacot, *Le Bouddha* (1947), pp. 86–88 (from 10th c. Ti Ms).

J. Thamar, *Etudes Asiatiques* (1949) pp. 12–14.

A. David-Neel, *La connaissance transcendante,* 1958, pp. 95–101 (from Ti)

G: *Im Zeichen Buddha's* (1957), pp. 125–6 (after E. Conze, 1954).

Dutch: J. Ensink, "De Essentie van de volmaakte deugd der wijsheid", in: *De grote weg naar het licht* (1955), pp. 89–91.

The immense popularity of this Sūtra is attested by the abundance of translations and commentaries. Avalokiteśvara, normally inconspicuous in the Prajñāpāramitā Sūtras, here explains the essence, or "heart", of the doctrine to Śāriputra. Nine tenths of the content are borrowed from the large Prajñāpāramitā (*P* 43–47=*Ś* i 136–141; *P* 242–269=*A* i 24–32; and

Ś xix f. 293b), but the parts have been welded together into a convincing artistic unity. This is the *dharmacakrapravartanasūtra* of the new dispensation, which represents the "second turning of the wheel of Dharma" (*A* ix 203), and it sets out to give a restatement of the four Holy Truths in the light of the dominant idea of Emptiness. At the end the teaching is summed up in a famous *mantra,* i.e. *gate gate pāragate pārasaṃgate bodhi svāhā,* which shows some similarity to Sāṃkhyā teaching (cf. the comments on Sāṃkhyakārikā 50 in *Sāṃkhyapravacanabhāṣya* III 43 and *Sāṃkhyatattvakaumudī*).

Commentaries:

Cy 1: Vimalamitra, *-ṭikā.*
Ti: *rgya-cher bśad-pa.* mdo-'grel XVI, 285b–302b. —To 3818, trsl. Vimalamitra, Nam-mkha', Ye-śes sñiṅ-po.

Cy 2: Jñānamitra, *-vyākhyā.*
Ti: *rnam-par bśad-pa.* mdo-'grel XVI, 302b–309b. —To 3819.

Cy 3: Vajrapāṇi, *-ṭikārthapradipa nāma.*
Ti: *'grel-pa don-gyi sgron-ma shes bya-ba.* mdo-'grel XVI, 309b–319b. —To 3820, trsl. Phyag-na rdo-rje, Seṅ-ge rgyal-mtshan.

Cy 4: Praśāstrasena, *-ṭikā (deśārtha-prakāśikā).*
Ti: *rgya-cher 'grel-pa.* mdo-'grel XVI 319b–330b. —To 3821. —cf. IOSC no. 122, *bśad-pa,* 9ff, Ka 52–61. —Fragments of same cy no. 124, 125.
E: E. Conze: Praśāstrasena's Ārya-Prajñāpāramitā-Hṛdaya-Ṭīkā, in: *Buddhist Studies in Honour of I. B. Horner,* 1974, pp. 51–61.

Cy 5: Kamalaśīla, *-ṭikā.*
Ti: *'grel-pa.* mdo-'grel XVI 330b–333a, trsl. Kumāraśrībhadra, 'Phags-pa śes-rab. —Peking no. 5221

Cy 6: Dīpaṅkaraśrījñāna and Legs-pa'i śes-rab, *-vyākhyā.*
Ti: *rnam-par bśad-pa.* mdo-'grel XVI 333a–338b. —To 3823. trsl. Dīpaṅkaraśrījñāna, Tshul-khrims rgyal-ba.

Cy 7: Śrīmahājana, *-artha-parijñāna.*
Ti: *don yoṅs-su śes-pa.* mdo-'grel XVI 338b–350a. —To 3822, trsl. Seṅ-ge rgyal-mtshan.
Y. Hariba, *Chibetto-bun Hannya-shingyō Chūshaku Zensho* (A

collection of all the commentaries of the P. P. -hṛdaya-sūtra (contained in the Tibetan Tripitaka), 1938.

Cy 7a: *Ssa byūryimahāprajñāpārāme hiya haṃbeca.* Khotanese "Summary of the hundred myriad Mahāprajñāpāramitā".

Kh: ed. H. W. Bailey, *Khotanese Buddhist Texts* (1951), pp. 54–61.

Cy 8: K'uei-chi, *-yu tsan.*

Ch: T 1710 ii. T. vol. xxxiii, pp. 514, 2–542, 3.

Cy 9: Yüan-t'sê, *Abridged, or brief commentary.*

Ch: T 1711 i. T vol. xxxiii pp. 542, 2–552, 1.

Cy 10: Fa-tsang, *-lü shu.* Brief Commentary. 702 A.D.

Ch: T 1712 i. T xxxiii pp. 552, 1–555, 2.

E: F. H. Cook, "Brief Commentary on the *Heart Sūtra*", *Buddhist Meditation: Theory and Practice* (Honolulu 1976).

e: Summary in C. C. Chang, *The Buddhist Teaching of Totality,* 1971, pp. 197–206.

Cy 10–1: Shi-hui, *A pearl-chain of remarks to the "short explanation of the Heart Sūtra" in the Prajñāpāramitā* (So Forke 842).

Ch: T 1713 ii. T xxxiii 552, pp. 2–568.

Cy 10–2: Chung-hsi (Sung).

Ch: Zokuzōkyō I. 41. pp. 340–356.

Cy 10–3: Ch'ien Ch'ien-i (Ming).

Ch: Zokuzōkyō I. 41. pp. 357–390.

Cy 11: Tsung-lei and Ju-ch'i.

Ch: T 1714 i. T xxxiii pp. 569–571, 1.

Cy 12: Wu-ching-tsê.

Ch: cf. Beal, *Catena,* p. 279.

Cy 13: Han-Shan. *Hsin Ching Chih Shuo.*

E: Ch. Luk, "A Straight Talk on the Heart Sūtra", in *Ch'an and Zen Teaching,* First Series, 1960, pp. 209–233.

Cy 14: *Shin kyo kie,* A.D. 1839. 34 leaves. cy to T 251. (Bodl. chin. 505f/1; ser. d. 352).

Cy 15: *Hsin-ching Chuan-chu.* A Chinese cy to the Hṛdaya Sūtra. By Upāsaka Chou Chih-an (no. 14, 227th Lane, Shih-Men

1st Road, Shanghai, China).

Cy 16: Vairocana, of Pa-gor, after Śārisiṃha.

Ti: *śer sñiṅ 'grel-pa sṅags-su 'grel-pa (mantra-vivṛta-prajñāhṛdaya-vṛtti)*. mdo-'grel CXXIV 103a–108b. —An explanation addressed to King Khri-sroṅ lde-btsan.

Cy 16a: Hakuin Zenji, A.D. 1753 (or 1744), *Dokugo-chū Shingyō*. "A Venomous Commentary on the P. P. Heart Sūtra".

E: E. Nishimura, in D. K. Swearer, *Secrets of the Lotus,* 1971, pp. 190–211.

cf. R. H. Blyth, Hakuin's commentary on the Shingyō, in: *Zen and Zen Classics,* vol. VII, 1962, pp. 193–8.

Cy 16b: Kōbō Daishi, A. D. 830, *Hannya-shingyō hiken* (Secret Key to the Heart Sūtra).

E: Y. S. Hakeda, *Kūkai, Major Works,* 1972, pp. 262–275.

Cy 17: Hōgo, A.D. 1807.

J: *Bon-mon hannya-shingyō shaku.* cf. Nanjio, *Bodl. Ct.,* 1881, no. 37.

Cy 18: S. Shiraishi, "Hannya-shingyō Ryaku-bonpon no kenkyū", *Nihon Bukkyō Kyōkai Nempō,* xii (1940), 38 pp.

Cy 19: E. Conze, *Buddhist Wisdom Books* (1958), pp. 77–107. (Reprinted from *The Middle Way,* 1955 and 1956).

Cy 20: Abh[illegible] On the Heart Sūtra, trsl. T. Leggett, *The Tiger's Cave,* 1964, pp. 15–125.

Cy 21: J. Keyaerts, Le Hṛdaya Sūtra, *Samādhi* I 2, 1967, pp. 25–31.

Cf. Tun-huang: Lalou no. 495 and 496, both entitled *'grel-pa.*

Cf. Shiiba Yoshio, *Hannya-shingyō taisei,* 1932.

D. T. Suzuki, "The significance of the Prajñāpāramitāhṛdaya Sūtra in Zen Buddhism", *EZB,* III (1934), pp. 187–206. —E. Conze, "The Hṛdaya Sūtra; its scriptural background", *The Middle Way,* xx 6 (1946), pp. 124–7; xxi 1, (1946), pp. 9–11, 17. "Text, Sources and Bibliography of the Prajñāpāramitāhṛdaya", *JRAS,* 1948, pp. 33–51. Reprinted TYBS pp. 148–167. —J. Thamar, "*Prajñāpāramitā*", *Etudes Asiatiques/Asiatische Studien,* 1/2 (1949), pp. 7–29 (continued in *Etudes Traditionelles,* 1950, ca. p. 171). Reprinted in *Samādhi* IV 1, 1970, pp.

19–43. —C. C. Chang, *The Buddhist Teaching of Totality,* 1971, pp. 60–120. —Pai Hui, "On the word cittāvaraṇa in no. 11", *Sino-Indian Studies* 3, 1949, pp. 131–139. —Wu Pai-wei, "A discourse on the interpretation of cittāvaraṇa in the Sanskrit text of the PP-hṛdaya", *Xiandai Foxue,* Peking 1958, no. 11, pp. 5–16.

B. SPECIAL TEXTS

12. THE QUESTIONS OF NĀGAŚRĪ.

S: *Nāgaśriparipṛcchā.* Lost.

Ch: T 234 ii. trsl. Shih Hsiang-kung, ca. A.D. 420–479. —T VIII pp. 740–48. *Sūtra on the Bodhisattva Mañjuśrī's highest pure act of seeking alms, spoken by the Buddha.* —So "acc. to the present tradition, but presumably by someone between Dharmarakṣa and Kumārajīva" (Hikata p. xvi; cf. xxii).

T 220, 576. trsl. Hsüan-tsang, A.D. 660 (shorter than T 234).

f: Hōbōgirin, pp. 164–6.

e: E. Conze, *SPT* pp. 160–164.

This Sūtra applies the basic conceptions of the Prajñāpāramitā to the various aspects of begging for alms, eating, etc.

12a. THE QUESTIONS OF PRAVARA, THE DEVA-KING.

S: (*Devarāja-Pravara-prajñāpāramitā-sūtra*). Lost.

Ch: T 231 vii. Upaśūnya, A.D. 565, T VIII pp. 687–726.

T 220 (6), Hsüan-tsang, A.D. 660, f. 566–573.

13. PRAJÑĀPĀRAMITĀ SŪTRA EXPLAINING HOW BENEVOLENT KINGS MAY PROTECT THEIR COUNTRIES.

S: (*Kāruṇikā-rājā prajñāpāramitāsūtra?*). Lost.

Ch: *Jên-wang hu-kuo.* (*Ninnō*).

T 245 ii. Kumārajīva, A.D. 401, T VIII pp. 825–834.

T 246 ii. Amoghavajra, A.D. 765, T VIII pp. 834–845.

It has been suggested that no more than a small portion of this Sūtra is likely to go back to an Indian original, and that the remainder was composed in China. The Sūtra may be fairly early, since a Chinese translation, now lost, of a *Prajñā of the benevolent kings,* in 2 fasc., can, on the authority of 13 cy 1, ca. A.D. 600, be ascribed to Dharmarakṣa (A.D. 307–313).

e: Summary in: M. W. de Visser, *Ancient Buddhism in Japan* (1928–35), I, pp. 116–189 (cf. 12–13). —E. Conze, *SPT* pp. 165–183.

The following description of the contents of the *Ninnō* is based on Kumārajīva's translation, but I have noted the main variations in Amoghavajra's (=Am) translation.

I. Chapter 1. *Preface*: Description of the assembly, which includes 16 kings. Cosmic wonders. Appearance of 10 Bodhisattvas from the ten directions. —*Ch.* 2. *Considering emptiness* (Considering the Tathāgata, Am): Protection of the Buddha-fruit. 13 (18, Am) kinds of emptiness. Buddhahood explained. —*Ch.* 3. *Instructions and conversion of Bodhisattvas* (Actions to be performed (*caryā*) by Bodhisattvas, Am): Deals with the 14 kinds of forbearance (*kṣānti*). —*Ch.* 4. *The two truths:* Conventional and ultimate truth. Blessings derived from perfect wisdom. —Name of the Sūtra, and assurance of its power to protect beings who cherish it (Am omits this).

II. Chapter 5. *Protecting the country*: The worship and reading of the Prajñāpāramitā protects both countries and individuals from all calamities. A story describes how in olden times Śakra repelled whole armies by having the Prajñāpāramitā Sūtra read by a hundred priests. Another story tells of the conversion of a thousand kings by the recitation and explanation of the Sūtra. The kings present in the assembly should therefore keep and read this Sūtra, and have it explained. —*Ch.* 6. *Spreading flowers* (Miracles, Am): Flower miracles are described. Then the perfection of wisdom is praised. Finally the Tathāgata shows his wonderful miraculous power by means of five miracles. —*Ch.* 7. *Receiving and keeping this Sūtra:* The practice of the Dharma,—14 kinds of forbearance, 10 acts of virtue, 10 stages, 84,000 perfections. Prediction of 7 calamities, due to impiety, at the time of the decay of the Law. The kings should use this perfection of wisdom to establish Dharma, and to drive away the calamities. Perfect wisdom is a precious jewel which protects. The ceremony to be performed is described. Five Bodhisattvas will protect the virtuous countries. In Kumārajīva's translation they are called "roars" (*nāda*), whereas in Amoghavajra's their names differ, and all begin with *vajra-*. Amoghavajra at the end of this chapter adds 36 *dhāraṇis* which will protect. —*Ch.* 8. *The Buddha commits the Sūtra and the Triratna to the benevolent kings*: Prophecies concerning the extinction of the doctrine, and disasters to come. Name of the Sūtra, which is also called "deathless medicine of the Law", because, when one obeys it, it can cure all diseases.

Commentaries:

Cy 1:	Kuan-ting.	Ch: T 1705 v. On T 245.
Cy 1-1:	Shan-yüeh, *Record of Divine Treasures*.	Ch.: T 1706 iv.

Cy 2: Chi-tsang. Ch: T 1707 vi (on T 245).
Cy 3: Yüan-ts'ê. Ch: T 1708 vi (to T 245).
Cy 4: Liang-p'i. Ch: T 1709 vii (to T 246).
A commentary by Paramārtha (A.D. 548–69) is mentioned in *Bukkyō Daijii,* III, p. 3742, 1.

Cy 5–6: The *Bukkyō Daijii* (de Visser, I, 120) mentions, as written during the Northern Sung dynasty (960–1127), two commentaries to the *Ninnō* by members of the Avataṃsaka school. The authors are (5) Yü-yung, and (6) the Korean Ching-yüan.

Cy 7–17: Japanese commentaries by Gyōshi (Hossō), 750; Saichō, or Dengyō Daishi (Tendai), 767–822 (to T 245); Kūkai, or Kōbō Daishi (Shingon), 774–835: *Ninnō-kyō kaidai* (to T 246), and *Ninnō-kyō bō*; Enchin, or Chishō Daishi (Tendai), 814–891; Kakuchō (Tendai), ca. 1028; Shinkaku (Shingon) 1181; Dōhan (Shingon), 1184–1252; Raiyu (Shingon), 1226–1304; Ryōjō (Tendai), ca. 1299; Ryōta (Shingon), 1622–80; Kwōken (Tendai), 1652–1739.

14. EXPLANATION OF THE FIVE PERFECTIONS.

S: *Pañcapāramitānirdeśa.* Lost.

Ch: T 220 (11–15), Hsüan-tsang, A.D. 659–663. ch. I, fasc. 579–583, II 584–588, III 589, IV 590, V 591–592.

Ti: (*'phags-pa*) *pha-rol-tu phyin-pa lṅa bstan-pa* (*shes bya-ba theg-pa chen-po'i mdo*). trsl. Jinamitra, Ye-śes-sde.
In Mdo sde. —0 848. —To 181, Tsa 1b–76b.

Mo: Ligeti no. 937, vol. 77, 1–102v (Eldeb).

The chapter headings are: 1. *rjes-su yi raṅ-ba,* Rejoicing. —2. *sbyin-pa'i thabs-pa,* Skill in giving. —3. *dpe,* Similies. —4. *mtshan-ma med-pa,* Marklessness. —5. *sgyu-ma lta-bur bstan-pa,* Exposition of illusoriness. —6. *'jig-rten-gyi khams graṅs med-par byaṅ-chub sems-dpa' spyod-pa daṅ saṅs-rgyas bstan-pa,* The exposition by the Buddha of the practice of the Bodhisattvas in countless world systems (?). —7. *phyir mi ldog-pa'i sa,* The irreversible stage. —8. *byaṅ-chub sems-dpa' yoṅs-su sbyoṅ-bar bya-ba,* The preparations (*parikarma*) of a Bodhisattva. —9. *sbyin-pa'i pha-rol-tu phyin-pa.* The perfection of giving.

15. THE PRAJÑĀPĀRAMITĀ SŪTRA, SPOKEN BY THE BUDDHA, WHICH AWAKENS TO ENLIGHTENMENT ABOUT ONE'S TRUE NATURE.

Ch: T 260 iv, trsl. Wei-ching, ca. A.D. 981. —T VIII pp. 854–864.

16. SŪTRA WHICH DEALS WITH THE UNDERSTANDING OF THE SIX PERFECTIONS IN THE MAHĀYĀNA.

Ch: T 261 x. Prajñā A.D. 788. T VIII pp. 865–917. —N 1004: *mahāyāna-buddhi* (*=li-ts'ü*) *-ṣaṭ-pāramitā-sūtra.*

No one seems so far to have made a study of this Sūtra.

C. TANTRIC TEXTS[1]

CA. Sūtras

17. THE PERFECTION OF WISDOM IN 150 LINES.

S: *Adhyardhaśatikā prajñāpāramitā-sūtra.* Or: *Prajñāpāramitā-nayaśatapañcāśatikā.*

ed. E. Leumann, *Zur nordarischen Sprache und Literatur* (1912), pp. 92–99.

ed. Izumi, Toganoo, Wogihara (Kyōto, 1917), pp. 1–19.

ed. S. Toganoo, *Rishukyō no kenkyū* (1930), pp. 1–9.

ed. P. L. Vaidya, *MSS* I, 1961, pp. 90–91.

The Sanskrit text is based on a slightly incomplete Central Asian Ms. of 168 lines: 45 are missing, among them 10 at the beginning and 6 at the end.

Ch: T 220 (10), 578. Hsüan-tsang, ca. A.D. 660 ($16^1/_2$ columns).

T 240 i. Bodhiruci, A.D. 693 ($7^1/_2$ columns).

T 241 ii. Vajrabodhi, ca. A.D. 725 (10 columns).

T 243 i. Amoghavajra, A.D. 770 ($7^1/_2$ columns).

T 242 i. Dānapāla, A.D. 980 (7 columns).

T 244 vii. Dharmabhadra, A.D. 999 ($113^1/_2$ columns). —*Anuttaramūla - mahāsaukhya - vajrāmogha - samaya - mahātantrarājasūtra,* N 1037. With an imperial preface by Chên-tsung (A.D. 998–1022), vol. VIII pp. 786–824.

This greatly expanded version exists also in Tibetan as *Śriparamādyamantrakalpakhaṇḍa* (no. 120 in Peking Kanjur), trsl. ca. 1025. 17 of its verses are preserved in the Javanese ritual, Sang Hyang Kamahāyānan Mantranaya (no. 26–42): the best edition is that by J. W. de Jong in *Bijdragen* 130, 1974, pp. 465–482.

Ti: *śes-rab-kyi pha-rol-tu phyin-pa'i tshul brgya lṅa bcu-pa.*

1 Pages 79–91 of the Bibliography have first been printed, in an abbreviated form, in *Sino-Indian Studies,* V 2 (1956), pp. 107–112. With some additions and corrections they can well bear reprinting here.

0 121, —To 17, and 489 (Ka 133a–139b). —Narthang, Sna-tshogs 240–249. —IOSC no. 96. 97–8 inc. 99–100?. —Tun-huang, Lalou no. 53, 54, 98.

ed. in Izumi, etc., pp. 23–55, after Peking edition in Otani Library of East Hongwanji. —In Toganoo 11–33 (corrected with the help of two more editions).

Mo: Ligeti no. 121; vol. 9, 344r–353r (Dandr-a).

khot: After Central Asian Ms in Leumann, Izumi, Toganoo.

E: E. Conze in *SPT* pp. 184–195, repr. from *Studies of Esoteric Buddhism and Tantrism,* ed. by Kōyasan University, 1965, pp. 101–115.

g: E. Leumann, translation of Khotanese part in: *Taishō Daigaku Gakuhō* (1930), pp. 47–87, "Die nordarischen Abschnitte der Adhyardhaśatikā P.P. Text und Uebersetzung mit Glossar" (Wogihara Festschrift). Cf. S. Kanaoka, "The lineage of viśuddhi-pada thought", in no. 17, *Indogaku Bukkyōgaku Kenkyū* 16, 1968, pp. 982–976. —Yukio Hatta, *Index to the Ārya-Prajñā-Pāramitā-Naya-Śatapañcaśatikā.* Kyōto, 1971. xxiii+225 pp.

Commentaries:

Cy 1: Jñānamitra. *-ṭikā* Ti: To 2647. Jn 272b–294a.

Cy 2: K'uei-chi. Ch: T 1695 iii (to T 220 (10)).

Cy 3: Amoghavajra. Ch: T 1003 ii.

Cy 4: S. Toganoo, *Rishukyō no kenkyū* (Kōyasan, 1930), 584 pp. 82 pl.

Although it differs in style from the other Sūtras on Perfect Wisdom, and might well be reckoned among the Tantras, Candrakīrti and Haribhadra nevertheless quote this Sūtra as an authoritative Prajñāpāramitā text (*Prasannapadā* 238, 278, 444, 500, 504 quote no. 17 ch. 7, and *AAA* p. 132 quotes ch. 15).

The text falls into 15 chapters. The 15th consists of 10 verses. The first 14 chapters, each very short, except for the first, are spoken by a number of mythical Buddhas, who, successively, expound the various methods (*naya*) of the Prajñāpāramitā. Each exposition is really a small litany, similar in style to those at the end of *A,* in ch. 29 and 31. Germ syllables, like AṂ, BHYO, etc., sum up the message of each chapter. The terminology is largely esoteric, and abounds in terms like *vajra, guhya, siddhi, amogha, krodha,* etc. Our Sanskrit text does not contain the recommendations of the study of the Sūtra, which the Tibetan and Chinese translations give, in verbally differing forms, after chapters 1, 2, 3, 4, 5, 13 and 15, and which on the Central Asian manuscript appear in Khotanese.

18. PERFECT WISDOM IN A FEW WORDS.

S: *Svalpākṣarā prajñāpāramitā-sūtra.*

S: (1) From the Calcutta Ms, ca. 1,000 A.D.
ed. E. Conze, *Sino-Indian Studies,* V 2, 1956, pp. 113–115.
ed. P. L. Vaidya, *MSS* I, 1961, pp. 93–4 (=Conze+baseless conjectures).
(2) From the Nepalese Mss, ca 1,700 A.D. sq.
ed. A. Yuyama, in: *Buddhist Thought and Asian Civilization.* Essays in Honor of H. V. Guenther, 1977 (=BTAC), pp. 286–292.

Ch: T 258 i, trsl. T'ien-hsi-tsai (Dharmabhadra), ca. A.D. 982; T VIII pp. 852–3.

Ti: *śes-rab-kyi pha-rol-tu phyin-pa yi-ge ñuṅ-ṅu.* 0 159. —To 22=530. —Narthang, Sna tshogs, 258b–260b, Rgyud DA 89–92.
ed. A. Yuyama BTAC pp. 293–297.

Mo: Ligeti no. 161; vol. 12, 42–44r (Dandr-a).

E: From S (1): E. Conze, *SPT* pp. 144–147; cf. SS no. 128.
From Ch: A. Yuyama BTAC pp. 298–301. —Ch. Willemen, "A Tantric Heart Sūtra", *Samādhi* 7, 1973, pp. 2–11.

cf. A. Yuyama". BTAC pp. 280–301.

In many ways this Sūtra is a counterpart to the *Hṛdaya.* It is a dialogue between the Lord and Avalokiteśvara, whose future Buddhahood is here predicted. The Bodhisattva is enjoined to repeatedly recite the "heart of perfect wisdom". The appeal of the Sūtra is to the less endowed, to beings who have "but little capacity to act", who have "little merit", who are "dull and stupefied". The *Hṛdaya,* on the other hand, is addressed to the spiritual elite. It concerns itself with the removal of the *cittāvaraṇā.* By contrast no. 18 is content to promise a removal of the more elementary *karmāvaraṇā.* Here the Buddha enters into a *samādhi* which concentrates on the practical fruit of the Buddhist way of life (*sarvaduḥkha-pramocana*), whereas in the *Hṛdaya* his *samādhi* represents the glory of the transcendental dharma itself (*gambhīra-avabhāsa-dharmaparyāya*). In no.18 the teaching of the perfection of wisdom is expounded only insofar as it concerns one's attitude to other beings, whereas the *Hṛdaya* concentrates on the attitude to dharmas. The formula of the "heart of perfect wisdom" in no. 18, which also recurs in no. 23, implies a more *bhaktic* appeal to the power of the deity, whereas the *mantra* of no. 11 condenses the very struggle for spiritual emancipation into one short formula. The claims on the reader's capacities are also rather modest. Avalokiteśvara asks the Lord to give the perfection of wisdom "in a few syllables, a source of great merit; by merely hearing it all beings extinguish all hindrances which come from their past karma, and they are definitely turned towards enlightenment".

The Tantric element is more pronounced than in the *Hṛdaya.* One short mantra, and one long *dhāraṇi* are given. The Sūtra promises that as a result of it "the beings who labour zealously at the evocation (*sādhana*) of mantras, will find that their mantras will succeed (*sidhyanti*), without fail", and, "where it has been read aloud, there all the assemblies are consecrated (*abhiṣikta*), and all their mantras are realized face to face (*abhimukhā bhavanti*)." The Mantra concerns the Tathāgata Mahā-Śākyamuni, a Buddha of the remote past, who was in the world at the beginning of the first incalculable aeon of the career of the Bodhisattva who later became the Buddha Śākyamuni.

19. THE PERFECTION OF WISDOM FOR KAUŚIKA.

S: *Kauśika prajñāpāramitā-sūtra.*
ed: E. Conze, *Sino-Indian Studies,* V 2 (1956), pp. 115–118.
ed. P. L. Vaidya *MSS* I, 1961, pp. 95–96.

Ch: T 249 i. Dānapāla, ca. A.D. 980. vol. VIII, pp. 846–7 (*Buddhabhāṣita Indra-Śakra-prajñāpāramitā-hṛdaya-sūtra*).

Ti: *śes-rab-kyi pha-rol-tu phyin-pa Ko'uśika shes bya-ba.*
0 173. Rgyud PA 18b–20a. —To 19 (=554), KA 142a–143b. —Narthang, Sna-tshogs 256a–258a, Rgyud DA 505b–508a. —mdo-maṅ no. 103, f. 328a–333a. Ti, much shorter than S, gives only the items 1–5, 16, 6 and 7.

Mo: Ligeti no. 175; vol. 13, 26r–28r (Dandr-a).

Khot: 2 small fragments, Skr. and Khot., in H. W. Bailey, *Khotanese Texts,* III (1956), pp. 102 and 118–19.

E: E. Conze *SPT* pp. 157–159.

e: *SS* no. 57.

This is nothing but a compilation of 21 fragments, and is therefore likely to be a later sūtra. The fragments are: 1) a definition of the prajñāpāramitā by way of negations, probably from the later part of the Large Prajñāpāramitā

(Suv. III 36a–b also provides a close parallel); 2) a passage from a later chapter of *A* (xxxi 525), 3) a list of the six perfections, 4) a list of the 18 traditional forms of emptiness, 5) a quotation from the *Vajracchedikā* (ch. 32a), 6 and 7) two quotations from Nāgārjuna (*Madhyamakakārikā* I 1–2), and 8 to 21) a number of spells, all, except one, addressed to the prajñāpāramitā, among them (no. 11) an echo of the *prajñāpāramitā-dhāraṇī* (29A on p. 86) and (no. 21), the mantra of the *Hṛdaya.*

20. THE PERFECTION OF WISDOM FOR SŪRYAGARBHA.

S: *Prajñāpāramitā Sūryagarbha mahāyāna-sūtra.* Lost.
Ti: *ñi-ma'i sñiṅ-po.* –0 742, 179a–180a. To 26.
Mo: Ligeti, no. 774; vol. 47, 213r–214v.
E: E. Conze, *SPT* pp. 148–9.

This Sūtra first compares the concentration of a skilful Bodhisattva with the sun from seven points of view. It then sums up the metaphysics of Perfect Wisdom, enumerates the blessings derived from a study of the Prajñāpāramitā-sūtra, and ends up with a few *gāthās.*

21. THE PERFECTION OF WISDOM FOR CANDRAGARBHA.

S: *Candragarbha prajñāpāramitā mahāyāna-sūtra.* Lost.
Ti: *zla-ba'i sñiṅ-po.* –0 743, 180a–181b. To 27.
Mo: Ligeti, no. 775; vol. 47, 214v–216r.
E: E. Conze, *SPT,* pp. 149–151.

This Sūtra compares the perfection of wisdom with the moon, discourses on the difference between the perfection of wisdom which is with, and the one which is without outflows, proceeds to a litany in the style of Dharmaudgata's *dharmadeśanā* in *A* ch, xxxi, and concludes with a mantra and short verse.

22. THE PERFECTION OF WISDOM FOR SAMANTABHADRA.

S: *Prajñāpāramitā Samantabhadra mahāyāna-sūtra.* Lost.
Ti: *kun-tu bzaṅ-po.* –0 744, 181b–182a. To 28.
Mo: Ligeti, no. 776; vol. 47, 216r–216v.
E: E. Conze, *SPT,* pp. 151–152.

This Sūtra first describes a concentration of the Bodhisattva Samantabhadra and its consequences, gives a few verses spoken by the Gods, and adds a few words on the training in perfect wisdom.

23. THE PERFECTION OF WISDOM FOR VAJRAPĀṆI.

S: *Prajñāpāramitā Vajrapāṇi mahāyāna-sūtra*. Lost.
Ti: *lag-na rdo-rje*. –0 745, 182a–b. To 29.
Mo: Ligeti, no. 777; vol. 47, 216v–217v.
E: E. Conze, *SPT*, p. 152.

This Sūtra first explains how one should train in perfect wisdom, gives a great mantra of the mother of all the Buddhas, and enumerates a few blessings which result from aspiring for the dharmas of a Buddha. Vajrapāṇi, "the spirit who bears the thunderbolt", a symbol of irresistible strength, has always been closely associated with the Prajñāpāramitā. In *A* xvii 333 he is said to always follow closely behind an irreversible Bodhisattva, in order to protect him. In the list of the *Mahāmāyūrī* he is the Yakṣa of the Vulture Peak, near Rājagṛha, the scene of most of the sermons on Perfect Wisdom. In the Vajrayāna he becomes the Bodhisattva who corresponds to Akṣobhya, and belongs to the same family as the Prajñāpāramitā, i.e. the *dveṣa* family.

24. THE PERFECTION OF WISDOM FOR VAJRAKETU.

S: *Prajñāpāramitā Vajraketu mahāyāna-sūtra*. Lost.
Ti: *rdo-rje rgyal-mtshan*. –0 746, 182b–183b. To 30.
Mo: Ligeti, no. 778; vol. 47, 217v–218v.
E: E. Conze, *SPT*, pp. 152–3.

This Sūtra describes the perfection of wisdom by two sets of four dharmas with which it is endowed, and which cause it to be produced. It says that one should train in perfect wisdom, and concludes with a few verses.

CB. Litanies

25. THE 108 MARKS OF PERFECT WISDOM.

S: *Prajñāpāramitā nāma-aṣṭaśatakā*. Lost.
Ch: T 230 i., Dānapala, A.D. 982, pp. 684–5. —(*Ārya-aṣṭasahasra-gāthā-prajñāpāramitā nāma aṣṭaśata-satya-pūrṇārtha-dhāraṇi-sūtra*. N 999).
Ti: *śes-rab-kyi pha-rol-tu phyin-pa'i mtshan brgya rtsa brgyad-pa*. 0 172. —To 25 (=553), Ka 174–5. —Narthang, Sna tshogs 250a–252a, Rgyud Da 502–3. —mdo-maṅ no. 16. —Tun-huang: Lalou, no. 45.3. —ed. E.

Conze, *Sino-Indian Studies,* V 2 (1956), pp. 118–122.

Mo: Ligeti, no. 174; vol. 13, 23v–26r (Dandr-a).

E: E. Conze, *SPT*, pp. 196–8.

e: SS no. 129.

This text dispenses with both the introductory and the end formula of a Sūtra. After an initial poem the 108 names or epithets of Perfect Wisdom are given without any further introduction. In the Chinese translation the items are numbered. The Tantra knows many such litanies of 108 names, for Avalokiteśvara, Tārā, Mañjuśrī, Maitreya, etc. In this case the names describe either the objective counterparts of perfect wisdom, or the mental attitudes which lead to it. The second part gives a long *dhāraṇi* (no. 29 B) with some orgiastic elements, unusual in this kind of literature.

26. THE 25 DOORS OF PERFECT WISDOM.

S: *Pañcaviṃśati-prajñāpāramitā-mukha.* Lost.
Toganoo prints the list in Skr. on pp. 398–400.

ch: T 242. Dānapāla's trsl. of no. 17. p. 783, col. 2–3.
T 241. Bodhiruci's trsl. of no. 17. p. 781, col. 1–2.

Ti: *śes-rab-kyi pha-rol-tu phyin-pa sgo ñi-śu rtsa lṅa-pa.*
0 124. —To 20. —Narthang, Sna tshogs 216a–b. —Feer p. 307.

ti: Tibetan translation of no. 17, ch. 15 A.
Śrī-paramādya, acc. to Toganoo p. 398 (cf. 0 no. 119, ch. 13: *śes-rab-kyi pha-rol-tu phyin-pa'i tshul.*) cf. Hikata p. xvii.

Mo: Ligeti, no. 125; vol. 10, 106r–107r (Dandr-a).

E: E. Conze, *SPT*, pp. 199–200.

Without the framework of a Sūtra the 25 formulas themselves occur also in no.17. They constitute the doors to the entrance into transcendental wisdom or, alternatively, the faces or aspects of transcendental wisdom. These formulas express either a metaphysical truth, or a state of spiritual perfection, or a short mantra. Tantric features are the loving enumeration of the classes of supernatural beings in the preamble, as well as the constant references to *vajra,* terms like *nisumbhaḥ* and *mahārāga,* and the reference to the body, speech and mind of the Tathāgatas.

CC. Dhāraṇis

27. EXPLANATION OF THE DHĀRAṆĪS OF THE NINNŌ

S: Lost.

Ch: T 996 i. trsl. Amoghavajra. T. vol. xix, pp. 522, 1–524, 2.
cf. M. W. de Visser, *Ancient Buddhism in Japan* (1928–35), I, pp. 142 sq., 159.

28. RULES FOR THE CEREMONIAL RECITING OF THE DHĀRAṆĪS OF THE NINNŌ.

S: Lost.

Ch: T 995 i. trsl. Amoghavajra. T. vol. xix, pp. 519, 2–522, 1.
No. 27–28 deal with the dhāraṇīs, 36 in number, which were added to the seventh chapter of no. 13 in T 246 ii (see p. 76).

29. THE DHĀRAṆĪS FROM THE DHĀRANĪSAṂGRAHAS.

A number of very short dhāraṇīs are found in varying recensions in Nepalese and Tibetan Collections of Dhāraṇīs, e.g. in Calcutta, no. 10741, fol. 11+22; Asiatic Society B 5, B 65; Oxford, Bodleian 1449, A.D. 1819; Royal Asiatic Society, no. 55, A.D. 1791, 240 leaves, no. 79, A.D. 1820; Paris, Société Asiatique, no. 14; Cambridge, Add 1326, 225 l., A.D. 1719; 1343.

29A. S: *Prajñāpāramitā nāma dhāraṇī*; or: *āryaprajñāpāramitā dhāraṇī*; or: (*śatasāhasrikā-prajñāpāramitā-mantra*); or: *Prajñāpāramitā sahasra dhāraṇī*.

ed. J. Filliozat, *JAs*, 1941–2. —Also in no. 19.

Ti: *śes-rab-kyi pha-rol-tu phyin-ma'i sṅags*; or: *śes-rab-kyi pha-rol-tu phyin-pa stoṅ-phrag brgya-pa'i sṅags* (*gzuṅs*); or:....*brgya-pa gzuṅ-bar 'gyur-ba'i sṅags* (*gzuṅs*). 0 271, 557. —To 576, 932. -mdo-maṅ no. 53, 56.

ed. R. O. Meisezahl, in *Tribus*, 7 (1957), pp. 49, 50, 101–2.

It is the purpose of 29A to help us remember the *Śatasāhasrikā*.

29B. S: (*Pañcaviṃśatisāhasrikā-prajñāpāramitā-mantra*).

Ti: (*śes-rab-kyi pha-rol-tu phyin-pa*)(or: *śer phyin stoṅ-phrag ñi-śu lṅa-pa'i sṅags* (or: *lṅa-pa gzuṅ-bar 'gyur-ba*).

0 272, 558; To 577, 933. -mdo-maṅ no. 52 *gzuṅs*.

ed. R. O. Meisezahl, pp. 50, 102. –Also in no. 25.

29C. S: (*Aṣṭasāhasrikā-prajñāpāramitā-mantra*).
Ti: *Śer-phyin brgyad stoṅ-pa'i sṅags* (or: *stoṅ-pa gzuṅ-bar 'gyur-ba*).
O 273, 559; To 578, 934; mdo-maṅ no. 54.
ed. R. O. Meisezahl, pp. 50, 102.

29D. S: (*Vajracchedikāhṛdaya*).
Ti: *rdo-rje gcod-pa'i sñiṅ-po.*
cf. R. O. Meisezahl, p. 143, and the end of Schmidt's edition of no. 8.

29E S: (*Aṣṭasāhasrikā-hṛdaya*).
Ti: *brgyad-stoṅ-pa'i sñiṅ-po.* 12 lines. Cf. Meisezahl, pp. 84–5.

30. THE DHĀRAṆĪ OF THE HEART OF PERFECT WISDOM.

S: *Prajñāpāramitā-hṛdaya-dhāraṇi.* Ms, Cambridge Add. 1554, 15 lines.

This consists chiefly of invocations. It begins with: *Oṃ namaḥ Śri-Vajrasattvāya!* It has no connection at all with no. 11.

31. THE PERFECTION OF WISDOM IN SEVEN VERSES.

S: *Ārya-saptaślokikā Bhagavati Prajñāpāramitā-nāma-sūtra.* Lost.
Ti: *Bcom-ldan-'das-ma śes-rab-kyi pha-rol-tu phyin-pa 'phags-ma tshigs-su bcad-pa bdun-ma shes-bya-ba'i mdo.*
mdo-'grel XVI 3a–b. trsl. Sumanaśrī, Rin-chen grub.

32. PERFECT WISDOM IN ONE LETTER.

S: *Bhagavatī prajñāpāramitā sarva-Tathāgata-mātā ekākṣarā nāma.* Lost.
Ti: *Bcom-ldan-'das-ma śes-rab-kyi pha-rol-tu phyin-pa de-bshin gśegs-pa thams-cad-kyi yum yi-ge gcig-ma shes bya-ba.*
O 741. –To 23. –Narthang, *Sna-tshogs* 255b–256a.
Mo: Ligeti, no. 773; vol. 47, 212v–213v.
E: E. Conze, *SPT*, pp. 201.
e: *SS* no. 130.

The one letter, or syllable, is 'A', which has always in Buddhist tradition had a special affinity with emptiness. The text gives the usual preamble and conclusion of a Sūtra, which is addressed to Ānanda, and the body of the Sūtra is extremely short.

CD. Rituals

33. A. THE GREAT HEART SŪTRA OF THE GREAT PERFECTION OF WISDOM. B. METHOD OF MAKING AN IMAGE OF THE PRAJÑĀPĀRAMITĀ.

S: Lost.

Ch: *Dhāraṇisamuccaya,* trsl. Atigupta, A.D. 653–654. A) T 901, iii, 804c–805a.–B) ibd. 805a sq.

33A is in the form of a short Sūtra. The Lord explains to Brahmadeva the virtuous qualities which follow from a practice of perfect wisdom. The enumeration of the various advantages to be gained from the prajñāpāramitā resembles that given, at much greater length, in *A* ch. III to V, but special stress is laid in this outline of the inconceivable *dhāraṇi-mudrā-guṇā* on the winning of meditational quietude (*śamatha*), which is as immovable as Mount Sumeru. This continues without a break into 33B.

33B is our first dated source for the iconography of the Prajñāpāramitā. It describes how the figure of Mahāprajñā, who is reckoned among the Bodhisattvas, should be painted. She is white, and has two arms. The left arm is turned towards the breast, the left hand being raised with the five fingers extended; in the palm of the left hand one should paint a Sūtra-box made of the seven precious things, which contains the twelve categories of sacred texts, i.e. the *prajñāpāramitā-piṭaka.* The right hand hangs over the right knee, the five fingers extended, in the gesture of *abhayadada.* Mahāprajñā is beautiful like a heavenly maiden (*devakanyā*) and serene in her features like a Bodhisattva. She has three eyes, wears a deva-crown, and is seated on a lion-throne. Her dress and ornaments are described in great detail. She is surrounded by *devas* and *vidyā-rājās.* The text then proceeds to describe 13 ritual gestures (*mudrā*), 9 *dhāraṇis* and the *maṇḍala* of the Prajñāpāramitā with its ritual.

34. RULES ON THE PLACES OF WORSHIP AND THE CHANTING OF THE LITURGIES OF THE NINNŌ.

S: Lost.

Ch: T 994 i. trsl. Amoghavajra, T vol. XIX, pp. 513,3–519,2.

e: Summary of contents in: M. W. de Visser, *Ancient Buddhism in Japan* (1928) I, pp. 160–175.

35. EVOCATIONS OF THE PERFECTION OF WISDOM.

S: *Prajñāpāramitā-sādhana.* In: *Sādhanamālā,* ed. B. Bhattacharya, I (1925).

The *sādhanas* are distributed as follows:

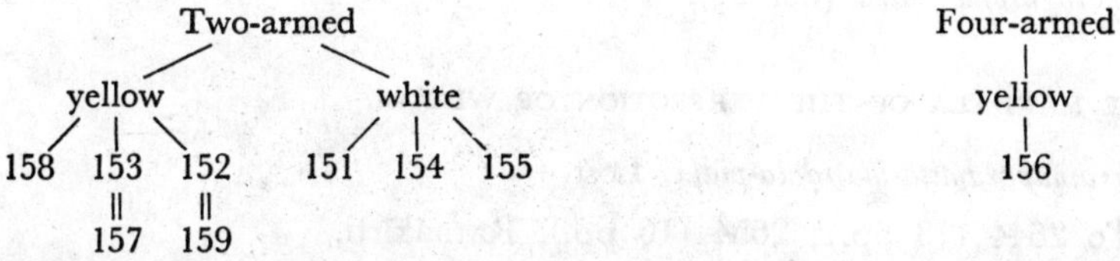

No. 151: Two-armed, white. R: red lotus and book. –152. Two-armed, yellow: R and L: blue lotus and book. –153: Two-armed, yellow: L. blue lotus and book. –154. Two-armed, white: R and L: red lotus and book. –155. Two-armed, white: R: red lotus, L: book held against heart. –156. Four-armed, yellow: two arms in *dharmacakra*; second L holds book on a lotus, second R in *abhaya*. –157, as 153. –158. Two-armed, yellow: L: red lotus and book. –159, as 152.

Ti: To 3400. Rgyud-'grel, DU 71 (trsl. of *Sādhanamālā*).

Also: To 2326 (by Kamalaśīla); 2640 (*prajñāpāramitā-hṛdaya-sādhana*) 2641; 3219–3222; 3352–3355; 3542 *śuklā*; 3542 *pītavarṇā*; 3544 *saṃkṣipta-pītavarṇā*; 3545 *śuklā*; 3547 *kanakavarṇā*; 3549 *kanaka-varṇā*; 3550.

The *Sādhanamālā*, which is earlier than A.D. 1100, gives nine *sādhanas* of the Prajñāpāramitā (one Ms gives in addition a hymn (*stuti*), i.e. no. 160). The most elaborate, no. 159, begins with a *maṇḍala* of the five Tathāgatas, with their female consorts. Later on the eight *yoginīs* are mentioned. The *sādhana* is attributed to Ācārya-Asaṅga. There is no reason to believe that the system of the five Jinas is much older than A.D. 750, and therefore this *sādhana,* which incidentally begins by quoting the first verse of Diṅnāga's *Piṇḍārtha,* is unlikely to be the work of the famous Asaṅga who lived more than three centuries before that date.

The procedure for conjuring up the Prajñāpāramitā is given only in an abbreviated form, being the same as that for the other deities. In addition each *sādhana* describes the distinctive visual appearance of the seven forms of Prajñāpāramitā envisaged here, and gives a germ syllable, and the mantra which corresponds to each form. 152, 158 and 159 have the same mantra (*oṃ āḥ dhīḥ hūṃ svāhā*), and so have 153 and 156 (*oṃ dhīḥ śruti-smṛti-vijaye svāhā*), and 151 and 155 (*oṃ picu prajñāvardhani jvala medhāvardhani dhiri dhiri buddha-vardhani svāhā*; this is also the mantra of Vajra-Sarasvatī in *sādhanas* 163, 165, 168). 157 has *oṃ prajñe mahāprajñe śruti-smṛti-vijaye dhīḥ svāhā.* This also forms part of the mantra in *Kauśika* ix, in the 108 *Marks of Perfect Wisdom,* and in the *Candragarbha Sūtra* (no. 21).

36. THE MAṆḌALA OF THE PERFECTION OF WISDOM.

S: *Prajñāpāramitā-maṇḍala-vidhi.* Lost.

Ti: To 2644 (13 pp.); 2654 (10 pp.), Ratnakīrti.

37. RITUAL CONCERNING A MAṆḌALA OF PRAJÑĀPĀRAMITĀ.

S: Lost.

Ch: T 1151. trsl. Amoghavajra.

An outline of this *maṇḍala* can be seen in *Mikkyō-daijiten,* p. 1840a. The Prajñā, in the centre, is surrounded by the 10 *pāramitās,* and by a number of deities, *rākṣasas,* etc.

38. SOME OF THE TEACHING ABOUT THE VAJRAMAṆḌALAVYŪHAPRAJÑĀPĀRAMITĀ.

S: *Śrīvajramaṇḍalālaṃkāramahātantrarājā.* Lost.

Ch: T 886, trsl. Dharmabhadra ca. 1000. (Nanjio adds: "agrees with Tibetan").

39. SŪTRA OF THE CONTEMPLATION OF THE BODHISATTVA PRAJÑĀPĀRAMITĀ, MOTHER OF THE BUDDHA.

S: Lost.

Ch: T 259 i, trsl. T'ien-hsi-tsai, A.D. 980–1000. T. viii 854.

40. RITUAL OF THE CONTEMPLATION OF PRAJÑĀ, MOTHER OF THE BUDDHA.

S: Lost.

Ch: T 1152 i, trsl. Dānapāla, ca. A.D. 1000.

39 and 40 both refer to a six-armed form of the Prajñāpāramitā of golden colour. In no. 39 the first right hand holds the rosary, the left the Sūtra-book; the second right an arrow, the second left a bow; the third right arm is in *varada,* and the third left holds a *cintāmaṇi.* The Prajñā has a body of pure golden colour, which emits millions of rays throughout the entire universe. The text also gives an initiation-*dhāraṇī*, a heart-*dhāraṇī* and a 'fundamental' *dhāraṇī,* and then enumerates the Buddhas and Bodhisattvas who surround the Prajñāpāramitā. In the case of no. 40 the two upper arms are in *dharma-*

cakramudrā, and the four others hold the Sūtra, *utpala, śakti,* etc.[1]

A few modern scholarly works

M. Lalou, "La version tibétaine des prajñāpāramitā", *JAs* 1929, pp. 82–102 (28 items).

T. Matsumoto, *Die Prajñāpāramitā Literatur,* 1932.

D. T. Suzuki, "The philosophy and religion of the Prajñāpāramitā", *EZB* III, 1934, pp. 207–288.

K. Kiyono, *Daihannya-kyō no kenkyū,* Hōun, 1937, 46 pp.

Kōun Kajiyoshi, *Genshi Hannya-kyō no kenkyū.* A study of the early versions of the Prajñāpāramitā Sūtra, Tōkyō 1944. 14+998 pp.

E. Conze, *Selected Sayings from the Perfection of Wisdom,* 1955, 133 pp. Repr. 1968, 1975.

R. Hikata, "An Introductory Essay on Prajñāpāramitā Literature" in *Suvikrāntavikrāmiparipṛcchā Prajñāpāramitā-Sūtra,* Fukuoka, 1958, pp. ix-lxxxiii and 5 Tables.

A. David-Neel and Lama Yongden, *La connaissance transcendante d'après le texte et les Commentaires Tibétaines.* Paris, 1958, 173 pp.

E. Conze, "The Development of P.P. Thought" (1960) = *TYBS* pp. 123–147.

R. O. Meisezahl, *Tibetische P.P.-Texte im Bernischen Historischen Museum,* 1964, 42 pp.

Shōyū Hanayama, "A summary of various research on the Prajñāpāramitā Literature by Japanese scholars", *Acta Asiatica,* Bulletin of the Institute of Eastern Literature, 10, The Tōhō Gakkai, Tōkyō 1966, pp. 16–93.

E. Conze, *Materials for a Dictionary of the Prajñāpāramitā Literature.* 1967, vii 447 pp. Repr. 1973.

G. Bugault, *La notion de 'prajñā' ou de sapience selon les perspectives du 'Mahāyāna',* 1968, 289 pp.

P. Beautrix, *Bibliographie de la littérature Prajñāpāramitā,* 1971 (324 items).

1 Although the last no. in this list is 40, there are in fact 42 P. P. texts. By some oversight I have on page 60 numbered one of two P. P.-s in 500 Lines as no. 7a instead of no. 8, and on p. 75 another Chinese text is numbered 12a instead of 13.

Prajñāpāramitā and Related Systems: Studies in Honor of Edward Conze, ed. by L. Lancaster (=*Berkeley Buddhist Studies Series*, 1), 1977.

Eleven contributors in the second part of this *Festschrift* (pp. 221–415) deal with the ideas of the P. P. Eleven contributions in the first part concern the literary documents, and will have to be noted in the next edition of this work, i.e. as follows:

no. 5, p. 48 Line 4: L. Schmithausen, Textgeschichtliche Beobachtungen zum 1. Kapitel der *Aṣṭasāhasrikā Prajñāpāramitā*, pp. 35–80.

no. 5, pp. 7–8: A. Rawlinson, The position of the *Aṣṭasāhasrikā Prajñāpāramitā* in the Development of Early Mahāyāna, pp. 3–34.

no. 5A, p. 53 line 12: A. Yuyama, The First Two Chapters of the *Prajñā-pāramitā-ratna-guṇa-saṃcaya-gāthā* (Rgs), pp. 203–218.

no. 6, p. 56 line 8: J. W. de Jong, Notes on Prajñāpāramitā Texts: 2. The *Suvikrāntavikrāmiparipṛcchā*, pp. 187–199.

no. 8, p. 62 line 2: R. E. Emmerick, The Concluding Verses of the Khotanese *Vajracchedikā*, pp. 83–92.

no. 8, p. 66 line 66: Y. Kajiyama, "Thus Spoke the Blessed One...", pp. 93–99 (on *āttamanāḥ* in *V* 32b).

no. 11, p. 68 line 9: L. Hurvitz, Hsüan-tsang (602–664) and the *Heart Scripture*, pp. 103–121.

no. 11, p. 74 line 2: A. Wayman, Secret of the *Heart Sūtra*, pp. 135–152 (see p. 70).

no. 11, p. 72 line 3: H. W. Bailey, *Mahāprajñāpāramitā-sūtra*, pp. 153–162;–L. Lancaster, A Study of a Khotanese *Prajñāpāramitā* Text: After the Work of Sir Harold Bailey, pp. 163–183.

no. 11, pp. 27–28: M. Pye, The *Heart Sutra* in Japanese Context, pp. 123–134.

THE COMMENTARIAL LITERATURE

Indian literary tradition regards a sacred text as incomplete without a commentary. The Prajñāpāramitā is no exception, and the majority of its versions have found a commentator, in India between A.D. 150 and 1200, and elsewhere until today.

1. The first two centuries of the Christian era produced a gigantic commentary, the *Mahāprajñāpāramitā-upadeśa-śāstra,* presumably on the version in 25,000 Lines, and traditionally ascribed to *Nāgārjuna.* It contains a staggering wealth of useful information, and reflects the attitude of the Mādhyamika school, which was in its tenets more akin to the Prajñāpāramitā than any other.

Lamotte (p. X) notes, however, that this work "does not occur in the lists of works attributed to Nāgārjuna by the *Lung-shu p'u-sa ch'uan* (T 2047), and the Tibetan historians Bu-ston and Tāranātha". The attribution of this work to Nāgārjuna is due to Kumārajīva, and his school, and probably Kumārajīva had obtained his information in Kashmir or Central Asia. The Sanskrit original is completely lost. We possess only the Chinese translation done by Kumārajīva between A.D. (402 or) 404 and 406, the *Ta-chih-tu-lun,* in 90 chapters and 100 *chüan.* Even Kumārajīva did not translate the entire work, which is said to have comprised 100,000 *ślokas,* or one million Chinese characters, and which would have been 1,000 *chüan* long. Only the first chapter (*parivarta*) of the Sanskrit is translated in full, in the first 34 *chüan.* That chapter covers the text of *P* until the last line of p. 34 in Dutt's edition. Of the remaining 89 chapters only an abstract is given.[1] The absence of a Tibetan translation suggests that around 800 A.D. the huge work was no longer obtainable in India.

The first part, i.e. chapters 1 to 48, has so far been translated by E. Lamotte. The text on which Nāgārjuna comments is, in that section, very similar to the one we have. The Abhidharma tradition is that of the Sarvāstivādins,

1 It is not quite clear from Demiéville's account whether the *shu* of Shih-hui-ying (ca 575), the *Szŭ-ch'uan,* in 30 *chüan,* which has been in part preserved and published in Japan, is an abbreviation of the *Ta-chih-tu-lun,* or an independent, though uninteresting work. See Bagchi p. 462. —Hui-Yüan, Abridgment of Mpp-s in 20 chüan, with Preface. See R.H. Robinson, *Early Mādhyamika in India and China,* 1967, 101 n .27, pp. 109–114, 200–205, and T 2145.

i.e. the Vibhāsā of Kashmir. The scriptural sources are those of the Sarvāstivāda-Vaibhāṣika of the North-West: the Sanskrit *Āgama,* the *Vinaya* of Sarvāstivādins and Mūlasarvāstivādins, the *Jñānaprasthāna* of Kātyāyana and the *Vibhāṣa* of Kashmir. The work was probably done by Sarvāstivādins converted to the Mādhyamika school. Kumārajīva, the translator, was himself such a convert. The authors belonged to the North West of India (E. Lamotte, *Asiatica,* 1954, 390–1). The Jātakas and Avadānas to which it refers are those which locate the events narrated in Gandhāra, Oḍḍiyāna, the Punjab and Swāt. (About 50 Mahāyāna Sūtras and Śāstras are quoted).

P. Demiéville[1] gives some interesting facts about the conditions under which the work was produced. The Emperor Yao Hsing (Wen-Huan) of the Later Ch'in (396–415), who had Kumārajīva fetched as war booty by one of his generals, personally organised the diffusion of Buddhism among the literati. The emperor himself presided over the sessions of the translation work, which took place in a hall, north of Ch'ang-an in the presence of a large audience. Several hundred monks and laymen, noblemen, literati, ministers, etc., were present when Kumārajīva, with the text in his hand, orally translated it into Chinese. The Emperor at the same time compared Kumārajīva's translation of the Sūtra with one of the older translations, while Kumārajīva accompanied his translation of the Śāstra with many explanations and discussions. After that the translation was written down, and many misunderstandings and interpolations may have arisen in the process. Often, in any case, the glosses of Kumārajīva are hard to distinguish from the Sanskrit original. Our present text of the *Ta-chih-tu-lun* contains sometimes the questions of the Chinese audience, and Kumārajīva's answers to them. Unlike Hsüan-tsang, Kumārajīva did not aim at literal exactness in his translations. He was inclined to the *ko-i* ("Search for the meaning") kind of translation, which aimed at finding some concordance of Buddhist beliefs with Taoism and Confucianism. The enormous influence of Kumārajīva's translations is largely due to the fact that he adapted himself to the understanding of his not always very well prepared audience, and that he remained intelligible to them. Further uncertainites are, incidentally, introduced into the text by its transmission.[2]

Rāhulabhadra[3], either a tutor[4] or a disciple[5] of Nāgārjuna, composed ca. A.D.

1 *JAs,* 1950, pp. 375–395.
2 About manuscripts and editions see *JAs,* 1950, pp. 390 sq. -See also Hikata LII–LXXV about the authorship of this work.
3 Matsumoto, *Suvikrāntavikrāmiparipṛcchā,* 1956, p. iii.
4 According to Tibetan sources.
5 According to Chinese sources. Hikata p. LXXI.

150 a "Hymn to Perfect Wisdom", the *Prajñāpāramitāstotra*, in 20 verses, to which a 21st was added at a later date[1]. In chapter 18 of the *Ta-chih-tu-lun* a *prajñāpāramitāstotra* is quoted, in 20 verses, of which 17 are identical with the Sanskrit of Rāhulabhadra's hymn[2]. The poem has also-been translated into Urdu[3], Gujarati[4] and, with a long Bengali commentary, into Bengali.[5] There is Newari paraphrase[6], an English translation by Swami Yatiswarananda[7], another one with Notes, by H.P. Shastri[8], and a rhythmical version by E. Conze[9]. Rāhulabhadra also composed a hymn on the *Saddharmapuṇḍarika Sūtra*[10], which shows many similarities with the one composed for the Prajñāpāramitā.

2. The fourth and fifth centuries saw the rise of the *Yogācārins*. Tāranātha claims (p. 122) that Vasubandhu wrote a commentary to *P*, and that Asaṅga, who found it difficult to understand the Prajñāpāramitā "without repetition and confusion" (p. 108) wrote the *Abhisamayālaṅkāra* (p. 112). According to Bu-ston (II 140)[11], Asaṅga composed the *Tattvaviniścaya* (*de-ñid rnam-ṅes*) "in which the subjects of the *AA* and the Prajñāpāramitā are demonstrated (en regard)". On page 1 of his *AAA*, Haribhadra says:

"The holy Asaṅga, endowed with translucent glory, and the foremost among those possessed of highest wisdom, has composed the commentary called "The Ascertainment of the True State of Things". Inspired by this work, the teacher Vasubandhu, exceedingly proud of his knowledge, skilful in making distinctions between what has reality and what has not, has

1 Printed in Aṣṭa, ed. Mitra, 1888, pp. 1–3. *Pañcaviṃśatisāhasrikā*, ed. Dutt, 1934 pp. 1–3. *Suvikrānta*-etc. ed. Matsumoto, pp. 1–2, ed. Hikata, pp. 1–2. –Useful variants can be found in the older Mss, i.e. for *A* the Ms Bodleian a. 7. R, B.M. Or. 6902 and 2203, and for *Rgs* the Ms. As. Soc. Bengal 10736.

2 *Traité*, pp. 1061–5.

3 Sanskrit-Urdu, Bulandshahi, 1904, pp. 8. 24.

4 *Gautam Buddha praṇita Prajñāpāramitāsūtram*, Sanskrit-Gujarati, with commentary in Gujarati, Ahmedabad, 1916, 15 pp.

5 K. Chatterji, Sanskrit-Bengali, with Bengali commentary. Calcutta, 1912, pp. 9+214, (Kishori-mohana Chaṭṭopadhyāya).

6 Ekaviṃśati-prajñāpāramitā. Nepalese Ms, 25 leaves.

7 In: *Altar Flowers*, published by Advaita Ashrama (S. Pavitrananda), 1934 (3rd ed. 1945), pp. 236–245 (Sanskrit-English).

8 The Prajñāpāramitā-Sūtra, Self-Knowledge, II 2, 1951, pp. 35–40.

9 "Hymn to Perfect Wisdom", The Middle Way, xxvi, 1951, pp. 24–5. Also: Buddhist Texts, 1954, no. 142. –Buddhist Scriptures, 1959, pp. 168–171 (with some corrections).

10 *Saddharmapuṇḍarīka*, ed. Wogihara and Tsuchida, pp. 37–9. Saddharmapuṇḍarīkastavaḥ, 20 vv.

11 See the comments of A. Wayman, *Analysis of the Śrāvakabhūmi Manuscript*, 1961, pp. 34–5.

composed the *Paddhati*, or "Guide Book", and won authority by his exposition of the meaning (of the Pañcaviṃśatisāhasrikā, according to Tsoṅ-kha-pa)". Tāranātha further gives interesting, though not always fully intelligible, details about a discussion between king Gambhīrapakṣa and Asaṅga, which resulted from the king's reading of the Prajñāpāramitā (p. 113). The king asked (pp. 114–5) three questions concerning the wording, and three concerning the meaning of the text. Asaṅga put his answers down in the *Trisvabhāvanirdeśa,* and other works. This work of 38 verses has been edited several times,[1] but its perusal shows that for the Yogācārins to interpret the Prajñāpāramitā often meant to introduce concepts quite alien to it.

We have three Yogācārin commentaries on the *Vajracchedikā.* Asaṅga's commentary (no. 8-cy 1) is a real masterpiece. The Sūtra, at first sight, gives an impression of incoherence. Asaṅga throughout shows how the different chapters are linked to one another, and Vasubandhu in his subcommentary (no. 8 cy 1–1) often explicitly asks the question or raises the problem, about what is behind the transition from one point to another. Sometimes the solution offered for the difficulties is more ingenious than convincing. For example, when ch. 12–14d are said to enumerate 11 points by which the gift of the Dharma is superior to any other gift (vv. 23–25), or when ch. 15b to 16c are represented as describing the 10 *dharme pratipatter karmāṇi* (vv. 39–41). At *V* ch. 17b, which is either too obvious or meaningless, Asaṅga (v. 43) finds refuge in obscurity.

Much light is also thrown on many of the technical terms employed. Vasubandhu attempts to account for the apparent repetitions, especially on the numerous occasions when the merit connected with Perfect Wisdom is stressed, and he maintains that in each case the subject is discussed in a different context and concerns a different aspect of *puṇya.* Nor is the difficulty entirely shunned why in chapter 17 the Sūtra should repeat what had been said before in almost the same words in ch. 3, 7, 8 and 10 (MBT I 112). This problem is solved by the assertion that the later passage considers the same problem on a much higher level. Ch. 17a and ch. 3, for instance, are verbally nearly identical, but ch. 3 is said to give the 4 aspects of the *upakārāśayaḥ* (v. 2), whereas ch. 17a concerns the removal of all *cittāvaraṇa* (*sems-kyi sgrib-pa*) (v. 42). Specific Yogācāra doctrines are almost completely ignored. At v. 20 we have the phrase *vijñaptimātratvāt,* which in this context, however, only means that the Buddhafields are a mere denomination, without material consistency (*avigrahatvād*). But in his comment on v. 76 Vasubandhu refers to the "store-consciousness". The commentary presupposes a text of the

1 Ed. S. Yamaguchi (1931); *MCB,* II (1933), pp. 154–7; Mukhopadhyaya (1939).

Vajracchedikā which does not differ materially from the one we find in our much later manuscripts. Only quite occasionally does it fail to fit our text, as at v. 47 where nothing in *V* ch. 17e-f seems to correspond to *dharmadhātāv akuśalaḥ,* or at v. 26 where *aparimāṇa* is understood of *guṇā* and not of *buddhā* as in *V* 14d.

Secondly there is Vasubandhu's, or Asaṅga's, prose commentary (no. 8 cy. 2). It falls into two parts. The first gives the division of the subjectmatter of the *Vajracchedikā* under seven topics. The second explains the text in detail, with constant reference to the divisions given in the first part.

The seven topics (*artha-padārtha, don-gyi gnas*) are:

1. Non-interruption of the lineage of the Buddha (*gotrānupaccheda*), in that the Perfection of Wisdom assures the continuity of the Buddha-family. –This refers to *paramānugraha* and *paramaparindanā* at ch. 2.

2. Characteristics of a Bodhisattva's training. –This refers to *kathaṃ sthātavyam,* etc., at ch. 2.

3. Eighteen supports of a Bodhisattva's practice, i.e. 1=*V* ch.3, 2=ch. 4, 3=ch.5, 4=ch.6–9, 5=ch.9–10a, 6=ch.10a, 7=ch.10b–c, 8=ch.10c, 9=ch.11–13b, 10=ch.13c, 11=ch.13d, 12=ch.13e–14d, 13=ch.14e-f, 14=ch.14f–16c, 15=ch.17a, 16=ch.17b–d, 17=ch.17e–f, 18=ch.17g–32a. Supports 1–16 concern the Path as *hetu,* 17 and 18 its *phala* (MBT I 163).

4. Antidotes. *V* ch. 3–4.

5. Non-delusion results from avoiding the two extremes, i.e. the imputation of either positive existence or of absolute non-existence to dharmas which are merely imagined (*parikalpita*). *V* ch. 8.

6. The 18 supports are distributed according to the stages (*bhūmi*) to which they correspond. 1–16 belong to the *adhimukticaryā,* 17 to the *śuddha-adhyāśayabhūmi,* which begins with the *pramudita* stage, and the 18th to the final stage of a Buddha.

7. The reasons why the book is called *Vajracchedikā.*

The third commentary, that by Śrīdatta (no. 8 cy 3), preserved only in Chinese, awaits further study.

Diṅnāga's *Prajñāpāramitā-piṇḍārtha* (no. 5 cy 5), ca. 450, is a short work of 58 memorial verses, which claims (in vv. 6, 22, 58) a special connection with the Aṣṭasāhasrikā. Actually, the bulk of it (vv. 5–54) is based on passages of the Large Prajñāpāramitā which have no parallel in it.

Dignāga sums up (*artha-samkṣepa*) (v.57) the teaching of the Prajñāpāramitā under 32 subjects, on which Bu-ston (I 51–52) has some comments, which are to some extent dependent on remarks of Asaṅga (in no. 8 cy 8?). I have added the comments, where significant, in brackets.

The 32 points are:

1. *āśraya*. The foundation, i.e. the Buddha as teacher.
2. *adhikāra*. The fitness for listening to the teaching, i.e. the Bodhisattvas (*bodhisattva-gaṇam adhikṛtya deśyate*).
3. *karma* (=*kriyā*). What should be done by the Bodhisattvas in accordance with the perfection of wisdom (*prajñāpāramitāyāṃ bodhisattvasya-anuṣṭhānam*).

4.–13. *bhāvanā*. Meditation—on the antidotes to the 10 imputations. vv. 19–54.

14.–29. *prabheda*. Classification—of the 16 varieties of emptiness. vv. 6–18. (*prajñāpāramitāyāḥ ṣodaśa-prakāraḥ. . . .ṣodaśa śūnyatā.*

30. *liṅgam*. Tokens[1]—two according to Bu-ston: 1) of the activities of the Evil One; 2) of a Bodhisattva having attained the irreversible state. This corresponds to *A* ch. xi and xvii, (*mārakarmāṇām avaivartikabodhisattvānāṃ ca.*)[2]
31. *āpad*. The faults into which one may fall. –According to Bu-ston one may fall into evil births as the consequence of abstaining from perfect wisdom (cf. *A* ch. vii) (*anarthaḥ saddharma-pratikṣepa-ādinā dharmavyasanasaṃvartaniyaṃ karma* (cf. *A* vii 178, 182) *saviṣayā* (cf. *A* vi 151–2) *ca prajñāpāramitā*. (cf. v. 56 on *prativarṇikā prajñāpāramitā*, cf. *A* v 112).
32. *anuśaṃsa*. The advantages gained from perfect wisdom; i.e. *A* iii-v. (*mahattvanirdeśaḥ prajñāpāramitāyāḥ*).

The bulk of this text is taken up with the items 4 to 29, which consist of two lists—one of the 16 forms of emptiness, and one of the 10 imputations. Both lists seem to derive from the Prajñāpāramitā itself, although presumably from some recension which has not come down to us.

S, *P*, *Ad*, and *D*, as we possess them, give a list of 20 forms of *emptiness*. Behind it we can infer that there were earlier lists of 18 and 16 forms. Asaṅga's (?) *Madhyāntavibhāga* gave a list of 16 kinds, and the explanations given by Vasubandhu and Sthiramati in their commentaries differ greatly from those in the text of the Prajñāpāramitā itself. Dignāga gives the same list as the *Madhyāntavibhāga*, but in a different order, perhaps in an endeavor to follow the argumentation of *A* ch.i. His explanation of the different items agrees closely with that of the *Madhyāntavibhāgaṭikā*. In one case he echoes the words of a *kārikā* in the *Madhyāntavibhāga*; i.e. verse 10 reads:

rūpa-ādy-abhāve tad-deha-pratiṣṭhā-lakṣaṇa-kṣatiḥ,

which can be compared with I 17:

1 Tucci trsl. as "logical argueing", perhaps owing to v. 55.
2 V. 55 does not correspond.

bhoktṛ-bhojana-tad-deha-pratiṣṭhā-vastu-śūnyatā,

i.e. the emptiness of enjoyer, enjoyed, the body thereof, and the receptacle.

The 16 kinds of emptiness never occur in the *Aṣṭa*. In his text Dignāga gives a number of quotations which are not easy to identify. I here give a survey of them:

verse/kind of emptiness	quotation	*A* ch. I
8 *adhyātma*	*bodhisattvaṃ na paśyāmi*	cf. 4. 25
9 *bahirddhā*	*rūpaṃ rūpa-svabhāvena śūnyam*	cf. 10
12 *atyanta*	*notpanno na niruddho vā*	cf. 11
anavarāgra	*sattva ity ādi*	
13 *sarvadharma*	*Buddhadharmāṃs tathā bodhisattvadharmān na paśyati*	
14 *paramārtha*	*dharmāḥ kalpitā*	cf. 15
15 *abhāva*	(*ātmadṛṣṭer ucchedam mahatyā*)= *mahatyā ātmadṛṣṭyaḥ prahāṇāya*	p. 19
16 *abhāvasvabhāva*	*sarvadharmā anutpannā*	

The list of the *ten vikalpa-vikṣepas* is derived from a text of the Prajñāpāramitā which seems to be lost. It plays a great part in Yogācārin writings. It is of interest as illustrating the considerable freedom with which the Yogācārins manipulated traditional texts in support of their doctrinal constructions. In the following survey I give six items; (1) the name, (2) the text of the *Śatasāhasrikā* (pp. 118, 7–120) (=Ś), to which the Tibetan *Pañcaviṃśatisāhasrikā* corresponds exactly, (3) the text of the revised *Pañcaviṃśatisāhasrikā* (ed. Dutt pp. 37–8) (=P), (4) Dignāga's quotation or paraphrase from the Prajñāpāramitā, after *Prajñāpāramitāpiṇḍārtha* (=D), (5) the text given in Asaṅga's *Mahāyānasūtrālaṃkāra* (XI 77) (=ML), and (6) that of *Mahāyānasaṃgrahaśāstra* (II 21–22; pp. 115–118 of Lamotte's translation) (=Ms).

1. *Abhāva-vikalpa.*
Ś: –P: bodhisattva eva samāno. D: bodhisattva san. v. 21. ML: iha bodhisattvo bodhisattva eva san. Ms: byaṅ-chub sems-dpa' ñid-du yod bshin-du.

2. *Bhāva-vikalpa.*
Ś, P, ML, Ms: bodhisattvaṃ na samanupaśyati. D: bodhisattvaṃ na paśyāmi aham......na-asti......buddha tathā bodhiṃ na paśyāmi. vv. 24, 28, 32.

3. *Adhyāropa-vikalpa.*
Ś, P, ML, Ms: bodhisattva-nāma-api na samanupaśyati......bodhisattvo mahāsattvaḥ svabhāvena śūnyaḥ......D: –(v. 33).

4. *Apavāda-vikalpa.*
Ś, P, ML, Ms: na śūnyatayā rūpaṃ śūnyam......D: na hi śūnyatayā śūn-

yam......māyopamas tathā buddhaḥ sa svapnopama (see no. 7). vv. 34, 35; cf. 36.

5. *Ekatva-vikalpa.*

Ś, P: –. D: (na rūpa ṃ śūnyatā) v. 40. ML, Ms: yā rūpasya śūnyatā na tad rūpam.

6. *Nānātva-vikalpa.*

Ś, P, ML, Ms: na-anyatra rūpāc chūnyatā......rūpam eva śūnyatā śūnyatā-eva rūpam......D: (na-anyat tad rūpam) v. 41.

7. *Svabhāva-vikalpa.*

Ś: nāmamātram idam yaduta bodhisattvaḥ......māyopamaṃ rūpam. māyā ca nāmamātram......svabhāvavirahitam. P: as Ś, but without the last word. D: (nāmamātram idaṃ rūpaṃ tattvato hy asvabhāvakam) v. 45. ML: (svalakṣaṇa-vikalpa). ML, Ms: nāmamātraṃ yad idaṃ rūpam......

8. *Viśeṣa-vikalpa.*

Ś: asvabhāvaś ca-anutpādo 'nirodhaḥ......na vyavadānam......; kasyacid dharmasya utpādaṃ na samanupaśyati, nirodhaṃ na samanupaśyati,...... P: māyādarśana-svabhāvasya hi na-utpādo na nirodhaḥ......na vyavadānam......; utpādam api na samanupaśyati, nirodham api na samanupaśyati. D: na-utpādaṃ na nirodhaṃ ca dharmāṇāṃ paśyati, v. 47. ML, Ms: rūpasya hi na-utpādo......na vyavadānam.

9. *Yathā-nāma-artha-abhiniveśa-vikalpa.*

Ś: kṛtrimaṃ pratipatti-dharmaṃ te kalpitā[1] āgantukena nāmadheyena-abhūta-parikalpitena vyavahṛyante, vyavahārāc ca-abhiniveśyante. P: kṛtrimaṃ nāma pratidharmam. te ca kalpitāḥ, āgantukena nāmadheyena vyavahṛyante. D: (kṛtrimaṃ nāma vācyāś ca dharmās te kalpitā) v. 48 ML: kṛtrimaṃ nāma......Ms: kṛtrimaṃ nāma. pratipatti-dharmaṃ te[2] āgantukena nāmadheyena vyavahṛyante, vyavahārāc ca-abhiniviśante.

10. *Yathā-artha-nāma-abhiniveśa-vikalpa.*

Ś: sarvadharmān na samanupaśyati na-upalabhate, asamanupaśyann an-upalabhamāno na manyate na-abhiniviśate......nāmamātram idam yad idaṃ bodhisattva iti......buddha iti......prajñāpāramitā-iti......P: as S, but abbreviated. D: prajñāpāramitā buddho bodhisattvo 'pi vā tathā nāmamātram ......bodhisattvasya no nāma paśyāmi. vv. 51, 54. ML, Ms: tāni bodhisattvaḥ sarvanāmāni na samanupaśyaty, asamanupaśyann na-abhiniviśate,—yathā-

1 Tib. Ś and P: chos-rnams so-so'i miṅ ni sgyu-ma ste, rnam-par brtags-pa de-dag, etc. —*AA* calls the whole passage the pratipatty-avavāda, and Haribhadra *AAA* 35 comments: bodhicitta-tad-ākṣipta-dharma-svabhāva prajñāpāramitāyāṃ yā pratipattir anupalambha-ākārā.

2 This is Lamotte's Sanskrit translation of the Tibetan: miṅ bcos-ma-la chos de-dag so-sor brtags-nas miṅ glo-bur-gyis, etc.

arthaya-ity abhiprāyaḥ.

This list, which occurs in Chinese in T 220 k. 4, pp. 17b, 25–17c, 16, is also mentioned in Hsüan-tsang's *Vijñaptimātratāsiddhi*, p. 521, and it had sufficient authority to be even inserted into one of the Sūtras, the *Nitārtha* (no. 10).

3. A number of thinkers took up an intermediate position between Mādhyamikas and Yogācārins, and they are known as Yogācāra-Mādhyamika *svātantrikas*. From the standpoint of this school we have the most influential commentary of all, the *Abhisamayālaṅkāra* (no. 2A cy 1). It was written in the fourth century A.D., or in the eighth century of the Buddhist era. We have no precise knowledge about the author, which is not surprising in view of the Buddhist passion for self-effacing anonymity. His identity has been much discussed in recent years. Tradition ascribes the work to Maitreyanātha. Some scholars, like Ui and, for a time, Tucci, assumed that this was the name of a teacher of Asaṅga,[1] to whom other treatises are also attributed.[2] Others believe that it was Asaṅga himself who wrote these verses.[3] To strengthen the authority of his words, tradition would then have claimed that he was inspired by Maitreya, the "saviour" (*nātha*), who revealed to him the inner meaning of the Prajñāpāramitā Sūtra, just as the Bodhisattva Mañjuśrī had revealed to Nāgārjuna the foundations of the Mādhyamika system. It may be apposite to quote what Haribhadra says in his *Abhisamayālaṅkārālokā* (p. 75):

"Asaṅga, although he knew the meaning of all the scriptures (*pravacana*) and had obtained understanding (*adhigama*), was nevertheless incapable of ascertaining (*unnetum*) the meaning of the Prajñāpāramitā, because of the great number of the repetitions and the difficulty of distinguishing the indivi-

1 Cf. *ZII*, 1928, p. 215. —*Madhyāntavibhāga*, ed. Yamaguchi, Introd. x-xviii, Obermiller in *IHQ*, ix, 1024 sq. —Demiéville in *BEFEO*, xliv, 2 (1954), pp. 377–382, 384–7.

2 Other works attributed to Maitreya are, in China, according to a tradition beginning with Tun-lun in his commentary to N 1170 (cf. Ui p. 221): *Mahāyānasūtrālaṅkāra, Yogācārabhūmiśāstra, Yogācāravibhaṅgaśāstra, Madhyāntavibhāgaśāstra* and *Vajracchedikāsūtraśāstra*. The Tibetan tradition differs: Obermiller (*AO* 81) gives another list of the *byams chos sde lṅa*, the five treatises of Maitreya; *Abhisamayālaṅkāra, Sūtrālaṅkāra, Madhyāntavibhāga, Dharmadharmatāvibhaṅga* and *Uttaratantra* (*rgyud bla-ma*). Bu-ston states that the five treatises are similar in style, and often the verses are the same (cf. also Tāranātha on the five dharmas of Maitreya).

3 So Tāranātha, p. 112. A. Wayman, *Analysis*, etc., 1961, pp. 37–9 regards this as quite out of the question. His attempt to totally dissociate Asaṅga from the *AA* is not confirmed by C. Pensa, *L'abhisamayālaṅkāravṛtti di Ārya-Vimuktisena*, I, 1967, p. xv and by pages 21 and 23 sq. of that work.

dual arguments, not to mention its profundity. He was in despair when the Lord (*Bhagavat*) Maitreya commented for him on the Prajñāpāramitā Sūtra, and made the treatise called *Abhisamayālaṅkāra*. After this treatise had been heard, it was subsequently commented upon by Asaṅga, by the master Vasubandhu, etc."[1]

Tradition claims that Maitreya descended from the Tushita Heaven to give a special revelation. In the *kārikās* of the *Madhyāntavibhāga* Maitreya is called *praṇetā*, "inspirer" (Yamaguchi, p. xi). He is the revealer of the hidden, as against the obvious, sense. Parahitabhadra (Yamaguchi, p. xiii) says that Maitreya, seeing that the Dharma is difficult to understand, taught Asaṅga, etc. The tradition that Nāgārjuna was inspired by Mañjuśrī would lead no one to infer that his works were written by a princely youth who was an historical person. Obermiller (*AO* 92) quotes the *Siddhānta* (*grub-mtha'*) of Jam-yaṅ bźad-pa (ca. 1800): "The teacher Nāgārjuna, having been inspired by the Bodhisattva Mañjuśrī, has laid the foundation to the Mādhyamika system in accordance with *Akṣayamatinirdeśa-sūtra*. The same has been done by the teacher Ārya-Asaṅga, in regard to the Yogācāra system through the inspiration of Maitreya, and on the basis of the *Saṃdhinirmocana-sūtra*". In view of what Demiéville has said, in *BEFEO* XLIV, 2, 1954, pp. 381, 434, it appears rather unlikely that Maitreyanātha should be regarded as an historical person.

In its doctrinal position the book shows some affinities with other Yogācārin works. The list of 22 forms of the "thought of enlightenment" in I vv. 18–20 is very similar, though not identical, with that in Asaṅga's *Mahāyānasūtra-alaṅkāra*, IV, 15–20, which, however, in its turn goes back to the *Akṣayamati-paripṛcchā*, the 45th work of the *Ratnakūṭa* collection. Chapter VIII is closely akin to chapter X of Asaṅga's *Mahāyānasaṃgraha*, and to the *Abhisamaya* chapter of his *Abhidharmasamuccaya* (pp. 92–99 in Pradhan's edition). The words of one verse, VIII 8, are almost identical with those of *Mahāyānasaṃgraha* X 13, and with regard to the preceding verse, VIII 7, the explanation of Asvabhāva to *Mahāyānasaṃgraha* X 12 points to a common substratum of ideas. The *Abhidharmasamuccaya* is also the source for the 16 *kṣaṇas* (Haribhadra pp. 169–170), and the defilements to be removed by the path (pp. 98–99, Haribhadra). *Abhisamayālaṅkāra* V 21 has its parallels in *Uttaratantra* I 152 and in the *Mahāyānasūtrālaṅkāra*. But it has been pointed out in *MCB*, I, p. 394 and *BSOAS*, viii, 1935, p. 81, that this verse was first elaborated by Aśvaghoṣa, then adopted and transformed by Nāgārjuna, and in that form frequently quoted in Mādhyamika and Vijñānavādin works.

1 Cf. also Bu-ston's quotation from no. 5 cy. 3 at II 139.

Two of the specific *doctrines* of the Yogācārins, i.e. the "storeconsciousness" and the three kinds of own-being (*svabhāva*) are quite ignored. On the other hand, the Yogācārin multiplication of the bodies of the Buddha is accepted, and at I 16 and VIII four such bodies are envisaged, whereas the Prajñāpāramitā itself, and with it the Mādhyamikas, never distinguished more than two, i.e. the Dharmabody and the "Form-body". Further, the author superimposes on the text the specific *categories* of the Yogācārins, particularly the "fourfold discrimination" (*vikalpa*), which plays a great part in the arrangement of the first and fifth *abhisamayas* (I vv. 25–36, 71; V 5–36). The Yogācārins teach that all error is due to the assumption, or invention, of a separate subject and object. To overcome that error one must remove a twofold false discrimination, first of the object, and then of the subject. In addition to being attuned to the Yogācāra way of thinking, this scheme has the advantage of being so elastic as to fit nearly any text. This fact is brought out in a startling way on two occasions when Maitreyanātha applies the scheme to passages from the large Prajñāpāramitā which are absent from the *Aṣṭasāhasrikā*. Yet Haribhadra, who sets out to co-ordinate the *Abhisamayālaṅkāra* with the *Aṣṭasāhasrikā*, can read exactly the same division of *vikalpas*, with all their details, into the words of other portions of the *Aṣṭasāhasrikā* which, in their turn, are absent from the text of the revised *Pañcaviṃśatisāhasrikā*. The first case is *A* ch. 29, pp. 475–477, where Haribhadra finds the fourfold *vikalpa* on the path of development (V 6b–e of *AA*). In the *Pañcaviṃsati* the same scheme is applied to the totally different passage *P* 465–479, which has no counterpart in *A*.

The second case concerns *AA* V a-g, the bulk of which Haribhadra and *P* assign to completely different passages of the *Prajñāpāramitā*. The following Table will show the position at a glance: The first column shows the section of *AA* according to Haribhadra; the second the pages of *A* in which these sections are explained; the third the pages of *P* which correspond to these pages of *A*; and the fourth the sections of *AA* to which *P* assigns its own text.

Haribhadra *AAA*	*A*	*P*	*P-AA*
V 5a 1	xxvi 436; cr. to:	429	=V 4
2	437;	429–30	=V 4
5b 1	437;	429–30	=V 4
2	438;	429–30	=V 4
	——	430a2	=V 5a 1
	——	430a4–b9	=V 5a 2
V 5c	xxvi 438–43; cr. to:	433b4–	=V 5c
V 5d	xxvii 444–; cr. to:	430b9–	=V 5b 1

V 5e	446–; cr. to:	431b4–	=V 5b 2
V 5f	451–; cr. to:	433b	=V 5b 2
V 5g	454–; cr. to:	445a7–	=V 5b g
		436b2–	=V 5d
	——	439a3–	=V 5e
	——	444b2–	=V 5f.

Maitreyanātha was, of course, hard put to it to combine into one coherent argument those parts of the Sūtra which had originated at different times, and which often constituted separate essays without any real connection between them.

In any case, it is not so much the plain and obvious sense of the Sūtra which this school tries to bring out. The Mādhyamika philosophy had been in complete harmony with the teaching of the Prajñāpāramitā Sūtras, and when Nāgārjuna and his school commented on them they could therefore be content with expounding the meaning of the text as its authors had plainly intended. It was different with the Yogācārins, who derived their doctrines from another set of Sūtras, like the *Saṃdhinirmocana,* and to whom the Prajñāpāramitā, as it stood, was a source not only of inspiration but also of some embarrassment. Not always quite at their ease with it, they were forced to postulate a hidden or indirect meaning of its sayings. It was the deeper meaning, as against the obvious and superficial sense, which Maitreya had revealed. In the words of Bu-ston, the aim of the *Abhisamayālaṅkāra* is to "give an analysis of the profound meaning" of the Prajñāpāramitā (I 41), and it "has for its principal subject matter the meaning of that which is taught indirectly, –namely the knowledge of the practical way (to attain the dignity) of a Buddha" (I 51).

We can therefore say that the *AA* has set out to do two things: 1. It gives an intelligible Table of Contents to the Large Prajñāpāramitā 2. It assigns to each section of the text its place on the path of spiritual progress which Buddhist tradition had mapped out as the way to Buddhahood. The text of the Sūtra is divided into eight sections, these again into 70 subsections, and these again into 1,200 different items. And the whole scheme, both in its general plan and in its particular details, views everything in its relation to the practical realization of salvation through wisdom.

This is already indicated by the word *abhisamaya* in the title. Etymologically derived from *abhi*+*sam*+the root *I* ("to go" *i-re*) *abhisamaya* can be translated as "coming together", or "reunion", or "communion". The true reality outside me comes together with the true reality inside me—that is the idea. In the Pali scriptures the term is used to designate the stage when we comprehend the four holy truths. In the *Abhidharmakośa* (VI 122) it is interpreted as the correct (*sam=samyak*) knowledge (*aya*) which is turned towards (*abhi*) Nirvāṇa. In the Prajñāpāramitā Sūtra itself it is invariably coupled with *prāpti*, "attainment". and in one place (*Su* i 7b) it is a synonym for *sākṣātkriyā* (realization).

The text of the Sūtra is divided up according to a list of eight kinds of *abhisamaya* which are not attested elsewhere. It is constructed on the following principles: The approach to enlightenment is viewed on three parallel *levels*, and four, or more, successive *stages*. In Sanskrit the one word *bhūmi* does duty for both "level" and "stage". The levels are distinguished by the type of person who stands on them, and there are three of these; the Buddha, the mahāyānistic Bodhisattva, and the hīnayānistic "Disciple", who is usually coupled with the Pratyekabuddha. Each one is capable of a particular range of insight, and the names for the three kinds of insight are taken from the Large Prajñāpāramitā where they occur with great regularity, and where they are also twice defined (*Ś* LIII f. 295=*P* f. 476a, and at *D* ch. 2, no. 50–52). The Buddha attains the *sarvākārajñatā*, "the knowledge of all modes", which is his clear and infallible cognition of all dharmas in all their aspects. Characterstic of the Bodhisattva is the *mārgākārajñatā*, the "knowledge of the modes of the path", which is his ability to know the decisive features of all the three careers coupled with his decision to reject the methods and aims of the Disciples and Pratyekabuddhas, and to strive to become a Buddha. The Disciples and Pratyekabuddhas finally achieve *sarvajñatā*, "all-knowledge", and their particular insight consists in that they perceive the absence of a self in all inward and outward dharmas. These three modes of insight constitute the first three *abhisamayas*, which occupy the first three chapters of *AA*, and are held to account for more than the first half of the Sūtra.

The remainder is then devoted to the Path and its Fruit, and the other four *abhisamayas* concern the Path, and the practical realization[1] of the above three forms of omniscience. IV, *sarvākārābhisaṃbodha*, "the full understanding of all modes", deals with the 173 modes, or aspects, of the three forms of omniscience. IV is then further subdivided into; V—*mūrdhābhisamaya*, "the full understanding at its summit", VI—*anupūrvābhisamaya*, the progressive, or gradual, understanding, and VII—*ekakṣaṇābhisamaya*, the "single-instantaneous" understanding,[2] followed by VIII—*dharmakāyābhisaṃbodha*, the full understanding of the Dharmabody. In the form of a diagram:

1 *Prayoga*, which is the *hetu* (IV–VII), in IX v. 2; and the *phala* (VIII) of IX v. 2, or *vipāka* of IX v.l.

2 See A. Coomaraswamy, *Time and Eternity*, p. 46, who compares Śaṅkara's *sadya* in *sadyo-mukti*, Brahmasūtrabhāṣya 1, 1, 11.

Method: I, II, III — Path: IV (V, VI, VII) — Fruit: VIII

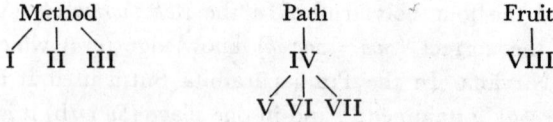

V concerns the culminating points[1] of a Bodhisattva's intuition of the Path; VI refers to the progressive contemplation[2] of the elements constituting the Path; VII, the result and final conclusion[3] of VI, refers to the final momentary intuition, which directly precedes the attainment of Buddhahood, which is reached in VIII, the realisation of the cosmical body of the Buddha being the final result of the Path.

The *AA* treats the contents of the *Prajñāpāramitā* as statements of spiritual experiences. While general scientific propositions can be considered in the abstract, experiences derive their meaning and significance from the concrete circumstances in which they take place, and the spiritual maturity of the observer is a decisive factor in the situation. The spiritual world is an essentially hierarchical structure, and the Absolute must appear different on different levels of attainment. Buddhist tradition had by 350 A.D. evolved a clear and detailed picture of the Path which a Buddhist Saint would have to traverse through countless aeons. The *AA* assigns an appropriate place on that Path to each meditation found in the *Prajñāpāramitā.* The reader of the *AA* must constantly bear in mind the position from which events are observed. What at first sight seems to be a dry and scholastic treatise then becomes a fascinating contribution to transcendental psychology.

The information about the Path envisaged here is scattered in many diverse publications. Its condensation into a diagram will be helpful to some readers. I have been content to give the Sanskrit terms. The English equivalents can be easily found in my translation of the *AA*.

In the diagram we have three columns. The central one draws up the pattern of the Path as outlined in common for all Vehicles. The lefthand column, based chiefly on the *Abhidharmakośa,* shows how it applies to the Method of the Disciples and Pratyekabuddhas. The seven *bhūmis* of the *śrāvakas* are given in italics. The term *gotrabhūmi* is here, incidentally, interpreted by Mahāyānists as denoting the stage where the Disciple definitely knows that he belongs to the spiritual lineage of the *śrāvakas*. Each of the 81 stages of the *bhāvanāmārga* is again divided into two steps, the *ānantaryamārga,* which corresponds to the *prahāṇa* of the corresponding *kleśa*, and the *vimukti-*

1 *Prakarṣa* in IX v. 1.
2 *Anukrama* in IX v. 1.
3 *Niṣṭhā* in IX v. 1.

mārga which corresponds to its *nirodha*. The *Abhidharmakośa* counts the elimination of the *kleśas* differently from the *Prajñāpāramitā*,[1] in that it envisages a reduction of the *kleśas* of each of the nine *dhātus* in turn from "very strong" to "very weak". The righthand column indicates the peculiarities which apply to the path of the Bodhisattvas, and they are derived from Haribhadra. In the subdivisions of the *Bhāvanāmārga* I have been forced to employ abbreviations for the terms expressing the relative strength of the *kleśas* (which slowly diminishes) and of the Path (which slowly increases), "a" standing for *adhimātra,* "m" for *madhya,* and "u" for *mṛdu.*

I append a few hints for the distribution of the text of the *AA* among these divisions: A=I 1, I 2, I 7, I 8, IV 6. –B=I 3, II 2, II 3, 2, IV 7, IV 8, 1. –B no. 4=I 9, 1–15. –A-C 16=VI. –C=II 4, III 9, IV 8, 2, V 5. –C-D, 10 *bhūmis,* =I 9, 16–17. –D=II 5–11, IV 8, 3, V 6. –D, *bhūmis* 8–10, =I 10, IV 9, IV 10, IV 11. –D, *vajropamasamādhi*=V 7[13]. –D, *ekakṣaṇābhisamaya*= VII. –B-E=I 4, I 5, III 7, III 8. –E=I 6, VIII.

1 See *AA* IV 8, 3, C and D, on pages 71 and 73 of my translation.

Disciples and Pratyekabuddhas	The Path	Bodhisattvas Mārgākārajñatā
śraddhā-bhūmi dharma-abhisamaya	A. SAMBHĀRAMĀRGA	ādikarmikabhūmi bodhicittotpāda
I. Śuklavidarśanabhūmi	5 mokṣabhāgīya: 1. śraddhā 2. vīrya 3. smṛti 4. samādhi 5. prajñā	
artha-abhisamaya dharmasmṛtyupasthāna	B. PRAYOGAMĀRGA	adhimukticaryābhūmi
II. Gotrabhūmi	4 nirvedhabhāgīya: 1. ūṣmagata 2. mūrdhan 3. kṣānti 4. laukikāgradharma ānantaryasamādhi	

lokottarasatyadarśana satya-abhisamaya	dhātu	C. DARŚANAMĀRGA	pāramitā	bhūmi
III. *Aṣṭamakabhūmi* srotāpattiphala-pratipannaka. 1st mārga	kāma	1. duḥkhe dharmajñānakṣāntiḥ		
	kāma	2. duḥkhe dharmajñānam		
	rūpa	3. duḥkhe 'nvayajñānakṣāntiḥ		
	arūpa	4. duḥkhe 'nvayajñānam		
	kāma	5. samudaye dharmajñānakṣāntiḥ		
	kāma	6. samudaye dharmajñānam		
	rūpa	7. samudaye 'nvayajñānakṣāntiḥ		
	arūpa	8. samudaye 'nvayajñānam		
	kāma	9. nirodhe dharmajñānakṣāntiḥ		
	kāma	10. nirodhe dharmajñānam		
	rūpa	11. nirodhe 'nvayajñānakṣāntiḥ		
	arūpa	12. nirodhe 'nvayajñānam		
	kāma	13. mārge dharmajñānakṣāntiḥ		
	kāma	14. mārge dharmajñānam		
	rūpa	15. mārge 'nvayajñānakṣāntiḥ		
	arūpa	16. mārge 'nvayajñānam		
IV. *Darśanabhūmi* 1st phala			dāna	1. pramuditā

anāsrava			D. BHĀVANĀMĀRGA				
	kleśa	dhātu		kleśa	mārga	pāramitā	bhūmi
	1. aa	kāma		aa	uu	śīla	2. vimalā
	2. am						
	3. au						
	4. ma						
	5. mm						
V: Tanubhūmi	6. mu						
2nd phala	7. ua						
	8. um						
VI: Vītarāgabhūmi	9. uu						
3rd phala							
	10.-18.	1st rūpa		am	um	kṣānti	3. prabhākarī
	19.-27.	2nd rūpa		au	ua	vīrya	4. arcismatī
	28.-36.	3rd rūpa		ma	mu	dhyāna	5. sudurjayā
	37.-45.	4th rūpa		mm	mm	prajñā	6. abhimukhī
	46.-54.	1st arūpa		mu	ma	upāyakauśalya	7. duramgamā
	55.-63.	2nd arūpa		ua	au	praṇidhāna	8. acalā
	64.-72.	3rd arūpa		um	am	bala	9. sādhumatī
	73.-80.	4th arūpa		uu	aa	jñāna	10. dharmamegha
	81.uu	bhavāgra	vajropamasamādhi				
				ekakṣaṇābhisamaya			

THE FRUIT				
vimuktimārga; viśeṣamārga Sarvajñatā		E. AŚAIKṢAMĀRGA	dharmakāyābhisamaya Sarvākārajñatā	
ARHAT	PRATYEKABUDDHA		BUDDHA	
VII: kṛtavībhūmi 4th phala kṣayajñāna anutpādajñāna			1. svābhāvikakāya 2. dharmakāya 3. sambhogakāya 4. nirmāṇakāya	Buddhabhūmi

4. BIBLIOGRAPHY OF SUB-COMMENTARIES TO ABHISAMAYĀLAṄKĀRA.

(A. In connection with *P*:)

AA-Cy 1: Ārya-Vimuktisena. *Pañcaviṃśatisāhasrikā-prajñāpāramitopadeśa-śāstra-abhisamayālaṅkāra-vṛtti.*

S: Manuscript of A.D. 1100 from Nepal. (In Rome).

s: ed. C. Pensa, SOR, I, 1967.

Ti: mdo-'grel I, 15b–249a. *ñi-khri snaṅ-ba.* –To 3787, *rgyan-gyi 'grel-pa.* trsl. Go-mi 'chi med, (Amaragomin), lotsāva Blo-ldan śes-rab (ca. A.D. 1100).

This is a commentary to both *P* and *AA*, side by side, and it is chiefly concerned with showing, point by point, the correspondence which exists between the division and verses of *AA* (quoted as *ity āha*) and the text of no. 2A (quoted as *yad āha*). The verses of *AA* are usually explained (prefaced by *yad uktam*), and so are difficult words occurring in the quotations from no. 2A, such as *kṛtajñatā, akūṭastha,* etc. cf. D. S. Ruegg, "Ārya and Bhadanta Vimuktisena on the gotra-theory of the Prajñāpāramitā", *Beitraege zur Geistesgeschichte Indiens,* 1968 (Frauwallner Festschrift = *WZKSO* 12–13), pp. 303–317. –C. Pensa, "Note di lessicografia buddhista", *Rivista degli Studi Orientali* xxxix, 1964, pp. 61–67. According to the colophon the author belonged to the Kauru-kulla branch of the Ārya-Saṃmitīyas.

Cy 2: Bhadanta Vimuktisena, *-abhisamayālaṅkārakārikā-vārttika.*

Ti: mdo 'grel II, 1–207a. –To 3788. *tshig-le'ur byas-pa'i rnam-par 'grel-pa.* Author: Rnam grol sde; transl. Śāntibhadra, 'bro Śākya 'od.

Cy 3: Ratnākaraśānti, *Śuddhamatī.*

Ti: mdo 'grel IX, 87–240. –To 3801. *tshig-le'ur byas-pa'i 'grel-pa dag-ldan.* trsl. Śrīsubhūtiśānti, Śākya blo-gros, Dge-ba'i blo-gros.

(B. In connection with Ś:)

= no. 1, cy 1.

(C. In connection with no. 1–3, and no. 1, 2, 5:)

=no. 1 cy 4.

AA-Cy 4: Bu-ston, *Rgyas 'briṅ bsdus gsum-gyi skabs brgyad don bdun-cu'i mtshams 'byed-par byed-pa'i Śer-phyin-gyi lde-mig ces bya-ba.* –To 5176, vol. 19, pp. 1–22.

(D. In connection with *A*:)

=no. 5, cy 1. cy 2. cy 3.

(E. In connection with *Rgs*:)

=no. 5A, cy 1, cy 2, cy 3.

(F. Without concordance with Sūtras:)

AA-Cy 5: Haribhadra, *Sphuṭārtha.*

S: Manuscript from Nepal. (In Rome).

Ti: mdo 'grel VII 93–161. *Don-gsal 'grel-pa ('grel chuṅ).* –To 3793. *vṛtti. 'grel-pa.* trsl. Vidyākaraprabha, Dpal-brtsegs (R). –Also: To 6794. ——Romanized text in H. Amano (see p. 28) facing the Sanskrit of *AAA.*

Cy 5–1: Prajñākaramati, *Abhisamayālaṅkāra-vṛtti-piṇḍārtha.*

Ti: mdo 'grel VII 289–315. –To 3795. *'grel-pa'i bsdus don.* trsl. Sumatikīrti, Blo-ldan śes-rab.

This is a summary of AA-Cy 5.

Cy 5–2: Dharmamitra, *-ṭikā Prasphuṭapadā nāma*

Ti: mdo 'grel VIII 1–128. –To 3796. *tshig-le'ur byas-pa'i 'grel-bśad tshig rab-tu gsal-ba shes bya-ba.* trsl. Abhyuktaka Ttaraśrīmitra, Chos-kyi śes-rab.

Cy 5–3: Phyā-pa chos-kyi seṅ-ge: –

Cy 5–4: Bu-ston rin-chen grub.

Ti: *Śes-rab-kyi pha-rol-tu phyin-pa'i man-ṅag-gi bstan-bcos mṅon-par rtogs-pa'i rgyan shes bya-ba'i 'grel-ba'i rgya-cher bśad-pa, Luṅ-gi sñe-ma shes bya-ba* (=Bu-ston's Phar-phyin). A.D. 1319. –To 5173. vol. 18, 1–363. –Refers to AA-Cy 3, no. 5A Cy 2, AA–Cy 9, no. 5–Cy 3, To 3790, no. 5–Cy 1, no. 5A Cy 1, AA-Cy 6, AA-Cy 5–1, AA-Cy 5–2, AA-Cy 7.

Cy 5–4–1: Ti: *Śes-rab-kyi pha-rol-tu phyin-pa grub-pa'i rab-tu byed-pa, Lta-ba ṅan-sel shes bya-ba.*

Appendix to Cy 5–4, defending the AA against adverse criticism. To 5174, vol. 19, Dza 1–31.

Cy 5–4–2: Ti: *Luṅ-gi sñe-ma'i skabs skabs-su mkho-ba'i zur-'debs, Mthoṅ-lam stoṅ-thun.*

Explanatory notes on important words and sentences in Cy 5–4. To 5175, vol. 19, Dza 1–14.

Cy 5–5: Re mda'-pa gshon-nu blo-gros.

Ti: (ṭīkā).

Cy 5–6: Dar-ma rin-chen, rgyal-tshab.

Ti: *Rnam-bśad sñiṅ-po'i rgyan. –Śes-rab-kyi pha-rol-tu phyin-pa'i man-ṅag-gi bstan-bcos mṅon-par rtogs-pa'i rgyan-gyi 'grel-ba don gsal-ba'i rnam-bśad, Sñiṅ-po'i rgyan.* To 5433, Kha 1–346: – LSOAS 82796. Based on cy 15.

Cy 5–6–1: Mkhon-ston Dpal-'byor lhun-grub.

Ti: *Bstan-bcos mṅon-par rtogs-pa'i rgyan-gyi 'grel-ṭik, Rnam bśad sñiṅ-po'i rgyan-gyi tshig-don rab-gsal shes bya-ba-las:*

a) skabs daṅ-po'i rnam-par brad-pa. Ka 1–125;
b) gñis-pa'i Kha 1–36; c) gsum-pa'i Ga 1–17;
d) bshi-pa'i Ṅa 1–48; e) brgyad-pa'i Ca 1–31.
To 6816.

Cy 5–7: Mkhas-grub bstan-pa dar-ba.

Ti: *Bstan-bcos mṅon-par rtogs-pa'i rgyan 'grel-pa daṅ bcas-pa'i mtha'-dpyod, Legs-par bśad-pa padma dkar-po'i 'phreṅ-ba-las skabs daṅ-po.* To 6819, 77ff. Critical study and refutation of different interpretations of ch. 1 of Cy. 5.

Cy 5–8: Mkhas-grub Dge-legs dpal bzaṅ-po.

Ti: *Śes-rab-kyi pha-rol-tu phyin-pa'i man-ṅag-gi bstan-bcos mṅon-par rtogs-pa'i rgyan-gyi 'grel-pa don-gsal-ba'i rnam-bśad, Rtogs-dka'i snaṅ-ba shes bya-ba.* To 5461, Ka 1–223.

Cy 6: Dharmakīrtiśrī, *Dur(ava)bodha-āloka-nāma ṭikā.*

Ti: mdo-'grel VII 161–289. –To 3794. *'grel-pa rtogs-par dka'-ba'i snaṅ-ba shes bya-ba'i 'grel-bśad.* trsl. Dīpaṃkara-śrījñāna, Rin-chen bzaṅ-po.

Cy 7: Kumāraśrībhadra, *Prajñāpāramitāpiṇḍārtha.*
Ti: mdo-'grel VIII 128–133. To 3797. *don bsdus-pa.* trsl. Kumāraśrībhadra, Bkra-śis rgyal-mtshan.

Cy 8: (Atīśa? Ratnākaraśānti?), *Prajñāpāramitāpiṇḍārthapradipa.*
Ti: mdo-'grel X 253a–264a. –To 3804, attr. to Mar-me mdzad ye-śes. trsl. Mar-me mdzad ye-śes, Tshul-khrims rgyal-ba.

The "Blue Annals" (p. 258) mention an "extensive exposition" of *AA* which Atīśa gave, and which "was written down by Phya-dar ston-pa, and became known as the "Prajñāpāramitā according to the method of Khams" (*Phar-phyin Khams-lugs-ma*).

Cy 9: Buddhaśrījñāna, *Prajñā-pradipa-āvali.*
Ti: mdo-'grel IX 1–87. – To 3800. *'grel-pa śes-rab sgron-ma'i phreṅ-ba,* trsl. Buddhaśrījñāna, Grubs Byams-pa'i dpal.

Cy 10: Ratnakīrti, *Kirtikalā.*
Ti: mdo-'grel IX 223–310. – To 3799, *'grel-pa grags-pa'i cha,* trsl. Ratnakīrti, Chiṅs yon-tan 'bar.

Cy 11: Abhayākaragupta, *Munimatālaṅkāra.*
Ti: mdo-'grel XXIX 71–398. –To 3903 (Independent work, but last three chapters on *AA*).

Cy 12: Rṅog blo-ldan śes-rab:–

Cy 13: Gtsaṅ-nag-pa brtson-'grus seṅ-ge: – (Concordance between the 70 topics of *AA* and the Prajñāpāramitā Sūtra).

Cy 14: Dol-po-pa śes-rab rgyal-mtshan:–

Cy 15: Tsoṅ-kha-pa: *Śes-rab-kyi pha-rol-tu phyin-pa'i man-ṅag-gi bstan-bcos mṅon-par rtogs-pa'i rgyan 'grel-pa daṅ bcas-pa'i rgya-cher bśad-pa, Legs-bśad gser-gyi phreṅ-ba shes bya-ba.* –To 5412 Tsa 1–405,ch. 1–3, Tsha 1–367, ch. 4–8. –Cy to AA and AA-cy 5.

Cy 15a: *Shugs-pa daṅ gnas-pa'i skyes-bu chen-po rnams-kyi rnam-par bshag-pa, Blo gsal bgrod-pa'i them-skas shes bya-ba.* To 5413. Tsha 1–42. – Cy to AA I 2, 3c.

Cy 15a–1 Ti: *Dge-'dun ñi-śu bsdus-pa, Bshugs gnas skyes-bu chen-po'i dka'-gnad.* To 5420, Tsha 1–7.

An explanation and abridgment of Cy–15a, by one of Tsoṅ-kha-pa's disciples.

Cy 15b: *Bsam gzugs zin-bris.* To 5417, Tsha 1–10. – A note on *dhyāna* and *ārūpyasamāpatti* in *AA*.

Cy 15b–1: Chos-kyi rgyal-mtshan, rje-btsun.

Ti: *Bsam-gzugs-kyi mtha'-gcod.* To 6823. 36 ff.

Cy 16: Dar-ma rin-chen, rgyal-tshab.

Ti: *Mṅon-par rtogs-pa'i rim-pa ñams-su len-tshul, Theg mchog sgo 'byed ces bya-ba.* To 5439, Ca 1–61.

Explanation of the importance of main sections in the *AA* and Cy–5.

Cy 16a: Ti: *Mṅon-par rtogs-pa brgyad-don bdun-cu daṅ bcas-pa'i 'grel-pa ñams-su len-tshul mdo-tsam daṅ bcas-pa.* To 5440 Ca 1–25.

Explanation of 8 subjects and 70 topics.

Cy 16b: *Mṅon-par rtogs-pa'i rgyan-gyi bsdus-don, Rin-po-che'i phreṅ-ba.* To 5441, Ca 1–14.

Summary of *AA*, cy 5 and cy 15.

Cy 17a: Ye-śes rgyal-mtshan.

Ti: *Śes-rab-kyi pha-rol-tu phyin-pa'i man-ṅag-gi bstan-bcos mṅon-par rtogs-pa'i rgyan-gyi bsdus-don shib-tu bkod-pa, Śer-phyin mdzod-brgya 'byed-pa'i lde-mig.* To 5996. Ja 1–47. Outline explanation of *AA*.

Cy 17b: Ti: *Śer-phyin stoṅ-phrag brgyad-pa daṅ mṅon-rtogs rgyan sbyar-te byaṅ-chub lam-gyi rim-pa'i gnad-rnams gsal-bar ston-pa'i man-ṅag, Śer-phyin gsal-ba'i sgron-me.* To 5997, Ja 1–80.

Upadeśa elucidating the main points of the *Lam-rim chen-mo* according to the views of *A* and *AA*.

Cy 18: Mkhas grub Dge-legs dpal bzaṅ-po, and Chos dbaṅ grags-pa'i dpal.

Ti: *Śes-rab-kyi pha-rol-tu phyin-pa'i man-ṅag-gi bstan-bcos mṅon-par rtogs-pa'i rgyan-gyi mthar-thug-pa'i lta-ba thal-'gyur-du 'grel tshul, Gnad-don gsal-ba'i zla-zer.* To 5460, Ka 1–14.

Shows that essential meaning of *AA* should be interpreted in light of Prāsaṅgika school.

Cy 19: Roṅ-ston śā-kya'i rgyal-mtshan. – (Cf. *Blue Annals* p. 340, 1080?). *Sa-skya-pa'i mkhas-pa Roṅ-ston śes bya kun-rig-gi mṅon rtogs rgyan 'grel daṅ, gYag ston-gyi 'grel-pa rgyas bsdus gñis, gor mas pas mdzad-pa'i sbas don zab-mo, yum don rab gsal, ña dpon kun-dga' dp(b)al-gyi 'grel-pa yod. yaṅ. roṅ-ston-gyi stoṅ-phrag brgya-ba'i 'grel-pa yod.*

Cy 20: Dge-'dun grub-pa.

Ti: *Rgyal-po zla-ba bzaṅ-po'i rnam-'phrul Ta'i-si-tu chen-po rnam-rgyal grags-pa'i: dri-ba* and *dri-ba'i lan.* To 5538–9.3 and 24ff. Record of Ta'i-si-tu chen-po Rnam-rgyal grags-pa's questions on *AA*, and of the answers to them.

Cy 21: Ṅag-dbaṅ blo-bzaṅ ryal-mtsho.

Ti: *Bstan-bcos mṅon-par rtogs-pa'i rgyan-gyi rtsa-'grel-rnams gsal-bar byed-pa blo-bzaṅ dgoṅs-rgyan gdoṅ-lṅa'i dbaṅ-po'i sgra-dbyaṅs-las:*

a) skabs daṅ-po'i tshig-don mtha'-dpyod, Pa 1–138; b) skabs gñis-pa'i, Pa 1–49; c) gsum-pa'i, Pa 1–22; d) bshi-pa'i, Pa 1–63; e) lṅa-pa daṅ drug-pa'i, P 1–36; f) bdun-pa daṅ brgyad-pa'i, Pa 1–44.

Sub-cy to *AA* and cy 5. Textbook of Bde-dbyaṅs College in 'bras-spuṅs temple. To 5647.

Cy 22: Chos-kyi rgyal-mtshan, blo-bzaṅ.

Ti: *Śes-rab-kyi pha-rol-tu phyin-pa'i man-ṅag-gi bstan-bcos mṅon-par rtogs-pa'i rgyan-gyi sñiṅ-po'i sñiṅ-po gsal-bar legs-par bśad-pa'i rgya-mtsho-las skabs-daṅ-po'i rnam-par bśad-pa.* To 5942, Ṅa 1–41. Explanation of essential points of ch. 1 of *AA*.

Cy 23: Chos-kyi rgyal-mtshan, rje-btsun.

Ti: *Bstan-bcos mṅon-par rtogs-pa'i rgyan 'grel-pa daṅ bcas-pa'i rnam-bśad rnam-pa gñis-kyi dka'-ba'i gnad gsal-bar byed-pa, Legs-bśad skal-bzaṅ klu-dbaṅ-gi rol-mtsho shes bya-ba las:* a) skabs daṅ-po'i spyi-don, Ka 1–116; b) skabs daṅ-po'i spyi-don-gyi smad-cha, Kha 1–185; c) skabs gñis-pa'i spyi-don, Ga 1–85; d) gsum-pa'i, Ña 1–34; e) bshi-pa'i, Ca 1–147; f) lṅa-pa'i, Cha 1–36; g) sgom-lam rtse-sbyor 'chad-pa skabs lṅa-pa'i spyi-don, Cha 1–27; h) drug-pa'i, Ja 1–5; i) bdun-pa'i, Ña 1–7; j) brgyad-pa'i, Ta 1–68; k) brgyad-pa'i; Chos-sku 1–71.

To 6814. Mainly based on cy 15 and 5–5.

Cy 23a: a) Skabs daṅ-po'i mtha'-dpyod, Legs-bśad gser-gyi phreṅ-ba mkhas-pa'i mgul-rgyan. Rnam-mkhyen 1–164. b) Skabs gñis-pa'i mtha'-dpyod, Dri-ma med-pa. Lam-śes 1–71. c) Skabs gsum-pa'i mtha'-dpyod, Gshi-śes, 1–23. d) Skabs bshi-pa'i mtha'-dpyod, Legs-bśad nor-bu'i 'phreṅ-ba. Rnam-rdzogs 1–63. e) Skabs lṅa-pa, drug-pa, bdun-pa rnams-kyi mtha'-gcod. Rtse sbyor. Mthar-gyi, Skad-cig-ma, 1–18. f) Skabs brgyad-pa'i mtha'-gcod. Chos-sku 1–15.

To 6815. A critical study and refutation of different interpretations of the AA and Cy 5.

Cy 23b: Ti: *Bstan-bcos mṅon-par rtogs-pa'i rgyan-gyi brjod-bya dṅos brgyad don bdun-cu ṅes-par 'byed-pa'i thabs dam-pa.*

To 6827 16 ff.

On 8 subjects and 70 topics.

Cy 23c: Ti: *Dge-'dun ñi-śu'i mtha'-gcod.*

To 6824, 45 ff. On *AA* I 2, 3c.

Cy 24: 'jam-dbyaṅs bśad-pa ṅag-dbaṅ brtson-'grus. – The 8 subjects of *AA*. A manual of the monastic schools. Part 1 is devoted to the refutation of others, part 2 to the explanation of his own standpoint, and part 3 to the refutation of objections.

Cy 25: Mkhas-grub bstan-pa dar-ba.

Ti: *Bstan-bcos mṅon-par rtogs-pa'i rgyan rtsa-'grel-gyi spyi-don rnam-bśad, Sñiṅ-po rgyan-gyi snaṅ-ba shes bya-ba las:*

a) skabs daṅ-po, 1–141. b) 4th chapter, 1–65.

To 6817, 6818.

Cy to *AA* and AA-cy 5.

Cy 26: Dbyaṅs-can dga'-ba'i blo-gros.

Ti: *Skabs lṅa-pa'i gshuṅ-don tshigs-su bcad-pa, Blo-gsal mgul-rgyan.*
To 6580. Ka 1–10.
Explanation of ch. 5 of *AA*.

Cy 27: Dharmabhadra.
Ti: *Mṅon-rtogs rgyan-gyi bsdus-don, Śer-phyin lde-mig.*
To 6367. Ṅa 1–12.
Cy to *AA,* on basis of cy–15.

Cy 28: Kloṅ-rdol bla-ma ṅag-dbaṅ, blo-bzaṅ.
Ti: *Phar-phyin-las byuṅ-ba'i miṅ-gi rnam-graṅs.*
To 6539. Ña 1–35.
On 8 subjects and 70 topics.

Cy 29: 'jam-dpal rgya-mtsho.
Ti- *Śes-rab-kyi pha-rol-tu phyin-pa'i mtha'-dpyod 'khrul sel gaṅgā'i chu rgyun mi pham shal luṅ.*
Skabs 3, 4, 5, 8 in LSOAS 41606. 41525. 41633. 41524.
Also by authors unknown or unascertained.:

Cy 30: Ti: *Śes-rab-kyi pha-rol-tu phyin-pa'i man-ṅag-gi bstan-bcos mṅon-par rtogs-pa'i rgyan-gyi 'grel-pa yum don gsal-ba.*
LSOAS 82797.

Cy 31: Ti: *Rgyal-dbaṅ 'phags-mchog dam-pa'i sku shabs-nas phar-phyin-gyi gshuṅ-gi dka'-gnas rnams-la bka'-'dri phebs-pa'i lan gshuṅ-don sñiṅ-por sgril-nas phul-ba.*
To 6863. Ms. 22 ff.
Explanation of difficult passages in *AA*, written in answer to an enquiry.

Cy 32: Ti: *Bstan-bcos mṅon-par rtogs-pa'i rgyan-gyi don gsal-bar byed-pa'i luṅ daṅ rigs-pa'i gter-mdzod.*
Detailed cy (mtha'-dpyod) on *AA* (8 chapters, *skabs,* with separate titles and headings) LSOAS 82833.

Cy 33: Ti: *Śes-rab-kyi pha-rol-tu phyin-pa'i mtha'-dpyod mkhas-pa'i mgul rgyan nor-bu'i 'phreṅ mdzes.*
Detailed cy to *AA*: ch. 2 (ff. 32) and ch. 6 (ff. 5) in LSOAS 41607, 41632. Cf. also LSOAS 41608 (dge-sloṅ

blo-bzaṅ Dam-chos, *skabs gsum*) and 82839 (blo-bzaṅ Bstan-pa'i ñi-ma, *Legs-par bśad-pa mkhas-pa'i mgul-(b)rgyan*).

Bstan-pa'i ñi-ma, blo-bzaṅ. 1689–1746.
Ti: *Phar-phyin skabs brgyad-kyi mtha'-dpyod legs-par bshad-pa mkhas-pa'i mgul rgyan*. ff. 506
Guṅ-thaṅ-pa Dkon-mchog bstan-pa'i sgron-me. 1762–1823.
Ti: *Phar-phyin skabs daṅ-po'i mtha'-dpyod mchan-'grel rtsom-'phro*. ff. 128.

For additions and corrections see: Lokesh Chandra, *Materials,* etc. III, 1963, pp. 528–534.
e.g. A-khu rin-po-che's *Tho-yig*.
rṅog lo-tsā-ba blo-ldan śes-rab-kyi phar-phyin tika chen. de'i phar-phyin.

INDICES

1. ALPHABETICAL LIST OF SANSKRIT TITLES

This list covers only the texts, and a few of the commentaries. Among the texts it omits those of which the Sanskrit titles are definitely lost, i.e. no. 15, 27 and 28 (about *dhāraṇīs*), 33b (iconographical), 34 (liturgy), 39 and 40 (iconographical).

2. ALPHABETICAL LIST OF INDIAN COMMENTATORS

Atīśa: see Dīpaṃkaraśrījñāna.

Abhayākaragupta: 5-cy 3; AA-cy 11.—Died 1125. He worked in Vikramaśīla and Nālandā, and later on in Tibet, where he helped in about 100 translations.

Amoghavajra: 17-cy 3.—See page 22.

Asaṅga: 8-cy 1-ca 350. Systematized Yogācāra thought.

Kamalaśīla: 7-cy 2; 8-cy 4; 11-cy 5.-A.D. 713–763. Pupil of Śāntarakṣita (A.D. 705–762), who had received the tradition of the Yogācāra-Mādhyamika-Svātantrikas through Śrīgupta and Jñānagarbha (cf. Tāranātha pp. 199 and 213).

Kambalāmbara: 5-cy 6; 5-cy 6–1.–A Siddha, perhaps a teacher of Indrabhūti, mentioned in the cy to the *Dohākoṣa*.

Kumāraśrībhadra: AA-cy 7.
Jagaddalanivāsin: 5-cy 4.
Jñānamitra: 11-cy 2; 17-cy 1.—ca. 1000. Teacher of Atīśa?
Triratnadāsa: 5-cy 5–1.—A Pupil of Vasubandhu, who learned Prajñāpāramitā from Dignāga.
Daṃṣṭrasena: 1-cy 2; 1-cy 4.—ca. 750. From Kashmir. Under Devapāla.
Dignāga: 5-cy 5.—ca. 450. See pp. 97–101.
Dīpaṃkaraśrījñāna: 1-cy 6; 11-cy 6; AA-cy 8 (?).—Born 1079.
Dharmakīrtiśrī: AA-cy 6.—From Suvarṇadvīpa?
Dharmamitra: AA-cy 5–2.—Mādhyamika.
Dharmaśrī: 1-cy 1; 5A-cy 3.–11th century. From Kashmir. Disciple of Vajrapāṇi. Follower of the Mahāmudrā tradition. Tsoṅ-kha-pa in AA-cy 15: 1-cy 1 not authentic; 5A-cy 3 was composed either by a translator or a Tibetan author.
Nāgārjuna: 2-cy 1.—See pp. 93–94.
Prajñākaramati: AA-cy 5–1.—ca. 1075.
Praśāstrasena: 11-cy 4.
Buddhaśrījñāna: 5A-cy 2; AA-cy 9.—Or Buddhajñānapāda? Pupil of Haribhadra, voluminous author on Guhyasamāja.
Mahājana: 11-cy 7.—Teacher of Atīśa.
(Maitreyanātha:) 2a-cy 1.—See pp. 101–102.
Ratnakīrti: AA-cy 10.—ca. 1050.
Ratnākaraśānti: 5-cy 2; AA-cy 3; AA-cy 8 (?).—ca. 1100. Teacher of Atīśa.
Rāhulabhadra: p. 94–95.
Vajrapāṇi: 11-cy 3.—Born 1017.
Vajraṛṣi: 8-cy 1–1–1.
Vasubandhu: 7-cy 1; 11-cy 1.—ca. 350.
Vimalamitra: 7-cy 1; 11-cy 1.—ca. 760.
Vimuktisena, Ārya: AA-cy 1.—ca. 450. According to Tāranātha (pp. 138–140) he came from the South. He understood the Prajñāpāramitā Sūtra and the Upadeśa from Ācārya Saṅgharakṣita, a pupil of Vasubandhu. According to others he heard the Abhisamaya (=*AA*?) from Ācārya Dharmadāsa, and the Upadeśa (=*AA*?) from Bhavya. Bu-ston (II 155) says that he was a pupil of Vasubandhu, and excelled his teacher in the knowledge of the Prajñāpāramitā which he taught for 30 years. "He was the principal of many great monasteries, belonged (at first) to the sect of the Kaurukullakas and was the nephew of the teacher Buddhadāsa. He attained the stage of *pramudita,* and heard the word of the Buddha himself".
Vimuktisena, Bhadanta: AA-cy 2.—ca. 580. Some considered him as a pupil of Ārya-Vimuktisena (Bu-ston II 156), Tsoṅ-kha-pa has, however, expressed doubts on the authorship of this work.
Śrīdatta: 8-cy 3.
Smṛtijñānakīrti: 1-cy 3.
Haribhadra: 5-cy 1; 5A-cy 1 (?); AA-cy 5.—ca. 770. Learned the Mādhyamika from Śāntarakṣita, the Prajñāpāramitā and *AA* from Vairocanabhadra. Bu-ston (II 157–9) and Tāranātha (pp. 219–20) describe how he was instructed by Maitreya to compose the *AAA*.

3. ALPHABETICAL LIST OF TIBETAN COMMENTATORS

Kloṅ-rdol bla-ma ṅag-dbaṅ blo-bzaṅ: 1-cy 7; AA-cy 28.—Born 1729. Tucci *TPS* pp. 149, 728.
Mkhas-grub Dge-legs dpal bzaṅ-po: AA-cy 5–8, 18. –A.D. 1385–1438. Pupil of

Tsoṅ kha-pa. Third abbot of Dga'-ldan.
Mkhas-grub bstan-pa dar-ba: AA-cy 5–7, 25.
Mkhon-ston dpal-'byor lhun-grub: AA-cy 5–6–1.
Dge-'dun grub-pa: AA-cy 20.—A.D. 1391–1474. Pupil of Tsoṅ-kha-pa. First Dalai Lama.
Ṅag-dbaṅ byams-pa: 5-cy 7.
Ṅag-dbaṅ blo-bzaṅ rgyal-mtsho: AA-cy 21.—A.D. 1617–1682. Fifth Dalai Lama.
Rṅog blo-ldan śes-rab: AA-cy 12.—A.D. 1059–1109. He lived, acc. to Dr. Haarh, under Sad-na-legs and Ral-pa-can, and he should not be mistaken for the translator of the same name, who lived at the time of king rTse-lde, ca. 1050.
Chos-kyi rgyal-mtshan, rje-btsun: AA-cy 15b–1, 23, 23a–c.
Chos-kyi rgyal-mtshan, blo-bzaṅ: AA-cy 22.—A.D. 1569–1662. First Panchen Lama.
Chos dbaṅ grags-pa'i dpal: AA-cy 18.
'Jam-dpal rgya-mtsho: AA-cy 29.—(8th Dalai Lama. A.D. 1759–1804) (cf. Tucci *TPS* pp. 343, 409).
'Jam dbyaṅs bśad-pa ṅag brtson-'grus: AA-cy 24.—A.D. 1648–1742.
Dar-ma rin-chen, rgyal-tshab: AA-cy 5–6, 16, 16a-b,—A.D. 1364–1432. Pupil of Tsoṅ-kha-pa. Abbot of Dga'-ldan since A.D. 1419.
Dol-po-pa śes-rab rgyal-mtshan: AA-cy 14.—A.D. 1292–1391 (Jo-naṅ-pa).
Dharmabhadra (Chos-bzaṅ): AA-cy 27.—Tibetan translator. See Tucci *TPS* p. 96.
Phyā-pa chos-kyi seṅ-ge, Ācārya: AA-cy 5–3.—A.D. 1109–1169. Studied Prajñāpāramitā under blo-gros 'byuṅ-gnas of Gro-luṅ, the chief disciple of rṄog blo-ldan śes-rab, and then composed his extensive commentary.
Bu-ston rin-chen grub: AA-cy 4, AA-cy 5–4, 5–4–1, 5–4–2.—A.D. 1290–1364.
Vairocana: 11-cy 16.—Of Pa-gor.
Dbyaṅs-can dga'-ba'i blo-gros: 5-cy 1–1; AA-cy 26.—Disciple of Rva-sgreṅ blo-bzaṅ ye-śes bstan-pa rab-rgyas.
Gtsaṅ-nag-pa brtson-'grus seṅ-ge: AA-cy 13.—ca. 1160. Pupil of Phyā-pa.
Tsoṅ-kha-pa: AA-cy 15, 15a-b.—A.D. 1357–1499. Learned Prajñāpāramitā from Re-mda'-pa.
Ye-śes rgyal-mtshan, blo-bzaṅ: 8-cy 14, AA-cy 17a, b.—Teacher of Tsoṅ-kha-pa.
Re-mda'-pa gshon-nu blo-gros: AA-cy 5–5.—A.D. 1349–1412. Studied Prajñāpāramitā under the mahāpaṇḍita Ña-dpon Kun-dga' dpal.
Roṅ-ston Śā-kya'i rgyal-mtshan: AA-cy 19.—ca. 1420.

4. ALPHABETICAL LIST OF CHINESE COMMENTATORS

Chi-tsang: T 1696, 1699, 1707; 2-cy 2, 8-cy 6, 13-cy 2.—A.D. 549–632. Founder of San-lun.
Chih-i: T 1698: 8-cy 5.—A.D. 531–597. Chi-chê Ta-shih, founder and 4th patriarch of T'ien-t'ai.
Chih-yen: T 1704; 8-cy 11.—A.D. 602–688. Hua-yen.
Fa-tsang: T 1712; 11-cy 10.—ca. 695. Hua-yen.
Han-shan: 8-cy 13.11-cy 13.—A Ch'an master. A.D. 1546–1623.
I-ching: T 1817; 8-cy 1–1–3.—ca. 700.
Ju-ch'i: T 1703, 1714; 8-cy 10, 11-cy 11.—ca. 1380.
K'uei-chi: T 1695, 1700, 1710; 8-cy 1–1–2, 8-cy 7, 11-cy 8, 17-cy 2.—A.D. 632–682. Fa-hsiang, disciple of Hsüan-tsang.
Kuan-ting: T 1705; 13-cy 1.—A.D. 561–632. 5th patriarch of T'ien-t'ai. This cy contains the oral explanation of his teacher Chi-chê Ta-shih (i.e., Chih-i). It

consists of five chapters: The 3rd and 4th explain the 2nd and 3rd ch. of the Sūtra, and the 5th explains ch. 3–8.
Liang-pi: T 1709; 13-cy 4.—A.D. 717–777. Mi-tsung. Disciple of Amoghavajra.
Lü-tsu: 8-cy 12.
Shan-yüeh: T 1706; 13-cy 1–1.—A.D. 1230. T'ien-t'ai.
Shih-hui: T 1713; 11-cy 10–1.—N: died 946; T: trav. 1165.—Hua-yen.
Tsung-lei: T 1703, 1714; 8-cy 10, 11-cy 11.—ca. 1380.
Tsung-mi: T 1701: 8-cy 8.—Died 841. Hua-yen.
Tzü-hsüan: T 1702; 8-cy 9.—Died 1030. Hua-yen.
Wu-ching-tsê: 11-cy 12.
Yüan-hsiao: T 1697; 2-cy 3.—Born 617. Hua-yen.
Yüan-ts'ê: T 1708, 1711; 11-cy 9, 13-cy 3.—A.D. 613–696. Korean.

5. ABBREVIATIONS

A	*Aṣṭasāhasrikā*
AA	*Abhisamayālaṅkāra*
AAA	*Abhisamayālaṅkārālokā*
Ad	*Aṣṭādaśasāhasrikā*
Ad-N	Ad, Narthang edition of Tibetan translation
AK	*Abhidharmakośa*
AM	*Asia Major*
AMG	*Annales du Musée Guimet*
AN	*Aṅguttara Nikāya*
AO	*Acta Orientalia*
Asl.	*Atthasālinī*
B	Bagchi
Bagchi	P. Ch. Bagchi, *Le Canon Bouddhique en Chine*, I (1926), II (1938)
Beckh	H. Beckh, *Verzeichnis der tibetischen Handschriften*, etc., Berlin, 1914
Ch	Chinese
ch	Chinese in part
Cy	Commentary
Da	*Daśasāhasrikā*
E	English
e	English in part
EB	*The Eastern Buddhist*
EZB	*Essays in Zen Buddhism* (Suzuki)
F	French
f	French in part
FBS	*Further Buddhist Studies* (E. Conze), 1975
ff	folios
Forke	A. Forke, *Katalog des Pekinger Tripitaka der kgl. Bibliothek zu Berlin* (1916)
G	German
g	German in part
GOS	Gaekwad's Oriental Series
H	Haribhadra
Hs	Hsüan-tsang
IIJ	*Indo-Iranian Journal*
IIR	Indo-Iranian Reprints
IOSC	India Office Stein Collection
J	Japanese

JAs	*Journal Asiatique*
Lalou	M. Lalou, *Inventaire des manuscrits tibétains de Touen-houang conservés à la Bibliothèque Nationale, Fonds Pelliot Tibétain,* I (1939), II (1950), III (1962)
Ligeti	L. Ligeti, *Catalogue du Kanjur mongol imprimé,* I (1942)
LSOAS	London School of Oriental and African Studies
M	Masuda
MBT	*Minor Budddist Texts* (Tucci)
MCB	*Mélanges Chinois et Bouddhiques*
mdo-'grel	P. Cordier, *Catalogue du fonds tibétain de la Bibliothèque Nationale,* II (1909), III (1915)
mdo-maṅ	M. Lalou, *Catalogue du Fonds Tibétain de la Bibliothèque Nationale,* IV 1. *Les Mdo-Maṅ* (1931)
Mhvy	*Mahāvyutpatti*
Mo	Mongol
Mpp-ś	*Mahāprajñāpāramitopadeśa*
MSS	P. L. Vaidya *Mahāyānasūtrasaṃgraha* I, 1961
MZB	*Manual of Zen Buddhism* (Suzuki)
N	Nanjio=B. Nanjio, *Catalogue of the Chinese translation of the Buddhist Tripitaka* (1883)
Ninnō	no. 13
O	Ōtani Catalogue of Kanjur, by Sakurabe (1930–32)
OA	*Oriental Art*
OLZ	*Orientalistische Literaturzeitung*
P	*Pañcaviṃśatisāhasrikā* (Quoted by the pages of Dutt's edition, or the folios of Cambridge Add. 1628).
Pa	*Pañcaśatikā*
P-Dh	T 222
P-Ku	T 223
P-Mo	T 221
Rgs	*Ratnaguṇasaṃcayagāthā*
Ś	*Śatasāhasrikā*
S	Sanskrit
s	Sanskrit in part
Sa	*Saptaśatikā*
SBE	*Sacred Books of the East*
SN	*Saṃyukta Nikāya*
SOR	*Serie Orientale Roma*
SPT	*The Short Prajñāpāramitā Texts* (E. Conze), 1974
SS	*Selected Sayings* (Conze), 1955
Su	*Suvikrāntavikrāmiparipṛcchā*
T	Taishō Issaikyō
Ti	Tibetan
ti	Tibetan in part
To	Tōhoku Catalogue of Kanjur and Tanjur, ed. H. Ui, etc. (1934.)—Extra-canonical works by Y. Kanakura, etc. (1953).
TPS	*Tibetan Painted Scrolls* (Tucci), 1949
TYBS	E. Conze, *Thirty Years of Buddhist Studies,* 1967
V	*Vajracchedikā*
WZKM	*Wiener Zeitschrift für die Kunde des Morgenlandes*
WZKSO	*Wiener Zeitschrift für die Kunde Süd- (und Ost-)Asiens*

Z	E. Zürcher, *The Buddhist Conquest of China*, 1959
ZII	*Zeitschrift für Indologie und Iranistik*

LIST OF EDWARD CONZE'S PUBLICATIONS ON THE PRAJÑĀPĀRAMITĀ LITERATURE

Editor's note: -At the last moment I decided to have a list of Professor Edward Conze's publications on the Prajñāpāramitā literature appended to this book. In consequence I was limited in time and unable to consult a number of works quoted herein, particularly reviews of Conze's books. I have however thought it better to include them rather than omit them or delay the publication. The full responsibility for any blame in regard to this List rests upon me. Prior to publication many translations and a few texts were distributed in typescript. Examples can be seen in the Libraries of the London School of Oriental and African Studies, of the India Office, and of the Buddhist Society in London. ......A. Yuyama

ABBREVIATIONS

I. Texts used:

AdP =Aṣṭādaśasāhasrikā Prajñāpāramitā: Palmleaf MS. Stein Ch 0079a (cf. No. 23), ed. E. Conze (Rome 1962–1974), and Tibetan Kanjur. -PPL 3.

Adhś =Adhyardhaśatikā Prajñāpāramitā: ed. S. Toganoo (Kōyasan 1930). -PPL 17.

ArŚ =Ardhaśatikā Prajñāpāramitā: ed. Narthang, Śer-phyin sna-tshogs KA 252a7–255b4.-PPL 9.

AŚ =Aṣṭaśataka: ed. Narthang, Śer-phyin sna-tshogs KA 250a–252a. -PPL 25.

AsP =Aṣṭasāhasrikā Prajñāpāramitā: ed. R. Mitra (Calcutta 1888).-PPL 5.

CG =Candragarbha: ed. Narthang, Śer-phyin sna-tshogs KA266a3–267b4.-PPL 21.

DsP =Daśasāhasrikā Prajñāpāramitā: edd. Tohoku 11, Peking 733.-PPL 4.

Eka =Ekākṣara: ed. Narthang, Śer-phyin sna-tshogs KA 255b–256a. -PPL 32.

Hṛd =Prajñāpāramitāhṛdayasūtra: ed. F. Max Müller and B. Nanjio (Oxford 1884: Larger and Smaller), and ed. E. Conze, JRAS 1948 (Larger and Smaller).-PPL 11.

JWHKC=Jên-wang-hu-kuo-ching: summarized after M. W. de Visser, Ancient Buddhism in Japan, I (1928), pp. 116–189.-PPL 13.

Kauś =Kauśika: Stein MS. 0044; ed. E. Conze (Santiniketan 1956). -

PPL 19.

NŚ =Nāgaśrī: extracted after P. Demiéville, Hôbôgirin, II (Tōkyō 1930), pp. 164–166.–PPL 12.

Pañc =Pañcaviṃśatisāhasrikā Prajñāpāramitā: ed. N. Dutt (London 1934) and Cambridge MSS.–PPL 2.

PM =Pañcaviṃśatimukha: ed. Narthang, Śer-phyin sna-tshogs KA 261 a1–262b1. –PPL 26.

PŚ =Pañcaśataka: ed. Narthang, Śer-phyin sna-tshogs KA 169b7–196b5. –PPL 7a.

Rgs =Prajñāpāramitāratnaguṇasaṃcayagāthā: ed. E. Obermiller (Leningrad 1937, repr. 1960).–PPL 5A.

Sapt =Saptaśatikā Prajñāpāramitā: edd. J. Masuda (Tōkyō 1930), G. Tucci (Rome 1923).–PPL 7.

SBh =Samantabhadra: ed. Narthang, Śer-phyin sna-tshogs KA 267b4–268b1.–PPL 22.

SG =Sūryagarbha: ed. Narthang, Śer-phyin sna-tshogs KA 264a4–266a3. –PPL 20.

ŚsP =Śatasāhasrikā Prajñāpāramitā: ed. P. Ghosha (Calcutta 1902–1913) and Cambridge MSS.–PPL 1.

Suv =Suvikrāntavikrāmiparipṛcchā Prajñāpāramitā: edd. T. Matsumoto (Stuttgart 1930, Leiden 1935); cf. T. Matsumoto (Tōkyō 1956), R. Hikata (Fukuoka 1958). –PPL 6.

Svalp =Svalpākṣarā Prajñāpāramitā: ed. E. Conze (Santiniketan 1956). –PPL 18.

Vajr =Vajracchedikā Prajñāpāramitā: edd. F. Max Müller (Oxford 1881), E. Conze (Rome 1957, repr. 1974). –PPL 8.

VK =Vajraketu: ed. Narthang, Śer-phyin sna-tshogs KA 269a5–270a5. –PPL 24.

VP =Vajrapāṇi: ed. Narthang, Śer-phyin sna-tshogs KA 268b1–269a5. –PPL 23.

II. Periodicals:

AA =American Anthropologist (Beloit).

ABIA =Annual Bibliography of Indian Archaeology (Leiden).

AM =Asia Major, new series (London).

AP =The Aryan Path (London).

AS =Asiatische Studien/Etudes asiatiques (Bern).

Bibl.bouddh. =Bibliographie bouddhique (Paris).

CAJ =Central Asiatic Journal (The Hague-Wiesbaden).

EB =The Eastern Buddhist, new series (Kyōto).

EW =East and West (Rome).
HJAS =Harvard Journal of Asiatic Studies (Cambridge, Mass.).
IIJ =Indo-Iranian Journal (The Hague, later Dordrecht).
IT =Indologica Taurinensia (Torino).
JA =Journal Asiatique (Paris).
JAOS =Journal of the American Oriental Society (Baltimore-NewHaven).
JAS =Journal of Asian Studies (Ann Arbor).
JIP =Journal of Indian Philosophy (Dordrecht).
JOI =Journal of the Oriental Institute (Baroda).
JRAS =Journal of the Royal Asiatic Society of Great Britain and Ireland (London).
LEW =Literature East and West (New York).
MB =The Mahabodhi (Calcutta).
MN =Monumenta Nipponica (Tōkyō).
MW =The Middle Way (London).
OA =Oriental Art (Oxford).
OLZ =Orientalistische Literaturzeitung (Leipzig-Berlin).
PEW =Philosophy East and West (Honolulu).
RHR =Revue de l'Histoire des Religions (Paris).
RO =Rocznik Orjentalistyczny (Warsaw).
SGZN =Suzuki Gakujutsu Zaidan Kenkyū Nenpō/Annual of Oriental and Religious Studies (Tōkyō).
SIS =Sino-Indian Studies (Santiniketan).
TLS =Times Literary Supplement (London).
TP =T'oung pao (Leiden).
UCR =The University of Ceylon Review (Peradeniya).
VDI =Vestink drevnej istorii (Moscow).

III. Otherwise:
PPL =E. Conze, The Prajñāpāramitā Literature ('s-Gravenhage 1960, 2nd ed. Tōkyō 1978).—Quoted by the numbers of sections of texts in the "Annotated Bibliography".

BOOKS

1. *Abhisamayālaṅkāra*. Introduction and translation from the original text with Sanskrit-Tibetan index (=*Serie Orientale Roma*, VI) (Roma: Istituto Italiano per il Medio ed Estremo Oriente, 1954), XI, 223 pp. -[PPL 2A]

Translation from U. Wogihara's ed. (Tokyo 1932–1935); vocabulary (Sanskrit index with Tibetan and English translations, pp. 107–178; Tibetan-Sanskrit index, pp.

179–233.

Reviews by J. W. de Jong, *Le Muséon,* LXVIII (1955), pp. 394–397; G. Roerich, *MB,* LXIII (1955), p. 301 f.

2. *Buddhist Texts through the Ages.* Newly translated from the original Pali, Sanskrit, Chinese, Tibetan, Japanese and Apabhramsa. Edited by E. Conze in collaboration with I. B. Horner, D. Snellgrove, A. Waley under the auspices of the Royal India, Pakistan and Ceylon Society (Oxford: Bruno Cassirer, 1954).

Conze's translation in full or part from the *Pañc, AsP, Vajr, Sapt, ŚsP,* Śāntideva's *Śikṣāsamuccaya* (ed. C. Bendall 1897–1902), Rāhulabhadra's *Prajñāpāramitāstotra* (edd. Mitra and Ghosha), and Larger *Hṛd.* Also appeared in the *Harper Torchbooks* (1964).

Reviews by A. L. Basham, *AP* (Dec. 1954), p. 568 f.; A. A. G. Bennett, *MB,* LXII (1954), p. 323–325; K. Ch'en, *HJAS,* XVIII (1955), p. 245f.; C. H. Hamilton, *JAOS,* LXXIV (1954), p. 168f.; D. G. Haring, *AA,* LVII (April 1955), p. 368; C. Humphreys, *MW,* XXIX (1954), p. 38 f.; M. Nagatomi, *LEW,*I, 4 (1954), p. 69f.; J. Nobel, *OLZ,* L (1955), Sp. 547–549; V. Rienacker, *Luzac's Or. List,* LXV, 3 (1954), p. 33; E. S. Semeka, *VDI,* 1956, 2, pp. 128–134; E. J. Thomas, *JRAS,* 1955, p. 98; G. Tucci, *EW,* V (1954), p. 230; O. H. de A. Wijesekera, *UCR,* XII, 3 (1954); A. H., *The Spectator,* 13 Aug. 1954.

2A. *Im Zeichen Buddhas: Buddhistische Texte,* herausgegeben und eingeleitet von E. Conze unter Mitarbeit von I. B. Horner, D. Snellgrove, A. Waley, übersetzt von M. Winder (=*Bücher des Wissens,* 144) (Frankfurt a. M.–Hamburg: Fischer Bücherei, 1957).

Review by R. B., *Einsicht,* 1958, p. 157f.

3. *Selected Sayings from the Perfection of Wisdom,* chosen, arranged and translated by E. Conze (London: The Buddhist Society, 1955, reprinted 1968, 1975), 131 pp., 1 frontisp.

Translated in full or part from the *ŚsP, Pañc, AdP, DsP, AsP, Suv, Sapt, Vajr, Hṛd* (Larger), *AŚ, Kauś, Eka.*

Reviews by C. H. Hamilton, *PEW,* VII (1957), p. 63; M. Scaligero, *EW,* VI (1956), p. 355f.; *The Theosophical Movement,* XXV, 4 (1956), pp. 77–79.

4. *Vajracchedikā,* edited and translated with introduction and glossary (= *Serie Orientale Roma,* XIII) (Roma: Istituto Italiano per il Medio ed Estremo Oriente, 1957), 113 pp. (Second edition with four pages of corrections and additions 1974, 118 pp.). –[PPL 8]

Reviews by J. W. de Jong, *IIJ,* IV (1960), p. 75 (with Conze's corrections on p. 75f.); M. Scaligero, *EW,* VIII (1957), p. 333f; A. Bareau, *RHR,* 1976, p. 191; L. O. Gomez, *JAOS,* XCVI (1976), p. 454; N. Poppe, *CAJ,* XX (1976), p. 150f.

5. *Buddhist Wisdom Books containing the Diamond Sutra and the Heart Sutra,* translated and explained by E. Conze (London: George Allen & Unwin Ltd., 1958, repr. 1966, 1970), 110 pp. (incl. a frontisp.). –[PPL 8 & 11]

The *Vajr* text based on Conze 's ed. (Rome 1957), and the smaller *Hrd* with Sanskrit text; American paperback——*Harper Torchbooks* (New York: Evanston/San Franciso: Harper & Row, 1972), and English paperback edition with a few corrections and a cover adorned with 35 Buddhas of Confession (London: Allen & Unwin, 1975); cf. Nos. 35 and 37, also 55.

Reviews by Kun Chang, *JAOS,* LXXXI (1961), pp. 163–165; H. Dumoulin, *MN,* XIV (1959), p. 198f.; Hiranmoy Ghoshal, *RO,* XXVIII (1964), pp. 144–148; I. B. Horner, *Luzac's Or. List,* LXIX, 3 (1958), p. 42; J. W. de Jong, *IIJ,* IV (1960), p. 76f.; Piyadasi Mahathera, *Forum,* XXXVIII (1958), pp. 36–38; M. H. R. (Robins), *MW* (Nov. 1958); G. Tucci, *EW,* IX (1958), p. 368; A. K. Warder, *AP,* XXX (1959), p. 220f.; F. Weller, *OLZ,* LIV (1959), Sp. 621–626; E. White, *AP,* 1976, p. 34f.

5A. *I libri buddhisti della sapienza.* Sutra del Diamante. Sutra del Cuore, trad. per G. Mantici (=*Civiltà dell' Oriente*) (Roma: Ubaldini Editore, 1976), 100 pp.

6. *Aṣṭasāhasrikā Prajñāpāramitā,* translated into English by E. Conze (The Perfection of Wisdom in Eight Thousand Slokas) (=*Bibliotheca Indica,* Work No. 284, Issue No. 1578) (Calcutta: The Asiatic Society, 1958; reprinted 1970), (v), v, 225 pp. –[PPL 5]

Translation from R. Mitra's ed. (Calcutta 1888); reappeared in No. 14 (Bolinas 1973, repr. 1975).

Reviews by Sangharakshita, *MB,* 1959, p. 286f.; G. Tucci, *EW,* XI (1960). p. 295.

7. *Buddhist Scriptures,* selected and translated by E. Conze (= *The Penguin Classics,* L–88) (Harmondsworth-Baltimore-Mitcham/Ringwood: Penguin Books, 1959, reprinted 1960, 1966, 1968, 1969, 1971, 1973, 1975), 250 pp.

Translated in full or part from the *Hṛd, Vajr,* Rāhulabhadra's *Prajñāpāramitāstotra,* also *Mahāprajñāpāramitāśāstra* attributed to Nāgārjuna.

Reviews by A. Bareau, *RHR,* CLVIII (1960), p. 226; Hiranmoy Ghoshal, *RO,* XXVIII (1964), pp. 144–148; P. Horsch, *AS,* XIII (1960), p. 154f.; S. Jivaka, *AP,* 1959, p. 149; M. Nagatomi, *JAOS,* LXXI (1960), p. 256; H. G. Porteus, *The Spectator,* 4 Oct. 1959; A. Robertson, *Daily Worker,* 6 Aug. 1959; M. Scaligero, *EW,* X (1959), p. 302f.; D. Snellgrove, *JRAS,* 1959, p. 186; F. Weller, *OLZ,* LV (1960), Sp. 415–417; *TLS,* 29 April 1960, p. 276

7A. *Scritture buddhiste,* trad. per G. Mantici (=*Civiltà dell' Oriente*) (Roma: Ubaldini Editore, 1973), 223 pp.

8. *The Prajñāpāramitā Literature* (=*Indo-Iranian Monographs,* VI) ('s-Gravenhage: Mouton & Co., 1960), 123 pp.

The present book is a revised and enlarged edition; a xeroxcopy of a revised version with corrections and additions up to August 1975 has been distributed to those scholars interested in it; an important supplement to this book is No. 43.

Reviews by A. Bareau, *JA,* CCLXIX (1961), p. 93f.; E. Frauwallner, *WZKSO,* V (1961), p. 170f.; F.-R. Hamm, *OLZ,* LVIII (1963), Sp. 187–189; G. Tucci, *EW,* XIII (1962), p. 64.

9a. *The Large Sutra on Perfect Wisdom with the Divisions of the Abhisamayālaṅkāra,* translated by E. Conze, Part I (London: Luzac & Co., for Oriental Studies Foundation Inc., 1961), li, 203 pp. –[PPL 2A]

"The translation normally follows the version in 25,000 Lines (*Pañcaviṃśati-sāhasrikā-prajñāpāramitā,* ed. N. Dutt, 1934). In some passages I have, however, translated the version in 100,000 Lines (*Śatasāhasrikāprajñāpāramitā,* ed. P. Ghosha, 1902–1913; and Ms Cambridge Add 1630), and the readings of the version in 18,000 Lines

(*Aṣṭādaśasāhasrikā-prajñāpāramitā*) and of various Chinese versions have occasionally been substituted, as representing an older text……" (Conze, p. vii).
Reviews by A. A. G. Bennett, *AP*, 1962, p. 30 f.; E. Frauwallner, *WZKSO*, V (1961), p. 170f. (esp. p. 171); L. Hurvitz, *ZDMG*, CXIX (1970), p. 403f.; U. Schneider, *IIJ*, IX (1966), p. 160f.; D. Snellgrove, *BSOAS*, XXV (1962), p. 376f.; F. Weller, *OLZ*, LX (1965), Sp. 593–596.

9b. *The Large Sutra on Perfect Wisdom with the Divisions of the Abhisamayālaṅkāra*, translated by E. Conze, Parts II and III (Madison: [Department of Indian Studies, University of Wisconsin], 1964), (ii), vii, 205–663 pp. (reprinted with corrected pages 584–587, 642–650 in Seattle 1966).

Offset printing from typescript.

9c. *The Large Sutra on Perfect Wisdom with the Divisions of the Abhisamayālaṅkāra*, translated by E. Conze. New edition in one volume (Berkeley-Los Angeles: University of California Press, 1975), XVIII, 679 pp.

Reviews by A. S. H., *MW*, L (1975); K. F. Leidecker, *Asian Student*, 27 Feb. 1976; A. Rawlinson, *Religion*, VII (1977), pp. 112–114; D. Seyfort Ruegg, *JIP*, V (1977), pp. 187–189; G. Schopen, *IIJ*, XIX (1977), pp. 135–152; F. J. Streng, *Religious Studies Review*, II 1 (1976); D. B. Zilberman, *JAS*, XXXV (1975), pp. 159–161; A. Wayman, *PEW*, XXVI (1976), pp. 483–485; *Choice*, July-Aug. 1975.

10a. *The Gilgit Manuscript of the Aṣṭādaśasāhasrikāprajñāpāramitā*. Chapters 55 to 70 corresponding to the 5th Abhisamaya, edited and translated by E. Conze, with a preface by G. Tucci (=*Literary and Historical Documents from Pakistan*, I) (=*Serie Orientale Roma*, XXVI) (Roma: Istituto Italiano per il Medio ed Estremo Oriente, 1962), XXV, 399 pp. –[PPL 3]

Cf. also No. 23 below.
Reviews by A. Bareau, *JAOS*, LXXXIV (1964), p. 461f.; J. E. S. D., *MW*, 1963, p. 177 f.; C. Pensa, *EW*, XIII (1962), p. 226f.; L. Schmithausen, *WZKSO*, VII (1963), p. 214.

10b. *The Gilgit Manuscript of the Aṣṭādaśasāhasrikāprajñāpāramitā*. Chapters 70 to 82 corresponding to the 6th, 7th and 8th Abhisamayas, edited and translated by E. Conze (=*Serie Orientale Roma*, XLVI) (Roma: Istituto Italiano per il Medio ed Extremo Oriente, 1974), XXIII, 254 pp.

Review by A. Bareau, *RHR*, CLXXXVIII (1976), p. 190.

11. *Materials for a Dictionary of the Prajñāpāramitā Literature* (Tokyo: The Suzuki Research Foundation, 1967, reprinted 1973), vii, 447 pp.

List of "Publications on Prajñāpāramitā" by the author, pp. 445–447 (written April 1966).
Reviews by A. Bareau, *RHR*, CLXXV (1969), p. 225f.; R. Hikata, *SGZN*, IV 1968), pp. 89–91 (in Japanese).

12. *Thirty Years of Buddhist Studies*. Selected Essays by E. Conze (Oxford: Bruno Cassirer, 1967 [1968]/University of South Carolina Press, 1968), xii, 274 pp.

Includes Nos. 19, 21–22, 25, 33, 43 and 48; cf. No. 16 below.
Reviews by J. W. de Jong, *IIJ*, XIII (1971), p. 143f.; A. Kunst, *BSOAS*, XXXIII

(1970), pp. 640–642; A. Wayman, *JAOS*, LXXXIX (1969), p. 192f.; F. Weller, *OLZ*, LXVI (1971), Sp. 76–79.

13. *The Short Prajñāpāramitā Texts*, translated by E. Conze (London: Luzac & Co./New Jersey: Rowman & Littlefield, 1973), (vi), viii, 217 pp.

Translated in full or part from the *Suv, Sapt, PŚ, Vajr, Hṛd, Svalp, SG, CG, SBh, VP, VK, ArŚ, Kauś, NŚ, JWHKC, Adhś, AŚ, PM, Eka*.

Review by G. Nagao, *EB*, n. s. IX (1976), pp. 139–142.

14. *The Perfection of Wisdom in Eight Thousand Lines & its Verse Summary*, translated by E. Conze (= *Wheel Series*, I) (Bolinas: Four Seasons Foundation, 1973), xxii, 327 pp.; reprinted with 3 pages of corrections, 1975. -[PPL 5 & 5A]

Translated from the *AsP* and *Rgs* (cf. Nos. 6 and 40, 47); includes "List of Topics", pp. 303–309; "Glossary", compiled by William Powell, pp. 311–325.

Reviews by A. Bareau, *RHR*, CLXXXVIII (1975), p. 103f.; J. W. de Jong, *IT*, II (1974), pp. 109–119; Nancy R. Lethcoe, *PEW*, XXIV (1974), p. 464f.

15. *Further Buddhist Studies*. Selected Essays by E. Conze (Oxford: Bruno Cassirer, 1975), xiv, 238 pp.

Includes Nos. 20, 42, 59–61; "Bibliography" of Conze's works, pp. 222–234.

Reviews by T. Ling, *TLS*, 29 July 1977, p. 941; Sangharakshita, *FWBO Newsletter*, XXXIII (1977), p. 15f.; M. O. C. Walshe, *MW*, LI (1976), pp. 127–129.

16. *Buddhist Studies 1934–1972* (San Francisco: Wheelright Press, Zen Center, 1977).

Nos. 12 and 15 reprinted in one volume as Parts I and II.

ARTICLES

17. "Prajñāpāramitā-hṛdaya-sūtra, translated from Sanskrit", *MW*, XX, 5 (1946), p. 105.-[PPL 11]

Reprinted in Nos. 2 (Text No. 146) and 3 (Text No. 54).

18. "The Hṛdaya Sūtra; its scriptural background", *MW*, XX, 6 (1946), pp. 124–127; XXI, 1 (1946), pp. 9–11, 17.-[PPL 11]

19. "Text, Sources and Bibliography of the Prajñāpāramitāhṛdaya", *JRAS*, 1948, pp. 32–51. -[PPL 11]

Reprinted in No. 12 (pp. 148–167: "The Prajñāpāramitā-hṛdaya-sūtra").

20. "Remarks on a Pāla Manuscript in the Bodleian Library", *OA*, I, 1 (1948–1949), pp. 9–12. -[PPL 5]

AsP MS.; cf. H. J. Stooke, "An XI Century Illuminated Palm Leaf MS.", *OA*, I, 1 (1948–1949), pp. 5–8, 3 figs., see also p. 190f.; cf. also *ABIA*, XVI Nos. 3809 and 3891.

21. "Prajñā and Sophia", *OA*, I, 4 (1948–1949), p. 196f.

Review-article of Helmer Ringgren, *Word and Wisdom* (Lund 1947); reprinted in No. 12 (pp. 207–209); cf. also No. 54.

22. "The Iconography of the Prajñāpāramitā", *OA*, II, 2 (1949–1950),

pp. 47–52, 4 figs., 1 pl.; III, 3 (1950–1951), pp. 104–109, 6 figs.

Reprinted in No. 12 (pp. 243–268 without figs. and pl.); cf. *ABIA,* XVI No. 108.

23. "Preliminary Note on a Prajñāpāramitā Manuscript", *JRAS,* 1950, pp. 32–36.

Stein MS. of *AdP:* Ch 0079a folios 535, 553, 574, 599, 611, 613; incorporated in his ed. of the Gilgit MS. of the *AdP* (No. 10); cf. A. Stein, *Serindia,* III (1921), p. 1449f.; used for translation in No. 3; cf. also M. T. de Mallmann, *Bibl. bouddh.,* XXI–XXIII No. 440.

24. "Hymn to Perfect Wisdom", *MW,* XXV, 1 (1951), p. 24f.

Rāhulabhadra's *Prajñāpāramitāstotra;* reprinted in Nos. 2 (Text No. 142), 2A (Text No. 137), 7 (Text No. II. 3. 4).

25. "The Composition of the Aṣṭasāhasrikā Prajñāpāramitā", *BSOAS,* XIV, 2 (1952), pp. 251–262.– [PPL 5]

Reprinted in No. 12 (pp. 168–184).

26. "The Worthy Audience", *Stepping Stones,* II, 10 (Kalimpong 1952), pp. 271–276.

Translations from the *Suv* I 4b–6a, II 19b–21a, 21b–24a; *Vajr* 15b; *Sapt* 27b; reprinted in No. 3.

27. "The Literature on Perfect Wisdom", *MW,* XXVII, 1 (1952), pp. 20–23.

Reprinted in No. 3 (pp. 11–16); cf. Nos. 28–29 below.

28. "The Teachings of Prajñāpāramitā", *MW,* XXVII, 3 (1952), p. 89f., 105.

Reprinted in No. 3 (pp. 16–19); cf. Nos. 27 and 29.

29. "The Doctrine of Emptiness", *MW,* XXVII, 4 (1953), pp. 124–127.

Reprinted in No. 3 (pp. 19–24); cf. Nos. 27–28 above.

30. "The Ontology of the Prajñāpāramitā", *PEW,* III, 2 (1953), pp. 117–129.

Incorporated in Conze, *Buddhist Thought in India* (1962).

31. "Maitreya's Abhisamayālaṅkāra", *EW,* V, 3 (1954), pp. 192–197.– [PPL 2A]

Incorporated in No. 8.

32. "A Prajñāpāramitā Rūpa", *MW,* XXIX, 2 (1954), p. 49f., 1 pl.

A bronze statue from Nepal; reprinted in No. 3 (frontisp., p. 7f.).

33. "Hate, Love and Perfect Wisdom", *MB,* LXII (1954), pp. 3–8.

Reprinted in No. 12 (pp. 185–190).

34. "The Frontispiece to the 'Diamond Sutra'", *MW,* XXX, 1 (1955), p. 1f., 1 pl.

The world's earliest dated printed book (868 A.D.) in the Stein Collection at the British Museum (British Library) of London; reprinted in No. 5 (pp. 72–74: Appendix I "The Frontispiece to the Tun Huang Print"; 1 pl. (frontisp.); cf. L. Giles, "Dated Chinese Manuscripts in the Stein Collection (IV)", *BSOS,* IX, 4 (1939), p. 1030f.; P. Pelliot, *Les débuts de l'imprimerie en Chine* (Paris 1953), p. 47f.;

Oriental Mansucripts, published by the Trustees of the British Museum (1973), p. 40f., pl. IX.

35. "The Heart Sutra Explained, I–IV", *MW,* XXX (1955), pp. 104–107, 119; XXX (1956), pp. 147–153; XXXI (1956), pp. 20–24, 76–81. –[PPL 11]

Reprinted in No. 5 (pp. 75–107).

36. "Tantric Prajñāpāramitā Texts", *SIS,* V, 2 (1956), pp. 100–122.

"Survey of the texts", pp. 100–107; "(Bibliography of) Tantric Prajñāpāramitā texts", pp. 107–112; "Three Late Prajñāpāramitā Texts", pp. 112–122: *Svalp* (PPL 18), *Kauś* (PPL 19), and *AŚ* (PPL 25).

37. "The Diamond Sutra Explained, I–IV", *MW,* XXXI, 3 (1956), pp. 109–114; 4 (1957), pp. 166–170; XXXII, 1 (1957), pp. 8–12; 2 (1957), pp. 48–53. –[PPL 8]

Reprinted in No. 5. (pp. 15–71).

38. "Marginal Notes to the Abhisamayālaṅkāra", *SIS,* V, 3–4 (=Festschrift Liebenthal) (1957), pp. 21–35. –[PPL 2A]

Incorporated in No. 8.

Review of the Festschrift by P. Demiéville, *TP,* XLV (1957), pp. 249–268, esp. p. 254.

39. "The Yogācārin Treatment of the Prajñāpāramitā Texts", *Proceedings of tle Twenty-Third International Congress of Orientalists (Cambridge 21–28 August 1954),* edited by D. Sinor (London: The Royal Asiatic Society, 1957; reprinted by Kraus Reprint, Nendeln, 1974), p. 130f.

Read on 25 August 1954.

40. "The Oldest *Prajñāpāramitā*", *MW,* XXXII, 4 (1958), pp. 136–141. –[PPL 5A]

English translation of Chapters I–II of the *Rgs;* incorporated in Nos. 47 and later 14.

41. "The Road to Omniscience", *MW,* XXXIII (1958–1959), pp. 8–12, 57–59, 99–101, 130–135, 129.–[PPL 5]

Translation of the *AsP,* Chapters I–II; reprinted in No. 6.

42. "The Buddha's Bodies in the Prajñāpāramitā", *Akten des vierundzwanzigsten Internationalen Orientalisten-Kongresses (München 28. August bis 4. September 1957)* (Deutsche Morgenländische Gesellschaft in Kommission bei Franz Steiner, Wiesbaden, 1959), p. 530f.

Reprinted in No. 15 (pp. 113–115).

43. "The Development of Prajñāpāramitā Thought", *Suzuki Daisetsu Hakushi Shōju Kinen Ronbunshū: Bukkyō to Bunka / Buddhism and Culture dedicated to Dr. Daisetz Teitaro Suzuki in Commemoration of his Ninetieth Birthday,* edited by S. Yamaguchi (Kyōto: Ōtani University/Tōkyō: Suzuki Research Foundation, 1960), pp. 24–45.

An important work supplementary to No. 8; reprinted in No. 12 (pp. 123–147).

44. "The Calcutta Manuscript of the *Ratnaguṇasaṃcayagāthā*", *IIJ,* IV

(1960), pp. 37–58. –[PPL 5A]

Cf. No. 45 below; also F. Edgerton, "The *Prajñā-Pāramitā-Ratna-Guṇa-Saṃcaya-Gātha*", *IIJ*, V (1961), pp. 1–18; A. Yuyama, *Rgs* (Cambridge 1976).

45. "Corrections of Obermiller's Text" and "Sanskrit-Tibetan-English Index" to the reprint edition of E. Obermiller, *Prajñā-Pāramitā-Ratna-Guṇa-Saṃcaya-Gāthā* (=*Indo-Iranian Reprints,* V) ('s-Gravenhage: Mouton & Co., 1960), pp. 127f. and 129–157. –[PPL 5A]

The glossary has been incorporated in No. 11; cf. also No. 44 above, and No. 47 below.

Reviews of Obermiller's reprint edition by R. O. Meisezahl, *Oriens,* XVII (Leiden 1964), pp. 289–301; J. Schubert, *OLZ,* LVII (1962), Sp. 524.

46. "Abhisamayālaṅkāra (1)", *Encyclopaedia of Buddhism,* edited by G. P. Malalasekera, Fascicule (I): A–Ac (Colombo: The Government of Ceylon, 1961), pp. 114b–116a.

47. "Verses on the Accumulation of Precious Qualities (*Ratnaguṇasaṃcaya-gāthā*)", *Indo-Asian Studies,* Part I (=*Śatapiṭaka Series,* XXXI) (New Delhi: International Academy of Indian Culture, 1962), pp. 126–178.–[PPL 5A]

Cf. Nos. 14 and 40.

48. "The Perfection of Wisdom in Seven Hundred Lines", *Kalpa: Journal of the Cambridge University Buddhist Society,* I, 2 (1963), pp. 4–10; 3 (1963), pp. 11–20. –[PPL 7]

First part only; reprinted in No. 12 (pp. 191–206), No. 13 (pp. 79–92).

49. "The Adhyardhaśatikā Prajñāpāramitā", translated by E. Conze, *Studies of Esoteric Buddism and Tantrism in Commemoration of the 1,150th Anniversary of the Founding of Koyasan/Kōyasan Kaisō 1150-nen Kinen: Mikkyōgaku Mikkyōshi Ronbunshū* (Kōyasan: Kōyasan University, 1965), pp. 101–115. –[PPL 17]

Reprinted in No. 13 (pp. 184–195).

50. "The Buddha's Lakṣaṇas in the Prajñāpāramitā", *JOI*, XIV (1965), pp. 225–229.

A critically edited text on the Buddha's 32 marks found in the *Pañc* (PPL 2A).

51. "'Maitreya's Questions' in the Prajñāpāramitā", by E. Conze and Shotaro Iida, *Mélanges d'indianisme à la mémoire de Louis Renou* (=*40e anniversaire de la fondation de l'Institut de Civilisation Indienne de l'Université de Paris 1967*) (=*Publications de l'Institut de Civilisation Indienne,* série in–8, fascicule 28) (Paris: E. de Boccard, 1968), pp. 229–242.–[PPL 2A]

"Maitreya's questions" found in the revised version of the *Pañc* (PPL 2A).

52. "La doctrine de la vacuité d'après la *Prajñāpāramitā*", *Hermès: Recherches sur l'expérience spirituelle,* VI: *Le Vide: Expérience spirituelle en Occident et en Orient* (Paris 1969), pp. 204–209.

A French translation of No. 29=No. 3 (pp. 19–24).

53. "Praśāstrasena's Ārya-Prajñāpāramitā-Hṛdaya-Ṭīkā", *Buddhist Studies in Honour of I. B. Horner* (Dordrecht: D. Reidel Publishing Co., 1974),

pp. 51–61.

'Phags-pa śes-rab-kyi pha-rol-tu phyin-pa'i sñin-po'i rgya-cher 'grel-pa (cf. Peking No. 5220 MA 319b8–330b6, Narthang MA 328b7–340a5), "giving the bulk of the direct comments on the *Short Text* only" (Conze p. 51).

54. "Buddhist *Prajñā* and Greek *Sophia*", *Religion: Journal of Religion and Religions,* V (Autumn 1975), pp. 160–167.

Cf. No. 21 above.

55. "Some More Comments on the Diamond Sutra", *Vajra,* III (1976), pp. 3–12.

This adds the explanation of chapters XIII to XXIX omitted in No. 5 (pp. 52–64).

56. "Notes on the Text of the *Aṣṭasāhasrikā*", *JRAS,* 1978, pp. 14–18.

This article rounds up what Conze has done on this text (PPL 5), and may well relieve some doubts about the validity of his translation.

REVIEWS

57. "Review of E. Lamotte, *Le traité de la grande vertu de sagesse de Nāgārjuna,* I, II (Louvain 1944, 1949)", *OA,* II, 4 (1950), p. 167f.

58. "Review of G. Tucci, *Minor Buddhist Texts,* I (Rome 1956)", *AM,* VI (1957), p. 122f.

This book includes "The *Triśatikāyāḥ Prajñāpāramitāyāḥ Kārikāsaptatiḥ* by Asaṅga"- 'Introduction', pp. 3–38; 'Comparison of Taishō 1510a and Taishō 1510b', pp. 39–50; 'Sanskrit text, Chinese, Tibetan and English translations', pp. 51–128; 'Analysis of the *Vajracchedikā* according to Vasubandhu (Taishō 1510) (compared with Kamalaśīla's commentary)', pp. 129–171; and "The Gilgit text of the *Vajracchedikā*", by N. P. Chakravarti, pp. 173–192; Conze uses the Gilgit text in his ed. of the *Vajr* (cf. No. 4 above).

59. "Review of Tokumyō Matsumoto, *Āryasuvikrāntavikrāmiparipṛcchāprajñāpāramitānirdeśasārdhadvisāhasrikābhagavatyāryaprajñāpāramitā* (Tōkyō 1956)", *IIJ,* II (1958), pp. 316–318.

60. "Review of Ryūshō Hikata, *Suvikrāntavikrāmi-Paripṛcchā-Prajñāpāramitā-Sūtra* (Fukuoka)", *IIJ,* III (1959), pp. 232–234.

61. "Review of C. Pensa, *L'Abhisamayālaṅkāravṛtti di Ārya-Vimuktisena: Prima Abhisamaya* (Roma 1967)", *IIJ,* XIV (1972), p. 123f.

Reprinted in No. 15 (p. 220f.)

MISCELLANEOUS

62. "A Personal Tribute", *EB,* n. s. II (1967), p. 84f.

Conze's short autobiographic note to the memorial number dedicated to D. T. Suzuki.

POSTSCRIPT

For the publications on other topics by Edward Conze (18 March 1904–) see *Further Buddhist Studies* [No. 15 above], pp. 222–234.